FAUSTIAN MAN IN A MULTICULTURAL AGE

RICARDO DUCHESNE

FAUSTIAN MAN
IN A MULTICULTURAL AGE

ARKTOS
LONDON 2017

ISBN	978-1-910524-84-8
EDITOR	Martin Locker
LAYOUT AND COVER	Tor Westman

ARKTOS MEDIA LTD.
www.arktos.com

CONTENTS

Preface

This is my second book. As the opening quote in Chapter 1 from Aldous Huxley suggests, it covers my intellectual journey some years after my first book was published in 2011, *The Uniqueness of Western Civilization*. The Huxley quote says (to me) that every intellectual who experiences significant changes in his outlook and continues to engage introspectively with the nature of these outlooks (e.g. Why is this thinker, previously dismissed, now at the centre of one's insights? Why are topics which were previously studied with great intensity now deemed irrelevant and repellent?) will realise that in the course of his long journey of questionings and re-evaluations, one may have been driven by impulses that were already there since childhood. These impulses may have been suppressed but they are now free to influence one's thinking.

Since my undergraduate years, I have travelled the full spectrum of both fashionable and unfashionable intellectual Western currents, starting with a strong attraction to Third World revolutionary writings, Soviet Marxism, then Marxist Humanism, New Left authors, a bit of existentialism, phenomenology, and materialism, middle of the road Liberalism, Hegel, Nietzsche and Weber. Throughout this process I have always read about the history of Western civilisation and the history of European ideas. All this culminated in *Uniqueness*, the product of a decade's work.

I was not overtly taken by the excessive rationalism of much of Western thinking, particularly in academia, and mistrusted, without knowing an alternative, the established interpretations of Western uniqueness with their focus on science, industry, law, and peaceful culture generally. Nietzsche gave me the psychological motivation (or aroused impulses within me) that led me to investigate the primordial historical roots of the West among barbarian, energising, horse-riding Indo-European speakers who came from the Pontic-Steppes to colonise the entire Occident and beyond with their aristocratic warlike culture. The presumption by safe academics that Western uniqueness was to be found in its great books, work ethic, and institutions struck me as the expression of the 'last men,' out of touch with what had already been understood by Oswald Spengler with his concept of the irrational Faustian spirit of Western creativity.

Reading James Burnham's *Suicide of the West: An Essay on the Meaning and Destiny of Liberalism* (1964) soon after *Uniqueness* was published further reinforced my sense that there was something wrong about the nature of contemporary liberalism and rationalism, not just in its inability to understand Spengler's idea of the West, but in actually accounting for its current decline and evident suppression in our culture of male affirmation and primordial identity. Hitherto I had been too 'progressive' in defending the uniquely Western idea of progress in liberal rather than Faustian terms, using the writings of Jurgen Habermas in *Uniqueness* to portray progress, in Burnham's words, as 'education generalised'. Finding the Alt Right finally allowed me to explore the biological and racial aspects of the West's Faustian Soul (as recounted in Chapter 1).

To return to Huxley's quote, my return to 'the obvious' was a slow but inevitable process, especially after 2011. This return stemmed essentially from what I had known instinctively since childhood; that race is a factor that must be taken just as seriously by social scientists as other 'big' factors such as 'economics', 'religion', 'ideas', 'greography', 'culture' and 'demography'. I am not a race determinist, and do think that these other factors are also essential to our understanding of history. But it is clear to me now that identifying the race of the peoples who founded Western civilisation and drove forward the 'rise of the West' (i.e. the Europeans whom I identify in this book as a sub-race of the White race) is essential in understanding both Western civilisation and its subsequent decline, a subject that has concerned me since *Uniqueness'* publication. We all know that 'non-intellectuals have never stirred' from the importance of race, but, as Steve Sailer likes to say, the educated liberals pretend not to notice. However it should be noted that in this book I don't view liberalism itself, as some in the Alt Right do, in negative terms as a form of 'rationalism' that is inherently disconnected from the tragic and dark side of human nature, the separation of peoples into races. I also don't think that Western liberalism is inherently suicidal, as Burnham first argued. In another book I will explore in more detail the relationship between Western uniqueness and liberalism; the responsibility of the West's major transformations and great epochs (i.e. ancient Greece and Rome, Christianity, Natural Rights, Bourgeois Revolutions, Modern Science, the Industrial Revolution and the Enlightenment) for the current suicidal path of the West. The argument will be that liberalism is inherent to Western identity; this civilisation cannot be traditional in the way other civilisations are, and although these great epochs are linked to current trends we dislike, they are not intrinsically and necessarily responsible for the decline of the West. As I point out in this book you are reading, decline is part of the natural cycles of cultures. What is really troubling today about the relative decline of the West is mass immigration, race-mixing, and the permanent marginalisation of Europeans *as a race* in the world, and for this we should blame cultural Marxism rather than liberalism.

There is no reason either to reject our rationalism just because we have realised the obvious reality of human irrationalism and the impossibility of educating humanity to behave in a non-interested, inclusive and non-ethnocentric way. Ethnocentrism is a rational and healthy human attribute explainable in Darwinian terms. Europeans are uniquely rational, and this disposition is itself a component of their Faustian psychology. Europeans, exponentially more so than any other people, have been singularly obsessed with unlocking the 'laws of nature,' in discovering the unknown and exploring the energy of nature to satisfy their infinite Faustian drives. We must be rational in the study of the irrational, but this does not mean we can do away with the irrational. Aldous Huxley already understood this: 'We cannot reason ourselves out of our basic irrationality. All we can do is to learn the art of being irrational in a reasonable way.'[1]

---

1   Bernfried Nugel, "'That Hideous Kind of Fundamentalism'": Aldous Huxley's View of "Righteous Indignation"'. *Aldous Huxley Annual: A Journal Twentieth Century Thought and Beyond.* Vol. 10/11 (2010/2011), p. 339.

The book starts in Chapter 1, with the importance of race in the historical identification of Western civilisation from prehistory to the present day, my own realisation of the importance of race and the domination of the West by cultural Marxism. It argues that the cycles of civilisational rise and decline have been a natural phenomenon in the history of cultures but never has a decline come along through the existence of a hostile elite breaking up the racial identity of a people, which would mean permanent decline and extinction. European peoples have conquered and dominated many territories, influencing their histories and cultures, and in return certain areas of the West have also fallen prey to non-European peoples. Nevertheless, we can identify the geographical location of the West culturally as long as we acknowledge the importance of race in this identification. Chapter 2 looks at the evolution of a European 'sub-race' (within the Caucasian race) in the continent of Europe after Homo sapiens arrived some 45,000 years ago, and how this sub-race evolved over the course of the Upper-Palaeolithic, Mesolithic, and Neolithic periods. Chapter 3 examines how the teaching of Western civilisation has been replaced by multicultural histories aimed at downplaying Western achievements, demonising Western actions, elevating the achievements of non-Western peoples. A case study is given using the rise of modern science which has been portrayed as a 'global affair' in which all the peoples of the world played an equal role. This demonstrated how this revisionism is being carried out in direct violation of the most basic protocols of scholarly research, evidence and standards. Chapter 4 makes a case for the importance of Spengler's concept of a Faustian soul for the understanding of Western creativity, with the intent of showing that the Indo-Europeans were the original Faustian men of the West, in a way that set them apart from all other peoples, Huns, Mongols, Turks, and other groups, from the Steppes. Finally, Chapter 5 uses the Faustian idea as part of an effort to show that almost all the explorers in history were European and that the driving motivation for European exploration was Faustian rather than economic.

Some of the contents of this book have appeared as articles. I am grateful to Kevin MacDonald for giving me the opportunity to publish my work at *The Occidental Quarterly* and for giving me permission to use a two-part article published in this journal for most of the content of Chapter 3, and other articles for some of the contents of Chapter 4, and some sections of Chapter 2.

1

Intellectual Journey after *Uniqueness of Western Civilization:* where is the European Race?

The course of every intellectual, if he pursues his journey long and unflinchingly enough, ends in the obvious, from which the non-intellectuals have never stirred.

ALDOUS HUXLEY

Decline of the West without a Concept of Race

In contrast to the central subject of *Uniqueness* (i.e. the West's rise), after its publication in 2011 I set about investigating the decline of the West. The idea of decline has a rich genealogy in the historiography of the West going back to the Greek historian of Rome, Polybius (c. 200–c. 118 BC), who observed that states experience a natural cycle similar to biological organisms, characterised by birth, growth, zenith, and decay. According to Polybius, primitive kinship first emerges and develops into monarchy, monarchy devolves in tyranny, and eventually tyranny is replaced by the aristocratic rule of the best men. This then degenerates into oligarchic privilege and excess, followed by democracy and finally, mob-rule. Polybius believed that the Roman state was superior to all prior forms of government in combining the best of three forms of rule, monarchical (the elected consuls), aristocratic (senate), and democratic (popular assemblies).[1] But in his estimation, while this mixed polity would slow down the constitutional cycle it would not stop it, and thus Rome too was bound to decay.

Giambattista Vico (1668–1674) was the first to extend this notion of cycles to the entire course of human history, arguing that there were three stages:

(1) Anarchy and savagery.

(2) Order and civilisation.

(3) Decay and a new anarchic barbarism.

The novelty in Vico was to suggest that the underlying mechanism of this recurrent cycle was human nature itself. When humans face anarchy and savagery, they feel the necessity of behaving in useful ways to protect themselves. They achieve this by creating order, which leads to civilised behaviour. But once they achieve comfort through civilisation they start to amuse themselves, growing dissolute in luxury and incapable of sustaining the discipline and seriousness required to sustain a civilisation.

Oswald Spengler is the most famous cyclical theorist. His book, *The Decline of the West* (1918), appealed to me for the obvious reason that it was about the West in contemporary times. The central arguments of his book are two-fold:

(1) All civilisations exhibit unique, self-contained identities nurtured 'on the soil of an exactly definable landscape to which plantlike it remains bound'.

(2) All civilisations follow a life-cycle of childhood, youth, manhood, old age, and then death, when they have 'actualised the sum of

---

1   Craige Champion, "Polybius on Political Constitutions, Interstate Relations, and Imperial Expansion." In *Blackwell's Companion to Ancient Greek Government*, H. Beck (ed.) (Oxford: Wiley-Blackwell Publishers, 2013).

possibilities in the shape of peoples, languages, dogmas, arts, states, sciences'.[2]

Spengler believed that in his time the West had reached old age and had already actualised its unique Faustian soul. But in reality there are 'two Spenglers': an earlier one who lamented the spreading of bourgeois philistinism and the exhaustion of Europe's majestic aristocratic tradition, and a later one who saw in science and technology a continuation (for some time) of the vitality and transformative energy of the West.[3] In his later writings, Spengler saw new forms of Faustian expression in modern industry and science, and new prospects for the imperial expansion of his native Germany. He remained however a pessimist in anticipating the eventual exhaustion of the West's energies in the rise of internationalism, quasi-pacifism, declining birth rates, hedonistic lifestyles, coupled with the spread of Western technology in the non-Western world and the rise of 'deadly competition' from Asia.

Yet, I was never fully persuaded by Spengler. For even if the West had been in a state of decline since Spengler's time, the historical record shows that a civilisation need not disappear completely, nor suffer permanent death. According to the theory of cycles, what civilisations experience are temporary downturns followed by renewals, unless they are conquered outright by stronger ones, absorbed within larger and more dynamic civilisations, or utterly destroyed. There are many examples throughout history of civilisation cycles which did not end in disappearance. This is what the famous 'dynastic cycles' in China are about. While China exhibited little creativity in the Arts and Sciences from the Sung Era to the end of the Qing Dynasty, in recent decades it has bounced back economically as one of the major producers of the world. It also maintains a demographic supremacy, with a population of 1.3 million within China (92% of which is ethnically Han), together with over 50 million overseas

---

2   Oswald Spengler, *The Decline of the West. Volume I: Form and Actuality.* (Alfred Knopf Publisher, 1980 [1922]), p. 106.

3   *The Uniqueness of Western Civilization* (Brill Publishers, 2011), pp. 333–339.

Chinese dominating the economies of Thailand, Singapore, Malaysia and Indonesia.[4] This is rounded off with their colonisation of Vancouver, Toronto, Melbourne, and other major Western cities.

It seemed to me that Western decline could no longer be framed in spiritual, political, economic, or geopolitical terms alone.[5] This civilisation was facing a previously unseen reality, with millions of non-Western immigrants being welcomed since the 1960's into almost all European-created nations. It seemed to me that decline could no longer be framed as a cyclical phenomenon, a mere question of the balance of powers in the world, or in terms of spiritual decline and political breakdown. Immigration was a new variable with truly permanent implications, for it concerned the possible ethno-cultural termination of the very people who modernised the West. But then I wondered: was not the West an ethnically diverse civilisation from the beginning? Did not the West include many lands in the Middle East, through the Hellenistic Era, and many areas of North Africa during Roman times? What about 'Asiatic' Russia, Mestizo/Christian Latin America, and the 'African American' population of the United States?

These questions led me into an investigation of the geographical history of the West. I wanted to know where the West had been located in the course of history; whether areas identified in historical maps as 'Western' but which were populated by a majority of non-Europeans were in fact 'Western' simply by dint of appearing so culturally and institutionally. The standard approach among historians, and in all 'Western Civ.' textbooks, was to attach the label 'Western civilisation' to lands and peoples that happened to be under the rule of 'Western' governments; hence, since Rome colonised Carthage, renaming it 'Africa,' this area was deemed Western during the time it was ruled by Rome. But was this area ever 'Western'? What about Greece under Ottoman rule? Sometime in 2011, I completed

---

4   Annabelle Gambe, *Overseas Chinese Entrepreneurship and Capitalist Development in Southeast Asia* (Palgrave MacMillan, 2000).

5   Michael Cox makes this mistake in 'Power Shifts, Economic Change, and the Decline of the West?' *International Relations* 26.4 (2012).

a 5000 word draft with the title, 'Where is the historical West?' trying to answer these interrelated questions. But I was never satisfied with the answers, and found myself unable to complete the paper, realising it was a mess. I was unsure where the West was at various points in history including the present, even though I had written over 500 pages on the uniqueness of this civilisation.

I realised that my unwillingness to fully acknowledge the concept of race accounted for this inability to determine, with any degree of certainty, the geographical boundaries and histories of the West. It was around this time, 2011 and 2012, that I started visiting such forbidden places as *VDare*, *American Renaissance*, *The Occidental Observer*, *Taki Magazine*, and *Counter-Currents*; from then on the idea grew in me that neither the rise nor decline of the West could be fully comprehended without acknowledging the reality of race. After visiting these sites I looked over the draft and it seemed inexperienced, even adolescent; one more paper carved out under the 'tyranny of liberalism'[6] and the belief that the Western world was different from the Rest only in its cultivation of universal values and its transcendence of ethnic identities. I could no longer accept the claim that non-Europeans could become Western *en masse* through proper guidance in the merits of civic equality, free markets, and tolerance. Nor could I accept the claim, as I had tended to do in *Uniqueness*, that these values alone, or the liberal-democratic way of life, fully covered the identity of the modern West. It now seemed obvious to me that not all the lands and peoples classified as belonging to 'Western civilisation' over the centuries were really Western or European.

It was not so much that I had never contemplated that the West was a civilisation developed by ethnic Europeans and that immigration posed a threat to this ethnic identity. It was more a matter of the environment in which I had studied the West — the university, where every student is taught right from the start that race is not just a construct but that

---

6   James Kalb, *The Tyranny of Liberalism: Understanding and Overcoming Administered Freedom, Inquisitorial Tolerance, and Equality by Command* (Intercollegiate Studies Institute, 2008).

discussions of white identity violate the very liberalism we have come to identify with the West. The first book I reviewed in my freshman year was *Man and Aggression* (1973), edited by Ashley Montagu, in which he flatly stated that 'it is nonsense to talk about genetic determinance of human behaviour...It is within the dimension of culture, the learned, the man-made-part of the environment, that man grows, develops, and has his being as a behaving organism.'[7] This view pervaded all the social sciences and humanities through my entire education, and it is still the dominant view today. In fact, it is a view enforced now more stringently than in Montagu's time, when Carleton Coon, well-known for his books on the biological differences of races in the world, could be president of the American Association of Physical Anthropology in the early 1960s.[8] The current official policy of the American Anthropological Association is that 'any attempt to establish lines of division among biological populations [is] both arbitrary and subjective.' This is also the policy of the American Sociological Association: 'race is a social construct,'[9] a position

---

7   Ashley Montagu (ed.), *Man and Aggression*. (New York: Oxford University Press, 1973), p. xvii.

8   Peter Sachs Collopy, 'Race Relations: Montagu, Dobzhansky, Coon, and the Divergence of Race concepts,' Joint Atlantic Seminar for the History of Biology at Drew University, https://collopy.net/projects/race.html. Montagu, born Israel Ehrenberg, was supervised as a grad student by Franz Boas. In 1940, he published *Man's Most Dangerous Myth: The Fallacy of Race*, after which he played a leading role in the United States against the use of the word 'race,' arguing that biologists should use the term 'ethnic groups' instead, and demanding that 'ethnicity' be defined in cultural terms only. A fanatic opponent of any study suggesting that races were biological realities, as testified by his acrimonious opposition to Carleton Coon's writings, Montagu once said that race 'is an area in which one must never let up, for the racists are ultimately the only genuine enemies of humanity' (as cited by Peter Sachs Collopy).

9   See 'Statement of the American Sociological Association' on 'The Importance of Collecting Data and Doing Social Scientific Research on Race,' adopted by the elected Council of the American Sociological Association (ASA) on August 9, 2002. While the concept of 'biological races' was rejected, the ASA insisted that the term 'race' should be used as a way of identifying and measuring 'racial inequalities' *in society*. It was stated: 'The purpose of the ASA statement is to support the continued measurement and study of race as a principal category in the organization of daily social life, so that scholars can document and analyse how race — as a changing social construct — shapes social ranking, access to resources, and life experiences.'

expressed to the letter in all the sociology texts I have used in my lectures over the last 20 years.

The Cultural Perspective of *Uniqueness*

It was within this climate[10] that I could not help writing in *Uniqueness*:

> At the heart of Western modernity — and here I am suggesting that the 'West' is a cultural term without *fixed* geographical and ethnic boundaries — is the idea of freedom, and the ideal of a critical, self-reflexive public culture.[11]

In *Uniqueness* I was opposing a different prohibition in academia, the notion that all cultures are the same and that it is racist to argue that Western civilisation modernised first on the strength of its own institutions and values. The accepted view was that the West modernised through the unfair colonisation of other continents, or through the 'lucky' acquisition of resources and geographical opportunities in the Americas and Africa. I was going against the academic grain arguing that the West had in fact been far more creative than all the other civilisations combined, and that

---

Likewise, the American Anthropological Association released a 'statement on race' (May 7, 1998) forbidding academic anthropologists from any notion that there are biological differences between population groups categorised as races, (http://www.aaanet.org/stmts/racepp.htm), and, on the other, it released a statement in 2003 — 'On the Importance of Collecting Data and Doing Social Scientific Research on Race' — allowing academics to use data categorising Americans in different racial groups as long as the intention was to show how certain groups were being discriminated and racialised: http://healthpolicy.unm.edu/node/49076.

10   This climate is not restricted to the social sciences; for example, the leading journal of medical research, *New England Journal of Medicine*, declared recently in an editorial that 'race is a social construct, not a scientific classification'. On this point, and similar ones, see Nicholas Wade, *Before the Dawn. Recovering the Lost History of Our Ancestors* (Penguin Press, 2006), pp. 183–184. I will return to Wade's book in chapter two. This journal felt a need to make this statement in light of an accumulating series of findings demonstrating that different races exhibit different genetic patterns of disease and drug response. They know it would be inconsistent with the medical profession to ignore findings pointing in the direction of better diagnosis and treatment.

11   *The Uniqueness of Western Civilization*, pp. 237–238.

it was the aristocratic heroic culture of the ill-reputed 'Aryans' which had initiated the West's creative dynamic.

Yet, as much as I emphasised in *Uniqueness* the ancient and medieval context upon which the rise of modern liberal institutions was predicated, the convergence of my view with mainstream liberalism was obvious: the triumph of the current ideals of freedom and democracy was the high point of the West. In my initial draft I thought that identifying the location of the West was a matter of tracing the historical evolution of the values, the 'learned' ideals, of this civilisation, beginning with the rise of citizenship and rational discourse in ancient Greek times, through the Roman invention of the legal persona, the Catholic fusion of reason and faith, the discovery of the individual in Renaissance times, the Newtonian Revolution, the Enlightenment, and so on, until the Allied victory in 1945, or even the fall of the Berlin Wall in 1989.

What concerned me above all was challenging the leftist idea that the *historic* West was a social construct without any cultural boundaries. I rejected the view that a proper liberal attitude required an egalitarian view of world history. I was struggling against the fact that only a handful of universities were teaching the history of this civilisation. Everyone was captivated by the postmodernist claim that 'no concept is by itself, and consequently in and of itself'[12], and that, accordingly, the term 'Western civilisation' must be conceived only in relation to the rest of the history of the world. Ancient Greece, according to Martin Bernal, was an outgrowth of the Near East; rather than founded by 'Aryan settlers, it was 'Afroasiatic', the product of Egyptian and Semitic influences.[13]

---

12   Jacques Derrida, *Positions* (University of Chicago Press, 1981), pp. 56–67.

13   Martin Bernal, *Black Athena: Afro-Asiatic Roots of Classical Civilization: The Fabrication of Ancient Greece, 1785–1985* Vol. 1 (Vintage, 1991). According to Bernal, European scholars in the 19th century maliciously traced the West's origins to Ancient Greece under the fabricated supposition that this was a land founded by white Aryans, thus cultivating the image of a purely white lineage from ancient to modern times, without any blemishes from Semitic and African influences. However, as David Gress argued in 'The Case against Bernal' (*The New Criterion*, December 1989), what Bernal had shown, at best, is that Greek culture came under Near Eastern influences in the early archaic period, 750–650 BC, not later. No one

In the academic world I inhabited even the landmass of 'Europe' was found suspect. How can a small straggling peninsula on the western end of a much larger and 'richer' Asian landmass be called a 'continent'? The 'the racist privileging of Europe' (on Mercator-derived maps) should not be allowed; the Peters projection, where Europe is 'considerably downgraded,' should be encouraged among students.[14] One of the projections world historians were most enthused about was the 'Hobo-Dyer Equal Area Projection Map,'[15] in which the world was turned upside down with Europe occupying a marginalised corner in the south east. No one cared

---

has ever proposed that Greeks were the creators of a self-contained civilisation. Jacob Burckhardt, like many others since, was plainly aware of the material tradition that the Greeks inherited from outside. In *The Greeks and Greek Civilization* (1898; New York: St. Martin's Press, 1998), he observes that the Greeks 'themselves did not generally begrudge other nations their inventions and discoveries' (p.136). Similarly, Will Durant, author of the eleven volume work, in collaboration with his wife Ariel Durant, *The Story of Civilization*, eagerly states in the second volume, *The Life of Greece*, that 'it was the belief of the Greeks that many elements of their civilization had come to them from Egypt... [I]n Egypt the Greeks acquired many new skills in pottery, textiles, metalworking, and ivory; there, as well as from the Assyrians. Phoenicians, and Hittites, Greek sculptors took the style of their early statues... Second to Egypt's was the influence of Phoenicia...' (New York: Simon and Schuster, 1939), p. 68.

The intention of Bernal was to go beyond claims of borrowings and instill upon his students the false idea that Greece was not 'original' at all. Yet Homer's epics were already (dated to about 750 BC) quite original, for all the 'orientalising' motifs that have been found in them. The heroic spirit in Homer, the individuality and free will of the characters are far more accentuated than in Near Eastern epics. Once we get to the pre-Socratics, the Sophists, Sophocles, Socrates, and Plato we are way past the Near East into another world of high culture (see *The Uniqueness of Western Civilization*, pp. 410–418).

14   These words from John Hobson's book, *The Eastern Origins of Western Civilization* (Cambridge University Press, 2004), are followed by: 'This present book in effect attempts to correct our perception of world history in the same way that the Peters projection seeks to correct our perception of world geography, by discovering the relative importance of the East vis-à-vis the West' (p. 6). For a systematic effort to refute Hobson's claim that the West owes almost everything to the East, see my article 'Asia First?' in *The Journal of the Historical Society*, 6 (1), 2006.

15   A recent example is Douglas Northrup, *A Companion to World History* (Blackwell Publishing, 2012), p. 2.

to mention that Europeans were the ones who discovered and mapped the entire geography of the earth.[16]

Facing this challenge, I wanted to identify the West (in the draft) as the one civilisation that gave birth to liberal-democratic values and modern industrial society. Thinking that the key was to identify the development of these values and technologies geographically, I concluded that Western Europe, the United States, Canada, Australia, and New Zealand were currently the most deeply Western; whereas Eastern (Catholic) European countries were closely Western but always 'lagging behind' the more advanced north-Western parts of Europe. Latin America was 'sort of' Western, unevenly progressing in a Western direction but not quite there yet due to its undeveloped democratic institutions, though Chile and Uruguay were closing in. The Orthodox Christian lands of Russia and the Balkans were also undeveloped, and out of the Western orbit during the Communist era, but nevertheless moving in a Western direction, notwithstanding their authoritarian traditions.

On what grounds did I exclude countries such as Japan, South Korea, Taiwan, and India with their 'emerging' representative institutions, scientific inquiry, and market economies? By insisting that these countries remained culturally different in the degree to which they lacked the Western background of Greco-Roman humanism, Christianity, Indo-European languages, and European high culture. At the same time, I was persuaded by Francis Fukuyama's 'end of history' argument that there was a growing convergence in the world toward a liberal democratic culture.[17] Samuel Huntington's observation that the world was becoming more modern

---

16   David Buisseret, *The Cartographic Revolution: Mapmaking in Western Europe, 1400–1800* (Oxford University Press, 2003). Northrup, without the slightest equivocation, states that 'the Hobo-Dyer Projection shows accurately the relative size of different land areas, while preserving north/south and east/west lines of bearing. It also gives the Southern Hemisphere visual prominence, imagining a globe that has been recentered Down Under' (p. 2). 'Imagining' is a word commonly used among historians, and academics, as well as 'imaginaries,' which essentially amounts to a call for historians to imagine history in multiple ways regardless of the documentary evidence and common sense.

17   *The End of History and the Last Man* (Free Press, 1992).

and less Western seemed inconsistent with the fall of the Soviet Union, the spread of Western popular culture, and the opening of China.[18] Non-Western countries needed to Westernise in order to modernise.

Samuel Huntington and the Ethnic Identity of Civilisations

Yet, by 2013, I found myself agreeing with Huntington's thesis that the very success of modernisation in non-Western countries was encouraging indigenisation and ethnic confidence, rather than Westernisation. Here was a mainstream scholar with a high reputation arguing that ethnicity was *not* a premodern phenomenon, a residue of parochial cultures incompatible with modernisation, but a living, pulsating fact about the nature of civilisations. Kinship, blood ties, common ancestry, tribalism, on a civilisational scale, could be re-energised with successful modernisation. Whereas in the West, it is true, modernisation had come with an emphasis on citizenship and individual rights 'regardless of ethnicity,' modernisation in many non-Western lands was occurring without this liberalism. Modernisation was not identical to Westernisation.

Not only was the West, Huntington explained in *The Clash of Civilizations*, 'the West long before it was modern,' but 'the more fundamental divisions of humanity in terms of ethnicity' had not been transcended but reinforced by modernisation. In contrast to Arnold Toynbee[19] and Fernand Braudel[20], both of whom defined civilisations, broadly speaking, in cultural, geographical, religious, and political terms, Huntington brought ethnic identity into the definition: 'A civilisation is an extended family and, like older members of a family, core states provide their relatives with both support and discipline.'[21] People in different

---

18 *The Clash of Civilizations* (Simon & Schuster, 1996).

19 Arnold Toynbee, *A Study of History, the first abridged one-volume edition* (Oxford University Press, 1972).

20 *A History of Civilizations*, trans. R. Mayne. (New York: Penguin Books [1963] 1995).

21 *The Class of Civilizations*, p. 156.

nations, he observed, felt a civilisational 'kinship' along blood lines, and 'in civilisational conflicts, unlike ideological ones, kin stand by their kin.' This leads to 'kin-country rallying,' which has political consequences and is discernible in 'efforts by a state from one civilisation to protect kinsmen in another civilisation.'[22]

Yet, I could tell that Huntington felt uncomfortable writing about the ethnic identity of Western civilisation; he seemed trapped in the belief that the West had transcended racial particularisms in its emphasis on civic equality 'regardless' of race. Huntington objected to the idea that the West was a civilisation in charge of universal values, and insisted that Western values were particular to the West and alien to other cultures. Yet, he could not quite conceive the idea that the West had an ethnic identity just like other civilisations, and the idea that the West, as a uniquely liberal civilisation, had transcended racial identities.

He noted that 'the concept of a universal civilisation is a distinctive product of Western civilisation...[T]he idea of a universal civilisation finds little support in other civilisations. The non-West sees as Western what the West sees as universal.'[23] But as much as Huntington insisted that Western liberalism consisted of values particular to a civilisation, he could not overcome the liberal notion that there was a universalism to the West in its advocacy of citizenship and democratic values regardless of racial identities. This is why, when writing about Western civilisation in particular, he downplayed the very ethnic identity he otherwise stressed in other civilisations, preferring instead to highlight purely cultural attributes: 'The crucial distinction among human groups concern their values, beliefs, institutions, and social structures, *not their physical size, head shapes, and skin colors*.'[24] But when it came to the way members of non-Western civilisations identified themselves, he readily insisted that racial ethnicity was crucial: 'To the Chinese government, people of Chinese descent, even if citizens of another country, are members of the Chinese community...

22   Ibid., pp. 217, 208.
23   Ibid., pp. 66–69.
24   Ibid., p. 42.

Chinese identity comes to be defined in racial terms. Chinese are those of the same "race, blood, culture," as one PRC scholar put it.[25]

Although Huntington concluded *Clash of Civilizations* with strong apprehensions about the ability of the West to retain its civilisational identity in the face of mass immigration, and called upon politicians 'to protect the cultural, social, and ethnic integrity of Western societies by restricting the number of non-Westerners admitted as immigrants or refugees,' he did not write with conviction or definite clarity about the ethnic European identity of the West. Instead he preferred to use cultural identifiers such as Christianity, rule of law, and the rights of individuals.[26]

Niall Ferguson: Western Universalism = Racial Mixing

I began to see the so-called defenders of 'Western values,' and the 'critics of multiculturalism,' in a whole new light. It became clear that many 'admirers' of the West were promoters of a civilisation with indefinite ethnic boundaries based on universal principles for the benefit of humanity. It became evident to me that what Niall Ferguson was advocating, for example, in his bestseller, *The West and the Rest*, was that historians

---

25   Ibid., p. 169.

26   Ibid., p. 186. Later Huntington went on to address directly the way immigration was radically altering the historic character of America in *Who are We? The Challenges to America's National Identity* (Simon and Schuster, 2004). He was called a racist by the mainstream media for arguing that America's culture was being threatened by Mexican immigration and 'Hispanisation'. But what appeared to be a strong set of arguments against immigration and multiculturalism in defense of the American Anglo-Protestant core — to the point that even neoconservatives felt very uneasy about his book — ultimately faltered in its lack of willful affirmation of the racial interests and identity of the American founding peoples.
     This observation was effectively made by John Attarian in a long review essay; Huntington's unwillingness to link the core Anglo-Protestant culture of America to the race of Europeans was the major flaw. As close to the race line as Huntington got (i.e. up to a concept of national membership based on ethnicity), he wavered throughout and, in the end, got entangled in contradictions, halfhearted measures, and ultimate acquiescence to the marginalisation of whites in America, under the illusion that masses of Mexicans, Muslims and Asians would, if properly assimilated, embrace the WASP heritage as their own. See Attarian's review-essay in *The Social Contract* (Volume 15, Number 1, 2004).

and schools should appreciate Europe merely for being the first place to witness industrialisation, mass consumption, and democratic institutions. The West was a showcase for a future in which different races would co-exist and interbreed in an atmosphere of liberal affluence. What made the West unique was its rise to modernity before other civilisations. The West became the West because it had initiated the development of modern science, together with a government based on property rights and the representation of property-owners in elected assemblies, and a capitalistic economy based on sustained innovations and mass consumer goods. It was a view of the West devoid of any particularity other than its modernity, which bespoke of 'human aspirations'. As Ferguson put it, Western civilisation is merely an idea, 'a set of norms, behaviors, and institutions with borders that are blurred in the extreme'.[27]

Coming across the writings of Paul Gottfried in 2013, I could see that Ferguson's idea of the West was consistent with the neoconservative notion that Western nations were different from other nations only in the degree to which they had customised 'natural rights' as political principles with a universal intent. These 'natural rights' were assumed to be inherent to all humans as humans regardless of location, religion, ethnicity, and historical background.[28] The only thing worrying Ferguson was the lack of assimilation by Muslims to Western values. 'Mass immigration is not necessarily the solvent of a civilisation,' Ferguson wrote, 'if the migrants embrace, and are encouraged to embrace the values of the civilisation to which they are moving.' The West is therefore a land open to everyone, based on individual rights, and opposed to any collective sense of ethnic and religious identity. The key to successful immigration is assimilation rather than multiculturalism. What was needed was nothing more than a more patriotic teaching of the West 'that can bolster our belief in the almost boundless power of the free individual human being'.[29] Aware

---

27   Niall Ferguson, *Civilization: The West and the Rest* (Allen Lane, 2011), p. 15.

28   In addition to his regular articles in *Taki*, *The American Conservative*, and *VDare*, I benefitted from his collection of essays in *War and Democracy* (Arktos, 2012).

29   Ferguson, p. 324.

as Ferguson was of the rapid growth of the Muslim population in the UK, he had no objections to immigration.[30] The West just needs to show resolve on Muslim assimilation...by teaching kids about freedom and the Enlightenment!

He actually extolled the role of mass migration in creating 'a single American civilisation,' by which he meant a mixed-race culture. He happily noted that the number of mixed-race couples in the United Sates 'quadrupled between 1990 and 2000', and that 'whites will probably be a minority of the US population.' Not to worry, he wrote, America will become like 'multi-colored Brazil...one of the most dynamic economies in the world.'[31] How could someone with Ferguson's educational background be swayed by the perception that Brazil is a paragon of racial harmony, when every city is a panorama of racial-income exclusion zones?[32] Ferguson even surmises that race mixing represented the fulfilment of Western egalitarianism, that the emergence of a 'homogenised humanity' through the 'democratic' blending of races, religions and cultures, is the ultimate end of history.[33]

However, upon gaining a better understanding in the differences between palaeo and neo-conservatism, I realised that these ideas have little in common with the same Edmond Burke that Ferguson otherwise defended against the Jacobins of the French Revolution. Burke rejected the claim that the French Revolution had generally come up with a set of philosophical principles — liberty, equality, and fraternity — that were applicable to all humans, as if humans could be abstracted from particular cultures. Calling for the merging of races, and the imposition of universal citizenry across the Islamic world is an extremely radical one, and at odds

---

30   Ibid., p. 290.

31   Ibid., pp. 138–139.

32   Edward Telles, *Race in Another America: The Significance of Skin Color in Brazil* (Princeton University Press, 2004). Stanley Bailey, *Legacies of Race, Identities, Attitudes, and Race in Brazil* (Stanford University Press, 2009).

33   Ferguson, p. 198. Apparently, so committed was he to this idea that he decided to abandon his white wife and three children, and marry Ayaan Hirsi Ali, the Somali-born feminist critic of radical Islam.

with Burke's emphasis on the particular customs and folkways of different cultures, and the 'ancient liberties' of Englishmen. Burke was a 'traditional conservative' and a liberal by the standards of his day. He would have rejected the rationalist contempt for the past contained in the anticipation that the United States will soon become a white-minority country. The core of Burke's conservatism is fear of rootlessness, and revolutionary agendas that disregard ancestry and hierarchy, loyalty and duty, inherited habits and prejudices.[34]

I could now see, around 2012–2013, that books I had enthusiastically used in past lectures — Walter Laqueur's, *The Last Days of Europe*, Pascal Bruckner's *The Tyranny of Guilt, An Essay on Western Masochism* (2010), Ayaan Hirsi Ali's *Infidel: My Life* (2007) — for their criticism of multiculturalism and the presence of radical Islam in the West, were actually defending a multiracial Western universalism. Muslims and Africans need not fear the West, Bruckner was saying: 'monochrome Europe, which was mostly white, is gone.'[35] Laqueur, for his part, was merely making a case for why assimilation was better than multiculturalism in the facilitation of mass immigration. Instead of perpetuating their 'separateness…by not mixing with the local population, only seldom marrying outside their community,' assimilation would encourage a true melting pot.[36] Hirsi Ali herself was warning against the radical threat that Islam posed to the West's culture of diversity and tolerance, defending the West as a civilisation that had produced values for all humans, including Muslims.

This 'patriotic' emphasis on assimilation no longer satisfied me one bit. I kept thinking about the Muslims who already made up over 25%

---

34   Even while George H. Nash's *The Conservative Intellectual Movement in America Since 1945* (Intercollegiate Studies Institute, 3rd ed. 2006) is rather mainstream, I benefitted from this highly regarded book. This was the first extensive book on conservatism I had read for the simple reason that conservatism is rarely discussed in academia except in a dismissive manner as a movement without any intellectual seriousness.

35   *The Tyranny of Guilt, An Essay on Western Masochism* (Princeton University Press, 2010), p. 154.

36   *The Last Days of Europe : Epitaph for an Old Continent* (St. Martin's Press, 2007), p. 71.

of the population in Marseilles and Rotterdam, 20% in Malmo, 19% in Leicester, 15 to 25% in Brussels and Birmingham and over 10% in London and Paris.[37] Could Europe really be identified as 'Western' once 'a fifth of Europeans' were designated as Muslim 'by 2050'? My apprehensions went beyond 'radical' Islam; I was coming across the writings of forbidden authors never mentioned in academia, and one of them, Guillaume Faye, persuaded me more than anyone in his valuation of Muslim immigration:

> Islam corresponds to nothing in the European soul and temperament. Its massive introduction into Europe would disfigure a European culture already damaged by Americanization. An assertive dogmatism, an absence of the Faustian spirit, a fundamental denial of humanism (understood as the autonomy of the human will) in favor of an absolute submission to God, an extreme rigidity of social obligations and prohibitions, a theocratic confusion of civil society, religion and the political State, an absolute monotheism, a profound ambivalence toward artistic freedom and scientific inquiry — all these traits are incompatible with traditional European patterns of thought, which are fundamentally polytheistic. Those who believe that Islam can be Europeanized, can adapt to European culture, can accept the concept of secularism, make a dreadful error. Islam, essentially, does not understand compromise. Its essence is authoritarian and bellicose.[38]

Paul Kersey's *Escape from Detroit*

I was also wondering about 'the colour of crime,' 'race and IQ,' 'race and heritability,' 'r and K strategies.' Having received a copy of the abridged version of Philip Rushton's *Race, Evolution, and Behavior* (2000) many years ago, but never caring to read what seemed to be a 'racist' tract, I finally read it in 2013, as well as articles by Steve Sailer and John Derbyshire.[39]

---

37   See Wikipedia: 'List of cities in the European Union by Muslim population'.

38   This passage comes from an excerpt of chapter IV of Faye's La colonisation de l'Europe: Discours vrai sur l'immigration et l'islam (Paris, 2000), collected (and translated?) in the website 'Racial Nationalist Library,' a 'Library of Essays/Racialist Texts'.

39   Some of Derbyshire's articles I was reading have been put together in a book format under the title *From the Dissident Right* (VDare.com Books, 2013). Sailer's articles can be easily obtained in the search engine of *VDare*.

I realised there was a substantial body of scientific work showing that over the course of thousands of years, inbreeding populations in different environmental areas of the earth had experienced different selective pressures, leading to the development of different racial groups. These racial groups could be roughly identified as European, Asian and African. These groups did exhibit innate statistical differences in behaviour, intelligence and personality, being either heritable or genetically passed from generation to generation.

I could not ignore the fact that trillions of dollars[40] had been spent by governments in the United States to close the educational/economic gap between whites and blacks, but that the gap had not changed much, if at all. Discrimination, or lack of social support, were not the main factors explaining this gap; genetic differences could not be ignored. I found Charles Murray's libertarian argument reasonable: that the black/white gap IQ score did narrow over the course of the 20th century with the end of segregation, better nutrition and educational facilities for blacks. However, this narrowing stalled around the 1970s. Once humans are provided an adequate environment in terms of health and educational opportunities, IQ scores barely change with additional improvements in that environment. There is extensive data showing that intelligence is highly heritable and that scores of white and black 18-year olds have not closed on tests administered after the 1970s. The gap remains at around 15 IQ points.[41]

---

40 Michael Tanner, 'The American Welfare State. How we Spend Nearly 1$ Trillion a Year Righting Poverty — and Fail' *Policy Analysis*, No. 694 (April 11, 2012). This essay writes of welfare generally rather than of transfers of resources from whites to blacks; still, it offers a very detailed assessment of the immense costs of equalisation programs. There is a study by Peter Brimelow and Leslie Spencer published in 1993 in *Forbes*, 'When Quotas Replace Merit, Everybody Suffers,' in which it was determined that the 'total shortfall' or cost attributed to federal compliance with affirmative-action policies and Equal Employment Opportunity Commission (EEOC) regulations was close to 4% of GNP or well over $225 billion.

41 I am not an expert on this issue; still, as scholars we must at least agree that there are empirically based arguments in the world of ideas pointing towards some important behavioural and general intelligence differences between racial groupings. For an interesting exchange on the black/white gap between James Flynn, who believes the

Paul Kersey's *Escape from Detroit: The Collapse of America's Black Metropolis* (2012) brought home to me the fact that a geographical location is deeply affected by its current racial makeup. There are two standard explanations in academia for the successes or failures of nations and cities. There is the geographical explanation popularised by Jared Diamond, which argues that the West modernised first because of the greater number of domesticable plants and animals in Eurasia (this giving the peoples of Eurasia a head start), and also because of the greater geographical balkanisation within Europe which encouraged competition and allowed it to surpass China later on. Whereas China was more connected geographically and thus regularly controlled by centralised governments, Europe was the lucky beneficiary of a balkanised geography, characterised by smaller political units eager to outdo each other through innovations. Then there is the institutional approach, which emphasises how values and beliefs are expressed institutionally, and how institutional frameworks regulate human behaviour.[42]

---

gap between blacks and whites has been closing over the last decades, and Charles Murray, see Ronald Bailey 'Closing the White/Black IQ Gap?' in *Reason.com* (December 1, 2006, https://reason.com/archives/2006/12/01/closing-the-black-white-iq-gap). I agree with Bailey, and this is a view Murray also endorses, that 'no matter who turns out to be right in the nature versus nurture debate over why there is a gap in black/white IQ scores…we must strive to treat every person as an individual.' However, I would add that from a sociological perspective we cannot ignore the statistical realities of group dynamics, just as we don't ignore statistical difference between groups on all sorts of other issues, when we talk about social classes or religious, sexual, or income group differences. There can be no sociological analysis without a consideration of group differences. Other academic sources which I have examined that look into IQ and other behavioural differences include: J. Philippe Rushton and Arthur Jensen, 'Thirty Years of Research on Race Differences in Cognitive Ability,' *Psychology, Public Policy, and Law* 11.2 (2005). Tarmo Strenze, 'Intelligence and socioeconomic success: A meta-analytic review of longitudinal research' *Intelligence* 35 (2007). Ian J. Deary, et al., 'Intelligence and educational achievement' *Intelligence* 35 (2007). Kevin M. Beaver and John Paul Wright, 'The association between county-level IQ and county-level crime rates' *Intelligence* 39 (2011). Angela S. Book, et al., 'The relationship between testosterone and aggression: a meta-analysis' *Aggression and Violent Behavior* 6.6 (2001).

42 Countless works by institutionalists have been published over the last decades by Europeans determined to solve poverty in the world; a recent one which gained

No doubt the geographic explanation carries weight when it comes to long term differences in the historical trajectories of civilisations and nations, but the institutional explanation has attracted the most attention. This is because it lends itself well to the Western hope that world poverty can be overcome with the right policies and institutional reforms. The institutional explanation agrees with the geographical explanation that biological differences among the peoples of the earth are too 'trivial' to have played a role in the divergent paths and state of modernisation of nations. It is only a matter of creating the proper institutional incentives, spreading 'inclusive institutions,' the free market, entrepreneurism, rational administration, and so on, in order for the peoples of the world to become modern. There is truth to this explanation; people will change their behaviour if large sums of money and effort are directed towards modernising their institutions.

But wouldn't it be unfair to ignore the racial nature of the people operating these institutions? As Kersey's research has shown, in the first half of the 20th century Detroit developed into one of the most dynamic cities of the world. Furthermore, whilst the black population had increased from slightly over 1% of the population in 1912 to about 25% in 1960, the city still thrived in the 1960's with a population that was 70% white, hosting museums, a symphony orchestra, splendid parks, beaches, skyscrapers, universities, libraries, good schools etc. But today, with blacks making up over 80% of Detroit (in fact around 92% of the city core) and having been in control of the city's government for over forty years, the city itself has collapsed. Half of all people are classed as being functionally illiterate and public schools are terrible and attended mainly by students in need of free lunch programs. There are countless dilapidated buildings and houses, a crime rate that from 1969 to 2012 has provided over 21,000 murders and the city as a whole is in regular need of massive federal handouts to avoid bankruptcy.

---

wide attention is Daron Acemoglu and James A. Robinson, *Why nations fail. The origins of power, prosperity and poverty* (Random House, 2012).

Against the often-heard claim that Detroit was the victim of a down-turn in the auto industry due to global market forces beyond its control, suffering a fate similar as Pittsburgh, for example, when its steel industry declined, Kersey shows that Pittsburgh's steel industry was in fact hit much harder than the auto industry in Detroit in the 1970s and 80s. And yet the loss of its main industry did not occasion Pittsburgh to deteriorate continuously. Instead, in the words of The Economist (2004), the city became 'the most liveable city in America.'[43] Pittsburgh, which happens to be 65% white and 25% black (90% white in the greater metro area), survived and prospered by diversifying its economy into higher education and health care fields, professional services, finance and wholesale trade.[44]

I could not help but ask, were Detroit, or Jackson, Miss (79.4% black), or Baltimore, Md (64.3%), or New Orleans, La (67%), or Flint, Mich (56.6%) places that could seriously be identified as Western?[45] Were these cities 'the end of history,' showcases of liberal-democratic achievement? How about the intense demographic transformation of Los Angeles (with its 48% Mexican population), of Houston, (41%), San Antonio (61%), or Phoenix (42%)? Were these places better identified as future members of the Nation of Aztlan?

But then I started wondering about the city of Vancouver in the province of British Columbia, Canada: a city that grew economically, maintaining low crime rates, and the same educational standards despite being overwhelmed by Chinese immigration in the last two decades. Still, all my instincts were telling me that these Chinese inhabitants were not Western, and that this city was fast losing its original Anglo-Saxon character. Studies showing that these Chinese immigrants had a higher average IQ

---

43   The Economist, 'A Summary of the Livability Ranking and Overview' (August 2004).

44   Kersey has written three more books narrating similar breakdowns in Atlanta, (Georgia), Birmingham (Alabama), and Chicago: Black Mecca Down: The Collapse of the City too Busy to Hate (2012); The Tragic City: Birmingham 1963–2013 (2013); Second City Confidential: The Black Experience in Chicago (2012).

45   'Ten Cities of 100,000 or More with Highest Percentage of Blacks or African Americans, 2000 and 2010,' http://www.infoplease.com/ipa/A0884135. html#ixzz2HPHxUAnO.

than average Eurocanadians were of no concern to me. There is much more to race than IQ. My senses were distinctly telling me that Chinese immigrants, even if they spoke perfect English, were fundamentally different in the way they looked and sounded; their overall morphology and behaviour was different. I did not need a scientific theory to explain this to me; the insights and feelings conveyed by my senses were more than enough.

The total number of Chinese in Vancouver in 1951 was still a meagre 8,729, in a population of roughly 345,000. In 1961, it increased slightly to 15,223, and then to 30,640 in 1971.[46] Then, during the 80s, the gates were thrown wide open and within a few years, by the mid-90s, the Chinese population suddenly shot up to 300,000, out of a total population of 1.8 million. The population with British ethnic origins was reduced from about 75% in the 1950s to 35.9% by 2006, whereas the Asian population overall climbed to 42%. Currently, as of 2011, non-Whites or 'visible minorities' constitute the majority in Vancouver, 51.8%, whereas Eurocanadians have been drastically reduced to 46.2% of the population, with projections showing that they will constitute only two out of five residents by 2031. As pollster Angus Reid concluded a few years ago, 'Vancouver is clearly an Asia Pacific city now.' As UBC history professor Henry Yu admitted with enthusiasm: 'Vancouver is no longer a Canadian city'; it is 'a global city that is one stop within the Pacific world, with two-thirds of male Canadians of Hong Kong origin between the ages of 25 and 40 living and working outside Canada.' The city now has a Chinese global lifestyle — one 'that is common in Hong Kong, where people know that a key to making money is not to view the place you make money as necessarily the same place you live.'

How, then, could anyone say that this city still remained Western when its non-white majority inhabitants view it as either Chinese or global? Even if the institutions were still functioning reasonably well, and even if

---

46   The following paragraph draws on my article 'Multicultural Madness,' *Salisbury Review* (Vol. 31, No. 1: 2012).

the place had experienced economic growth and scientific advancement, it seemed obvious to me that it could no longer be identified as European. Paul Kersey noted that in Detroit the average price of a home in 2009 was just $7,000 (since no one wanted to buy them in majority black neighbourhoods). In Vancouver we have the opposition situation: the average price of a home is currently over 1 million, with a recent study indicating that it will rise to 2.1 million by 2030, since a substantial number of the buyers are foreign Chinese millionaires, forcing the European founders into small apartments.

Race matters. The physiognomies of the people, their faces, colour, hair, mannerisms and temperaments are very important to the character of a nation and city. I started to realise as well that the non-European immigrants arriving into Canada were interested in assimilating only to those aspects of Canadian culture that allowed them to keep their ethnic identity and advance their own ethnic interests. I began to ponder the following question: How could a city or nation be called Western if most of its inhabitants were pursuing ethnic interests that stood in competition with the ethnic interests of Europeans? If large ethnic groupings were being formed inside Western nations with ethnic interests that competed with native Europeans, and these groups lacked any deep bonds, how could one classify these nations or regions as Western?

The Ethnic Phenomenon in a Cultural Marxist Society

With these questions in mind, sometime 2013–2014 I decided to read *The Ethnic Phenomenon* by Pierre L. van den Berghe. Published in 1981, *The Ethnic Phenomenon* was one of the earliest accounts of ethnocentrism from a sociobiological perspective.[47] The essential finding of sociobiology on the subject of 'ethnocentrism' is that all humans have a natural disposition to view other ethnic groups from within the standpoint of their own ethnic in-group. I was curious as to why only European ethnics were

---

47   Pierre L. van den Berghe, *The Ethnic Phenomenon* (New York: Elsevier North-Holland, 1981).

deemed 'racist' if they exhibited this preference, whereas non-Europeans were seen as rightfully proud of their heritage. *The Ethnic Phenomenon* is 35 years old, which is a very long time in a field that relies on genetics and neuroscience, and one where major findings have been made since. When van den Berghe wrote his book, sociobiology was a marginalised field, although it had already attracted major names including E. O. Wilson, William Hamilton, Napoleon Chagnon, and Richard Dawkins. To this day, in sociology (the discipline I teach) current textbooks offer a short section on sociobiology, but in a dismissive manner as a field that wrongly equates human behaviour with animal behaviour and ignores the preponderance of culture in human affairs.

Van den Berghe made two basic claims. Firstly, that 'ethnic and racial sentiments are an extension of kinship sentiment.'[48] Preference for individuals of the same ethnicity (Irish, German, Chinese, Mexican), or of the same race (White, Black, Asian) is part of our human nature. Ethnocentrism is simply a 'propensity' to favour kin, and this propensity, as actualised in politics, is a form of nepotism. Secondly, ethnic groups are extended families sharing distinctive genes. Of course, if we go 'back enough' in time, all humans have a common descent. However, ethnic boundaries have in fact been created socially through the course of time, as groups have diverged and developed distinctive genetic traits in different localities of the earth, and practiced preferential endogamy and physical territoriality. This argument, van den Berghe added: 'says nothing about racial differences between humans groups...On the contrary, it stresses a *common* biological propensity, not only of all humans, but also of all social animals, to favor kin over non-kin.'[49]

But instead of addressing this propensity as a naturally selected disposition, van den Berghe noted, social scientists decided to categorise ethnocentrism as a dysfunctional malady that must be removed from human behaviour. Social scientists decided to teach that humans do not in fact

---

48   *The Ethnic Phenomenon*, p. 18.

49   Ibid., pp. 29–30.

have a natural inclination to identify with their own kin. Rather, this inclination is a 'purely cultural product peculiar to certain types of society.'[50] Modern industrial societies must transcend this attribute through proper education, making humans behave in such a way that they judge others in terms of their personal attributes and merits regardless of ethnicity. Van den Berghe thus noted that sociobiology was 'in clash with the two dominant ideologies of industrial society — liberalism and socialism.' This moral demotion of ethnocentrism was particularly salient in the United States in the 60s and 70s, as the government was determined to encourage the integration of blacks and whites and the assimilation of immigrants from different racial backgrounds. The Civil Rights movement demanded a new cultural emphasis on the common goals of Americans against segregationist laws and the 'divisive' in-group attitudes of immigrant groups.

What admirers of van den Berghe's book have failed to notice is that he did not question the intentions of liberalism and socialism, but tried to argue that sociobiology was not inherently a counter-ideology to liberalism and socialism; it was an approach concerned with explaining nepotism and ethnocentrism from a scientific standpoint *in order to handle better its negative aspects and offer realistic policies for the resolution of ethnic conflicts.* He actually agreed with the need to 'stop' this ethnocentric behaviour for the sake of the survival of the human species. He just wanted social scientists to deal with it as a natural instinct and thereby create proper incentives to encourage new forms of identity: 'Ethnicity is not lightly shed. There must be powerful material incentives to make one change one's ethnic group. Furthermore, once shed, an ethnic affiliation is almost invariably replaced by a new one.'[51]

In many ways, contrary to the perception of many current proponents of sociobiology, van den Berghe's hope that the social sciences would start taking biology seriously has materialised in recent years. His observation that the 'study of human social behavior...is almost entirely disembodied from the evolution of the human organism in the social sciences' is no

---

50   Ibid., p. xi.
51   Ibid., p. xii.

longer accurate, notwithstanding the continued opposition of many social scientists to sociobiology. There is now a massive body of literature and an entire new field of research known as 'Evolutionary Psychology,' which studies the ways in which humans have evolved psychological disposi-tions and behaviours as adaptations to recurring survival problems in the environment. Numerous books have been published on a whole range of issues, from how humans discern kin from non-kin, identify and prefer healthier mates, cooperate with others and follow leaders, to matters such as infanticide, marriage patterns, promiscuity, the perception of beauty, parental investment, and cross-cultural differences.[52] Cultural perspec-tives are still dominant in academia, and feminists have reacted shrilly to theories explaining that males and females have evolved different repro-ductive strategies in regards to sexual accessibility, fertility assessment, commitment seeking, and parental investment. But we are way past a time when the established ideologies of liberalism and socialism were unwill-ing to accept anything coming from the unstoppable field of genetics.

What has transpired is far more sinister yet expressive of the abilities of our current establishment to assimilate counter-narratives within its wings, so long as these narratives are controlled and moderated opposi-tions that do not threaten the basic pillars of diversity. As I was reading about the subject of ethnicity, I was coming across a term gaining a lot of track in the blogosphere: 'cultural Marxism'. I was particularly influenced

---

52   The literature favouring sociobiology or evolutionary psychology is both abundant and populated by major figures. Following are some key authors and texts: Steven Pinker, *The Blank Slate: The Modern Denial of Human Nature* (New York: Viking, 2002); Robert Wright, *The Moral Animal: Evolutionary Psychology and Everyday Life* (1995); Jerome Barkow, ed., *Missing the Revolution: Darwinism for Social Scientists* (Oxford University Press, 2005); Jerome Barkow, Leda Cosmides, and John Tooby, eds., *The Adapted Mind: Evolutionary Psychology and the Generation of Culture* (Oxford University Press, 1992); David M Buss, *Evolutionary Psychology: the New Science of the Mind* (Boston, MA: Pearson Education; 2004); Richard Joyce, *The Evolution of Morality* (Cambridge, Mass: The MIT Press, 2006); Geoffrey P. Miller *The Mating Mind: How Sexual Choice Shaped the Evolution of Human Nature* (Garden City, N.Y: Doubleday, 2000); Azar Gat, *War in Human Civilization* (Oxford University Press, 2006).

by the essays and lectures of William Lind[53] and Paul Gottfried,[54] and by Patrick Buchanan's book, *The Death of the West: How Dying Populations and Immigrant Invasions Imperil Our Culture and Civilization*,[55] which I used as required reading for a course. I was captivated by the speeches of Jonathan Bowden on the Frankfurt School and other fascinating subjects. This simultaneous reading about the science of ethnocentrism and cultural Marxism illuminated for me the intersection of science and ideology in the West today, in ways beyond anything van den Berghe had observed in his time. This made me realise that it was no longer a matter of the suppression of sociobiology, but rather the incredible ability of cultural Marxism to accommodate much of what genetics had to say except those findings that went against the implementation of racial equality and mass immigration.

The standard definition of cultural Marxism is that, unlike classical Marxism, it is an ideology preoccupied with the transformation of Western culture generally rather than the replacement of Capitalism with Communism. Cultural Marxists are dedicated to gender equality through the abolition of male and female traditional roles in society; to sexual equality through the downgrading of heterosexuality and the celebration of polymorphous sexual relations; to the replacement of Christian morals with politically correct morals; and finally to the abolition of 'white supremacy'. But as I read about the many challenges of sociobiology to feminism, the genetics of human aggression, and in particular to the nature versus nurture debate occasioned by Steven Pinker's book, *The Blank Slate: The Modern Denial of Human Nature* (2002), I concluded that evolutionary psychology does not necessarily constitute a challenge to our cultural Marxist establishment as long as it avoids the subject of race.

---

53 For example, see speech delivered by William Lind to *Accuracy in Academia* under the title, 'The Origins of Political Correctness' (2000), available online: http://www. academia.org/the-origins-of-political-correctness/.

54 Paul Gottfried, 'Yes Virginia [Dare], There Is A "Cultural Marxism"' *VDare* (October 15, 2011).

55 *The Death of the West: How Dying Populations and Immigrant Invasions Imperil Our Culture and Civilization* (St Martin's Press, 2001).

Much as Pinker claims to be a politically incorrect risk-taker, in challenging the notion that our behaviours are socially constructed and that human inequalities are a product of differential distribution of resources, his exceptionally successful career and ability to speak and write in multiple venues tells us he does not pose a threat to the mainstream, but is in fact part of it.[56] The expectation by the proponents of evolutionary psychology that eventually our academic establishment would accept the 'corrective power of science' has proven correct, albeit in all studies of human behaviour *except* in the field of race differences.

Cultural Marxism has a left and a right side, if you will, with both sides reinforcing each other. The left push for more feminism and socialism, and the right for less government spending, less demonisation of traditional family values and Christianity. Both however agree on the need to overcome racial disparities and bring racial diversity upon all white nations. These two sides co-exist in a state of tension and debate, and while the left is clearly dominant in academia, the society at large welcomes mainstream conservative ideas. Both sides are committed to diversity; what cultural Marxism does not tolerate is a challenge to this commitment. We can talk about 'racialised' minorities or non-whites, and about black pride and Asian identity, and, as suggested above, about different medical diagnoses for different races, but never about white pride and white identity.

---

56   Steven Pinker's book, *The Better Angels of Our Nature: Why Violence has Declined* (Penguin Books, 2011) reveals a Pinker that views the West as nothing more than a civilisation that expresses universal values for humanity, which he endorses for nurturing the 'better angels of our nature' through its ideals of tolerance, science, and civic equality, in opposition to all forms of ethnocentrism. As critics have observed, this argument strains, or contradicts, Pinker's prior emphasis on human nature and biological constants, though he insists that it does not, and that he has always recognised that human nature is not fixed but flexible and with a 'good' side. But he never explains why mass immigration and imposition of diversity across the West is a demonstration of our 'angelic' nature. Israelites don't approve of mass immigration, does that mean they are still dominated by the 'bad' side of human nature? When all is said, Pinker's evolutionary psychology is consistent with the political expectations of cultural Marxism on the most profound question of our time: whether European peoples have a collective right to express their ethnocentric natural inclinations or not?

Politically Correct Evolutionary Psychology

I was curious as to how standard psychology texts were handling socio-biology or evolutionary psychology and how they were dealing with the issue of race and ethnocentrism. After examining about 10 texts, it was evident that these fields had become an integral part of the discipline of psychology. Every standard textbook I examined announced a commitment to scientific research, and identified psychology as 'the study of behaviour scientifically,' 'the biological foundations of behaviour.' The text *Psychology, Frontiers and Applications*, by Michael Passer et al., for example, stated that:

> No behavior by any organism can occur in the absence of biologically based mechanisms that receive input from the environment, process the information and respond to it. In humans, these inborn mechanisms allow us to, among other things, learn, remember, speak a language, perceive certain aspects of our environment at birth, respond with universal emotions, and bond with other humans. Evolutionary psychologists also believe that important aspects of social behaviour, such as aggression, altruism, sex roles, protecting kin, and mate selection, are the products of evolved mechanisms.[57]

The only behaviour not seen as a product of evolved mechanisms was ethnic prejudice. There is a section in *Psychology, Frontiers and Applications*, 'Prejudice and Discrimination', in which students are informed that one of the first characteristics we tend to notice about other people when we meet them is their ethnicity. But right away the text tells students that our first impressions may be prejudicial and should not be trusted. Students are warned: 'Prejudice refers to a negative attitude toward people based on their membership in a group.'[58] There is a picture of two Klansmen. The only examples of racial prejudice are of whites holding negative stereotypes of blacks.

---

57   Michael Passer, Ronald Smith, Michael Atkinson, John Mitchell, and Darwin Muir, *Psychology, Frontiers and Applications* (McGraw-Hill Ryerson, Second Edition, 2005), p. 139.

58   Ibid., p. 694.

Overall, racial prejudice is portrayed as an irrational disposition to be understood within the context of a cultural background, rather than a biological background, and to be eliminated through proper education and behavioural controls. Prejudice is caused by a 'constellation of factors, including historical and cultural norms that legitimate different treatment of various groups.' The text observes that humans tend to exhibit 'in-group favouritism' and 'out-group derogation,' but it does not anchor this tendency in evolutionary psychology, implying instead that this behavioural trait is immoral, due to 'cultural' influences in need of alteration and improvement by psychologists. Indeed, the text paints 'social constructivism' as the perspective best suited to explaining prejudicial behaviours. It tilts in a strong 'culturist' direction when it comes to race and prejudice, but then tilts the narrative back in a strong 'genetic' direction when it comes to politically safe behavioural traits such as memory, illnesses, anxiety and mating patterns.[59]

The issue, it seemed to me after examining these texts, is not merely that the vast majority of psychologists are liberals united by 'sacred values' that are hostile to non-liberals, as Jonathan Haidt noted a few years ago.[60] It is far more sinister; psychology is actually committed to the employment of scientific methods as a way of *altering many naturally selected behaviours that do not conform to diversity*. This is a discipline interested in 'unlocking the secrets of the brain,' 'improving' the mental state of humans, eliminating psychological 'disorders' through various controls, techniques and pharmaceuticals, and, in this endeavour, it has decided to promote the creation of a new type of human being in the

---

59   Actually, I searched for another text taught in psychology departments that would only follow a strictly biologically oriented approach and found this title: *Physiology of Behavior* (Allyn and Bacon, Seventh Edition, 2001) by Neil R. Carlson. This text does not have a section on racial prejudice, and so the entire text is committed to 'biological roots of behavior' and 'natural selection and evolution'.

60   See Haidt's homepage, 'Post Partisan Social Psychology.' (http://people.stern.nyu. edu/jhaidt/postpartisan.html). Another study on the lack of mainstream conservative professors in psychology is: Yoel Inbar and Joris Lammers, 'Political Diversity in Social and Personality Psychology.' *Perspectives on Psychological Science*, Vol. 7 (2012).

West that welcomes diversity. To give an example from another text, Karen Huffman's *Psychology in Action* specifically calls upon students to 'self-improve' themselves by overcoming their prejudices and celebrating diversity. She utilises the concepts of 'operant conditioning' and 'cognitive-social learning' to propose environments in which Westerners from childhood onwards will experience 'negative reinforcement' when they behave in prejudicial ways, and 'positive reinforcement' when they behave in ways 'appropriate' to a diverse environment. In a chapter on 'learning' entitled 'conditioned race prejudice' (containing numerous pictures of white racists), Huffman promises students that this chapter will teach them to 'expand their understanding,' 'control their behavior,' 'enhance their enjoyment of life' and help them 'change the world'.[61] In *Psychology, Frontiers and Applications*, students are actually offered a guideline on ways to reduce prejudice between people, by encouraging diverse groups to 'engage in sustained close contact,' giving 'equal status' to members of diverse groups, achieving 'common goals, and promoting social norms that validate and reinforce 'group contact' and equal status.[62]

---

61   Karen Huffman, *Psychology in Action* (John Wiley & Sons, Inc. Ninth Edition, 2010), pp. 202–239. Countless similar books can be cited here; just Google the words 'diversity in education'; it is the biggest industry, with thousands of bureaucratic 'educators' partaking in this brainwashing. The role of psychology in promoting diversity can be ascertained in Maykel Verkuyten's *Identity and Cultural Diversity: What Psychologists Can Teach Us* (Routledge, 2013). This book looks at ways in which psychologists can induce Europeans to view immigration and multiculturalism as a good thing, reduce tensions, bring harmony, and make diversity 'work'; racial mixing and assimilation is portrayed as something that must happen, but which requires psychological adjustments.

62   Ibid., p. 608. Another example (from Physical Anthropology, which happens to be the 'scientific' oriented side of Anthropology) of this effort to accommodate new scientific findings in ways consistent with the protocols of cultural Marxism was amply demonstrated at a symposium held in 2007 at the University of New Mexico, under the heading 'Race Reconciled?: How Biological Anthropologists View Human Variation'. An article on this symposium was published in *American Journal of Physical Anthropology* (2009) under the same title. Attended by specialists in human biology, genetics, forensics, bioarchaeology, and paleoanthropology, the goal was to get these experts to think about the way recent scientific findings were affecting their views on human origins, the relationship between biology and culture, forensic identification, 'whether or how to use the term "race" in research and teaching', and to identify common ground and points of disagreement.

Frank Salter on the Science of Genetic Interests

I realised that writing about the ethnic composition of Western civilisation would not be easy in the face of this prohibition against white racial identity and the absorption of evolutionary psychology within the matrix of cultural Marxism. Early in 2014, I read *On Genetic Interests, Family, Ethnicity, and Humanity in an Age of Mass Migration*, by Frank Salter.

Should we be surprised that the 'common ground' reached by the 'many participants' on the concept of race was consistent with the views held by Ashley Montagu decades ago, and the other members of the Bolshevik triumvirate, Stephen J. Gould and Richard Lewontin? They agreed that i) there is substantial biological variation among individuals within populations, ii) patterns of within (and among) group variation have been substantially shaped by culture, language, ecology, and geography, and iii) race is not an accurate or productive way to describe human biological variation; rather, current variations in levels of development and intelligence have been substantially shaped by the geography and culture in which children have grown.

Participants also debated 'sources of disagreement'. It becomes apparent in reading about these disagreements that, having shown their common acquiescence to the political expectations of their times, they had to find a way to sustain the authority of the science of genetics and what it teaches about group variations 'in the social and health-related' fields, for example. Race is a social construct, but should 'racial categories' be rejected altogether 'in medical genetic research'? There was 'one fundamental disagreement...which was over the precise nature of the geographic patterning of human biological variation.' Essentially this disagreement was over how to express this variation without using racial categories.

I would also encourage readers to watch 'The Great Debate — Xenophobia: Why Do We Fear Others?' This debate, which took place at Arizona State University, 31 March 2012, is about the human instinct to form in-groups and out-groups particularly along ethnic lines. The members in this panel (primatologist Frans de Waal, economist Jeffrey Sachs, psychologist Steven Neuberg, neuroscientist Rebecca Saxe, and physicist and mathematician Freeman Dyson) all recognised in varying ways the powerful drive within all living beings, including bacteria, to organise themselves into in-groups and out-groups. Yet the tenor and objective of the conference, as evident from the title, was to view this as a problem that needs to be transcended. But if it is a behavioural disposition selected by nature for its survival advantages, why is it a problem? Because this is a panel of Western scientists committed to diversity and mass immigration. This was not a conference, it should be restated, by academics belonging to programs in gender studies and critical race theory. It consisted of intelligent scientists who have produced research showing that organisms as diverse as amoebas, elephants, and humans survive inside groups in which there is competition between individuals, but also widespread in-group cooperation in competition with outside groups. Yet, all these scientists were advocating the idea that in-group preference is an immoral form of behaviour that must be eradicated as 'xenophobic'.

Reading this book, in combination with books and articles on the history of Canadian multiculturalism, I realised that multiculturalism was an asymmetrical system in which Europeans, and only Europeans, were expected to celebrate other cultures, feel guilty about their own ethnic identity, and behave as universal altruists; while at the same time non-Europeans inside the European homelands were being encouraged to practice their in-group ethnic interests. It became obvious that multiculturalism was not simply about 'understanding' different cultures but about accepting mass immigration into European lands. The dissemination of multiculturalism in academia was an effort, as Salter saw it, 'to break down or neutralise ethnocentric responses to diversity' among Europeans through 'diversity education' and 'by breaking down the correspondence between national and ethnic identity.'[63] The more this correspondence was diluted, both through the ideology of cultural Marxism and the actual effectuation of racial interbreeding in the West, the more difficult it would be to identify Western civilisation.

What made Salter's book all the more attractive was the framing of the question of genetic interests in 'an age of mass immigration'. Europeans could not go on ignoring the reality of genetic interests, especially in the face of the continuous expansion of other ethnic groups with divergent interests inside their own homelands. This was no longer a scientific inquiry about understanding human behaviour but a book that spoke about genetic interests as the 'ultimate interests' in the survival strategies of ethnic groups.[64] The social sciences were not only ignoring biological research; they had 'long been deployed to facilitate mass immigration, multiculturalism and thus, in effect, the partial replacement of native

---

63   Frank Salter, *On Genetic Interests. Family, Ethnicity, and Humanity in an Age of Mass Migration* (Transaction Publishers, 2007), pp. 145–147.

64   For an answer to the question why the concept of 'genetic interests' has been suppressed for so long in the West, see Ted Sallis, 'Why was the understanding of genetic interests delayed for 30 years?' *Counter Currents Publishing* (April 2011), http://www.counter-currents.com/2011/04/why-was-the-understanding-of-ethnic-genetic-interests-delayed-for-30-years/#more-11618.

born populations.'[65] Finding the location of Western civilisation was not a purely scholastic question but a metapolitical struggle against the effort of our elites to brainwash students into accepting the disappearance of this civilisation from the world's geography.

The following is what I took from Salter's book: To speak of the European 'ethny' in general, not of an actual group of Europeans organised in an ethnically conscious way as an in-group, but of Europeans generally as a geographic race, is to speak of a people with both a common cultural ancestry and a common constellation of genetic traits. Belief in European racial distinctiveness does not amount to a belief in racial purity, but a belief in an ethnic 'super family' that 'can number in the millions'. The question of which particular ethnic nations constitute a race and how we distinguish races, is a matter of their relative genetic distances against a 'backdrop' in which 'all humans share 99.9% of their genes.'[66] Europeans, the inhabitants of Europe in the last centuries and the settler nations of North America and Australia, have had (before the onset of mass immigration from the Third World) a close genetic relationship characterised by a unique package of genetic traits that distinguish them from other racial groups in the world. Ted Sallis, who has followed closely the work of Salter, expresses this well. A race 'is essentially a genetically distinct subpopulation that is characterised by a suite of heritable (genetic) phenotypic traits distinguished from other such groups.'[67]

Ethnic groups throughout history have exhibited a strong predisposition to employ symbolic markers and codes to acculturate members to attach themselves emotionally to their ethnic in-group. They associate 'positive emotions such as happiness, love, and respect for things that benefit the group' while associating 'negative emotions, such as anger,

---

65   *On Genetic Interests*, p. 147.

66   Ibid., p. 91.

67   Ted Sallis, 'Racial Purity, Ethnic Genetic Interests, and the Cobb Case,' *Counter-Currents Publishing* (November 2013). http://www.counter-currents.com/2013/11/racial-purity-ethnic-genetic-interests-the-cobb-case/. See also by Sallis, 'Ethnic Genetic Interests,' *Counter-Currents Publishing* (April 2011), http://www.counter-currents.com/2011/04/ethnic-genetic-interests/.

contempt, and disgust' for out-groups that threaten the group.[68] In doing so, ethnic groups are advancing their genetic interests. These interests are the 'ultimate interests' in that they are about the biological survival of ethnic groups. The fitness of individuals within ethnic groups and nations is increased by the reproductive success of their immediate families, since they have the closest genetic information. Favouring your own ethnic group is adaptive for the simple reason that it improves the standing of your ethny in competition with other groups. This applies as well to races, for members of a race share more genetic information with each other than with people from other races. The best strategy for the preservation and advancement of the genetic interests of an ethny is a well-defined territorial state. History is witness to ongoing wars between ethnic groups expanding against other groups or being conquered by armies and displaced by migrants. A 'central feature of ethnic competition' in the past was 'genocide and ethnic cleansing'.[69]

Immigration is not merely about the risk that alien *cultures* pose to the West, for example the inability of Muslims to assimilate. Mass immigration by non-Europeans involves ethnic displacement by people with different genetic interests. The greater the genetic distance between the native Europeans and the immigrants, the greater the genetic loss to the nation. Salter calculates that 'some ethnies are so different genetically' that if 12.5 million Bantu immigrants were to move to England, the genetic loss to the remaining English would be over 3 million children.[70] Plunging native birth rates, contrary to what conservatives say, is hardly as damaging to European natives as their replacement by genetically distant immigrants. A low birth rate merely reduces the number of natives, which can be increased by future generations, but once immigrants from non-European races are established within the European nation, their genes and genetic kinship become a permanent addition.

---

68   *On Genetic Interests*, p. 130.
69   Ibid., p. 127.
70   Ibid., p. 76.

Add to this the reality that Europeans tend to be more individualistic, less collective in their ethnic awareness, for complex historical reasons,[71] combined with the reality that non-Europeans are more collective and racially aware. These non-Europeans practice ethnic nepotism and engage in the highly threatening practice of free-riding ethnic behaviour by utilising welfare services, schools and national infrastructure created and sustained by Europeans, whilst at the same time being cheered on by a cultural Marxist establishment that prohibits whites any racial awareness. Slater thus calls for genetic interests to be 'explicitly incorporated' into Western political theory and for strong constitutional guarantees favouring the ethnic interests of European peoples:

> Existing constitutions are limited to defending the proximate interests. But the ultimate interest is not happiness, nor liberty, nor individual life itself, but genetic survival. A scientifically informed constitution that takes the people's interests seriously cannot omit reference to their genetic interests.[72]

The importance of race is not group differences 'in intelligence, cultural achievements, athletic performance, or health'.[73] It is the preservation of the racial distinctiveness of Europeans and other races in the world. Salter calls for a 'universal nationalism' in which all ethnies have a right to self-determination and all ethnies learn to co-exist peacefully through international organisations, trade, and diplomacy. Globalisation is consistent with ethnic national self-determination. This is evident in the intensive participation of non-Western nations in multiple global relationships without imposing on their people a form of globalism that calls for mass immigration, racial mixing, and civic constitutions based on supposedly universal values.[74]

---

71   Kevin MacDonald, 'What makes Western Culture Unique' *The Occidental Quarterly*, Vol. 2 (2): 2002.

72   *On Genetic Interests*, p. 229.

73   Ibid., p. 108.

74   Michael Polignano praises Salter's book as an 'immensely impressive book' but thinks it is flawed in emphasising ethnic preservation without considering ways to improve the quality of the European gene pool through eugenics, not by mixing

Although Salter does not frame his argument in terms of writings and theories proposed over the years on 'Western decline,' it became obvious to me after reading his book that the 'ultimate' factors in Western decline were not cultural, economic or even environmental, but the complete control of Western nations by elites dedicated to mass immigration and the dissolution of the racial interests of Europeans. Western nations, as Salter observes, are ruled by both corporate and liberal-minded elites who have little identification with their own people, live cosmopolitan lifestyles, intermarry across ethnic lines, and are committed to open borders, cheap labour, and diversification. The problem is not immigrants *per se*, since they are simply coming to lands welcoming them as cultural enrichers where they are encouraged to affirm their ethnic and religious identities.

With these ideas in mind, I decided to create a blog, Council of European Canadians, early in the summer of 2014 'dedicated to the promotion and defence of the ethnic interests of European Canadians.' I called for a strategy in which European Canadians would make use of the current policy of multiculturalism in Canada, using this policy for their own ends by asking for a seat at the table as a people concerned for the preservation of Canada's European heritage. As part of the 'beliefs and goals' of the Council, I stated:

Europeans with high quality genes from other races, since this would run against European interests, but by mixing Europeans genes within America, for example. He also criticises Salter's universal nationalism for ignoring the ways in which 'low IQ ethnies' can benefit, and have benefitted historically, from colonialism by high IQ ethnies. The colonisation of Africa by the British, which raised the life expectancy and productivity of Africans, increased their genetic power. Another assessment by Polignano can be quoted for its worthiness: 'Salter's universal nationalism is just another form of "live and let live" liberalism. But only Whites are susceptible to such schemes. Other races will be undeterred in pursuing their ethnic interests at the expense of others. Some, such as the Jews and the Chinese, will even pursue world hegemony. Thus I fear that Salter's universal nationalism, like all forms of unreconstructed liberalism, will only prove a disadvantage to Whites. Moralistic abstractions about fairness and rights will not secure our survival if a ruthless, predatory, and amoral race gains the power to make ultimate decisions about the destiny of life on this planet.' See 'The Ethics of Racial Preservation: Frank Salter's On Genetic Interests,' *Counter-Currents Publishing* (April 2011), http://www.counter-currents. com/2011/04/the-ethics-of-racial-preservation-frank-salters-on-genetic-interests/.

We believe Canada is a nation founded by Anglo and French Europeans. In 1971, over 100 years after Confederation, the Anglo and French composition of the Canadian population stood at 44.6 percent and 28.7 percent respectively. All in all, over 96 percent of the population was European in origin. We therefore oppose all efforts to deny or weaken the European character of Canada. We believe that the pioneers and settlers who built the Canadian nation are part of the European people. Therefore we believe that Canada derives from and is an integral part of European civilization and that Canada should remain majority European in its ethnic composition and cultural character. We therefore oppose the massive immigration of non-European and non-Western peoples into Canada that threatens to transform our nation into a non-European majority within our lifetime.

In subsequent months I posted articles on a whole range of subjects. From the beginning the blog became a subject of controversy with numerous complaints filed against me to the president of the university where I was working, The University of New Brunswick, and to other members of the administration, followed by TV interviews, many articles in the mainstream media, student university papers, and radio debates. It was obvious I had hit a nerve in the Western establishment. *You must not question mass immigration in the name of the ethnic interests of Europeans.*

But the question I started with right after publishing *Uniqueness* still remained unanswered: where was the historical West? Was it possible to identify this civilisation in a definite racial way, offering a deeper grasp of its historical genealogy, and address how the West was declining by being colonised demographically? This is the subject of the next chapter.

2

The Genetic and Cultural Location of the West

It's time to address that old chestnut that biological differences among human populations are "superficial," only skin-deep. It's not true: We're seeing genetically caused differences in all kinds of functions, and every such difference was important enough to cause a significant increase in fitness (number of offspring) — otherwise it wouldn't have reached high frequency in just a few millennia. ... Evolution has taken a different course in different populations. Over time, we have become more and more unlike one another as differences between populations have accumulated.

GREGORY COCHRAN and HENRY HARPENDING

What is a race?

The aim of this chapter is not to offer a scientific account of the geographical and historical distribution of the Caucasoid race. I am instead interested in Western civilisation, the geographical location of Europeans as racial group and as a cultural people. The objective is to delineate the historical geography of Western civilisation/culture without ignoring race. Thousands of books can be found on every aspect of Western history, but barely any books can be found addressing the emergence of the West from a racial perspective. In fact there are none which discuss the West in relation to its expansion into non-European lands, and its current immigration trends. Only one book borders on this subject: Carleton Coon's *The Races of Europe*, published in 1939. But this book is of limited use; not only is it dated scientifically, it does not draw a clear distinction between the general Caucasoid race and the peoples who inhabited the continent of Europe. The book classifies many groups outside Europe (i.e. Turks, Jews, Egyptians, Arabs and others) as members of the 'Mediterranean White Race', including many groups inside Europe bordering the Mediterranean Sea. It then identifies many other races inside Europe (i.e. Alpine, Lappish, Danubian, Dinaric and Nordic) as Caucasian, together with all the Mediterranean races.

It is not that I disagree entirely with Coon's categorisation of all these groups under the term 'Caucasoid'. The problem is that, given what we are now learning about the evolution of the historic inhabitants of Europe, the term 'Caucasoid' is not precise enough. Still, *The Races of Europe* remains an impressive book, with masses of details about the Neanderthals, Upper Palaeolithic Man, the Magdalenians, the Mesolithic peoples, the Neolithic and the Mediterranean races. It also contains descriptions of numerous specific ethnic groups located in Europe, such as the Illyrians, the Kelts, the Scythians, the Romans, and the Germanic peoples. The book makes effective use of the techniques of racial differentiation known at the time in Physical Anthropology; classifications, for example, based on stature of body form, head size and other metrical characters of the face and body, pigmentation, general morphology. Coon, in this respect, offers some valuable insights about what a race is, and what the major components are of the Caucasoid race:[75]

Recently, a number of books have appeared identifying the genetic history, the origins and movements of Europeans as a race, their principal racial features, and their physical, behavioural and mental characteristics; factors we need to know in our effort to identify Europeans as the makers of the West. These books are: *Before the Dawn: Recovering the Lost History*

---

75   I ordered *Race and History: An Ethnological Introduction to History*, by E. Pittard (Kegan Paul, 1913, republished in 2003), but this was somewhat of a disappointment as it makes no clear distinctions between ethnic groups and races and consists mostly of descriptive statements, superseded by Coon's book, *The European Races*. The fact that this book was republished so recently shows how sparse the literature on race and its relation to history is, if the issue is not the alleged racism of whites.

of our Ancestors (2006) by Nicholas Wade; *Understanding Human History* (2007) by Michael Hart; *The 10,000 Year Explosion: How Civilization Accelerated Human Evolution* (2010), by Gregory Cochran and Henry Harpending, and, more importantly, *Ancestral Journeys: The Peopling of Europe from the First Venturers to the Vikings* (2013) by Jean Manco. One key point we learn from the first three books listed here is that there have been biological changes in humans since they migrated out of Africa some 50,000 years ago. Different races evolved in different continents, and one of these races can be clearly classified as 'Caucasoid,' located in Europe, the Middle East, North Africa, and the Indian subcontinent. However, by relying on a number of additional articles published in the last few years, between 2013 and 2015, as well as the book *Ancestral Journeys* by Manco (despite its cultural Marxist framework), I would argue that European peoples constitute a distinctive subrace within the Caucasoid race that is unique to the continent of Europe. This subrace evolved in this continent, and is the one directly responsible for the development of Western civilisation. We need to think of Europeans as a subrace that evolved through thousands of years inside Europe in direct response to the unique ecology of Europe *and* in response to their own unique cultural activities.

But, first, what is a race?

Carleton S. Coon's answer to this question is surprisingly consistent with recent studies that rely on the new science of genetics. I shall therefore start with his definition, as expressed in *The Races of Europe*, and in *The Living Races of Man*, published a few decades later in 1965. He says that humans are members of the species Homo sapiens, and that all members of this species, regardless of geographic location, can breed together and produce mixed offspring. However, 'within this larger group [of Homo sapiens] there are many variations of superficially great importance' and thus it is possible to divide humans into sub-species of races.[76] Why these variations? The Homo sapiens 'spread into many environments', with 'extremely varied' selective pressures, producing a 'prodigious differentiation

---

76 *The European Races*, p. 3.

within the human species ... Man did not stop evolving once he became a man [Homo sapiens].'[77] These environments included both natural and cultural pressures and influences: 'Changes in type and complexity of civilisation, acting presumably through nutritional agencies', resulted in different statures and body forms generally. Groups evolved new traits in relative isolation, while others experienced 'great mixing and blending'. For this reason, 'it is not easy' to define and classify races. The classification of humans into races should not be according to a 'rigid scheme': the scheme 'must be elastic'.[78] Coon is obviously aware that races can be classified only along a continuum exhibiting either a gradual blending between groups located in proximate geographical regions or 'sharper' breaks between groups 'cut up by geographical barriers'.[79]

Contrary to claims by critics of racial schemes, this is a standard difficulty in all classification schemes used by the scientific establishment. Just as we classify animals and plants of the same species into different groupings, we can classify humans according to racial criteria. It should be noted that Coon does not rank the races but merely draws attention to the fascinating variety of human groupings in the planet with different racial traits. In this manner, Coon's system is the best suited to this chapter's objective; identifying the movements of the European peoples throughout the development of Western culture. According to Coon, there are three main sub-species of races (Caucasoid, Mongoloid and Congoloid), with four more races identified. He also draws further divisions within each of these main racial types to take account of important additional morphological differences, geographical variations, *and* the ways in which different environments engendered cultures which 'profoundly' affected the character of the races. The following succinct statement by Coon is worth quoting:

> A race is a major segment of a species originally occupying, since the first dispersal of mankind, a large, geographically unified, and distinct region, and

---

77   Ibid., p. 9.

78   Ibid., p. 5.

79   Ibid., p. 11.

touching on the territories of other races only by relatively narrow corridors. Within such a region each race acquired its distinctive genetic attributes — both its visible physical appearance and its invisible biological properties — through the selective forces of all aspects of the environment, including culture. After having become differentiated in this fashion, each race filled out its space, resisting, because of its superior local adaptation, the encroachment of outsiders with whom it mixed, from time to time if not continuously, along its borders.[80]

Hart, Wade, Cochran and Harpending offer an up-to-date scientific definition. Hart is the most succinct in pointing out that races are 'not unique to the human species', since many animal species consist of more than one type, though these types are called subspecies or breeds rather than races. This is his definition:

> A race...might be defined as a large group of individuals — all of them members of the same species — who have formed a partially or completely isolated breeding population for a significant period of time, and who consequently differ statistically from the rest of the species in various heritable traits by which they can be recognized.[81]

Hart emphasises geographic isolation as the major factor that caused humans to be differentiated into races. Breeding populations that are geographically separated for a long time will experience an accumulation of genetic differences between them, both by natural selection and by genetic drift. It has been imperative for those who believe that races are a social construct to insist that humans have been interacting and amalgamating since they evolved into Homo sapiens, for they know that the theory of natural selection cannot but support the existence of races if human populations across the earth were in isolation for thousands of years. This is down to the simple fact that a human population will experience different selective pressures in different environments. In turn, this will result in the evolution of distinct genetic traits, which is itself the basis of the argument for different races. As Wade observes:

---

80   *The Living Races of Man* (Alfred A, Knopf, New York, 1965), p. 10.

81   Ibid., p. 11.

The ancestral human population of 50,000 years ago differed greatly from the anatomically modern humans of 100,000 years ago [...] After the dispersal of the ancestral population from Africa 50,000 years ago, human evolution continued independently in each continent. The populations of the world's major geographical regions bred for many thousands years in substantial isolation from each other and started to develop distinctive features, a genetic differentiation which is the basis for today's races.

By 'ancestral' Wade means the humans of the Upper Palaeolithic who evolved in Africa and then began 50,000 years ago to spread into every continent. Hart believes that four principal races evolved in the major continents: Mongoloid, Negroid, Australoids, and Caucasoid. He divides the first two races into the following sub-races: i) Mongoloid: Amerian Indians and Asian Mongoloids. ii) Negroid: Negroes, Congoid Pygmies and Khoisan. He adds that there are also major population groupings which are admixtures of the principal races, that many of us today are hybrids and that within each of these races and subraces one finds multiple ethnic groups classified according to a whole host of cultural markers. Hart neatly sums up some of the key physical differences observed between the races under the following categories: 'surface differences' (skin colour, hair colour, shape of nose and lips, shape of eye lids); 'existence and susceptibility to various diseases' (sickle-cell anaemia, measles, malaria); 'rate of physical maturation' (age at which children can turn over, crawl, and walk); 'reproductive' (age at menarche, gestation period); 'body build' (height, stockiness, width of hips, lung capacity, fraction of quick-twitch muscle).

Hart also addresses 'behavioural differences' in studies of contemporary racial groups in terms of aggressiveness, impulsivity, divorce rates and finally differences between races in the r-K survival strategies. The latter are related to the interval times between births, offspring per female, parental care, onset of sexual activity, and infant mortality rate. However, as I indicated above, the main focus of Hart's book is on racial differences in intelligence and the role these differences have played in the cultural development of different civilisations. What interests me here is the biological changes that Homo sapiens underwent once they reached the continent of Europe some 45,000 years ago, replacing the Neanderthals. Neaderthals evolved in Eurasia from an earlier migration out of Africa of a species known as Homo heidelbergensis, which originated between 800,000 and 1,300,000 years ago.

A European subrace?

Let's start with Coon again. He writes in *The Races of Europe*:

> At any rate, the main conclusion of this study will be that the present races of Europe are derived from a blend of (A), food-producing peoples from Asia and Africa, of basically Mediterranean racial form, with (B), the descendants of interglacial and glacial food-gatherers, produced in turn by a blending of basic Homo sapiens, related to the remote ancestor of the Mediterraneans, with some non-sapiens species of general Neanderthaloid form. The actions and interactions of environment, selection, migration, and human culture upon the various entities within this amalgam, have produced the white race in its present complexity.[82]

He explains that the present races/ethnic peoples (using these terms interchangeably) of Europe (i.e. Germanic, Celtic, Danish, Baltic, Slavs, Iberians, etc.) are a product of Neanderthals, Upper Palaeolithic peoples, and Mediterranean races that originated in the Near East as Neolithic farmers. The contribution of the Neanderthals was small and in his estimation Europeans originated out of both Upper Palaeolithic and Mediterranean types. The Upper Palaeolithic peoples are the original modern sapiens of Europe, whereas the Mediterraneans came later as a more advanced Neolithic people. The Upper Palaeolithic and Mediterranean mixture occurred mainly along the Mediterranean coasts, producing a white crossbreed typified by what he calls 'the Dinaric race'.

Experts today agree that the Upper Palaeolithic peoples arrived in Europe some 45,000 years ago via the Near East after leaving Africa 50,000

---

82   This passage can be found in any edition of this book, in the section, 'Statement of Aims and Proposals'.

years ago. A recent study of the genetic material in a jawbone (of an Upper Palaeolithic Homo sapiens) found in 2002 in Romania estimated that between 6% and 9% of the individual's genome came from Neanderthal ancestors. Roughly speaking, it has been estimated that Neanderthals have contributed between 2% and 4% of the DNA of present-day Europeans, or 1–3% of the DNA of present-day people in Eurasia.[83] It should be noted that Coon did not only write of a Mediterranean sub-Caucasoid race, but identified two more white sub-races in Europe: Nordic and Alpine. He observed the predominance of the Nordic type in countries of Central and Northern Europe; and of the Alpine race in central/southern/Eastern Europe and parts of Western and Central Asia. Interestingly enough, Madison Grant had already offered a mapping of these three sub-white races in his book, *The Passing of the Great Race*, published in 1916.[84] Coon estimated that the greatest impact of the Mediterranean peoples from the Near East who invaded Europe 'in the latter part of the 4th millennium BC' was on southern Europe, Italy and Spain.[85] Coon also discussed the appearance of 'Corded or Battle Axe' people in most of north central Europe, originally from 'somewhere north or east of the Black Sea', whom he identified as Mediterranean Danubians.[86]

It is now believed that the 'true' Neanderthals, which by 200,000/250,000 years ago had evolved from Homo heidelbergensis, became extinct in Europe roughly 5,000 years after Homo sapiens reached the continent (i.e. between 41,000 and 39,000 years ago). Thus began the Upper Palaeolithic Era in Europe. I would argue that these Upper Palaeolithic peoples were not 'European' in race when they were already

---

83   Qiaomei Fu et. al., 'An early modern human from Romania with a recent Neanderthal ancestor' *Nature*, Vol. 524 (August 13, 2005). For a view that there is negligible or no evidence of Neanderthal genetic mixture with the Upper Paleolithic humans, see Richards M, et. al., 'Paleolithic and Neolithic lineages in the European mitochondrial gene pool,' *American Journal of Human Genetics* 59, 1 (1996).

84   See Wikipedia, File:Passing of the Great Race — Map 4.jpg 'Present Distribution of the European Races'.

85   *The European Races*, p. 54.

86   Ibid., pp. 107–109.

residing in Europe but rather they evolved into a European sub-race over the course of millennia as a response to new environmental pressures. Culture too acted as an important selective pressure. The following argument should be taken as a very tentative statement; it has been only in the last three years or so that a string of articles have appeared informing us about three major findings in the genetic history of Europeans:

(1)   It was not until about 5800 years ago that light-skin genes, as well as other genes for blue eyes and blonde hair, started to show up at a high frequency among the inhabitants of Europe.

(2)   A mass migration of Bronze Age pastoralists from southern Russia (or the Pontic steppes near the Black Sea) contributed up to 50% of ancestry in some north Europeans.

(3)   The genetic make-up of the 'people of the British Isles' has barely changed since 1400 years ago.

In this chapter we will see that the mainstream media is wilfully distorting the scientific content and political implications of these findings, all of which corroborate the long standing, but prohibited argument, that Europeans are a people with a unique evolutionary history inside the continent of Europe.

But firstly I would like to clarify the way in which the racial and cultural term 'European' is being used by all sides in this debate. The general wording in respect to the evolution of white skin, to start with, has been along the lines of 'when Europeans became white'. But the more accurate heading should be: 'when or how the inhabitants of Europe became European.' After all, Europeans emerged in time from a preceding people that were *not* European. This evolution, of course, was not simply a matter of when they evolved white skin; there were a number of other key traits, which did not emerge at once but in time, which means that it is difficult to state with any definiteness when the inhabitants of Europe became 'European.'

The question is not *when* Europeans evolved x or y traits, white skin or lactose tolerance, since this way of framing the issue supposes that the inhabitants of Europe were European the moment Homo sapiens arrived in this continent some 45,000 years ago. We need to think of Europeans as a race that evolved through thousands of years inside Europe, in response to the unique ecology of this continent and the cultural activities that emerged therein. The upper Palaeolithic peoples who first inhabited Europe, coming from Africa via the Near East, were not Europeans but a people still closely descended from the African Homo sapiens that left Africa some 50,000 (or 60,000 years ago), who retained many African genetic traits.

To this day it is common to find the Upper Palaeolithic peoples in Europe described absolutely as the 'original' or 'first Europeans'. But the succession of European cultures witnessed during the long Upper Palaeolithic epoch (i.e. the Aurignacian, 45,000 to 28,000 years ago; the Gravettian, 28,000 to 21,00 years ago and best known for its Venus figurines; and the Solutrean, 21,000 to 16,500 years ago), are best identified as a process of evolving into European peoples. Why should we not be free to narrow the term 'European', in light of evidence that the Homo sapiens who migrated out of African and into Asia, Europe, Australia and America evolved independent of each other and in response to environmental/cultural influences and genetic drift? Going beyond Wade, Cochran and Harpending, I would argue that just as we can speak of a new Caucasoid race evolving outside of Africa in general, we can speak of a 'European' subrace. This subrace evolved with its own anatomical, behavioural and IQ traits due to breeding within a relatively isolated geographical unit; Europe itself.

Below are a number of representations from various sources that depict the evolving race of Europeans. Bear in mind that they emphasise what Hard classifies as 'surface differences' in racial characteristics (i.e. skin colour, nose/eyelid shape, hair/eye colour etc.):

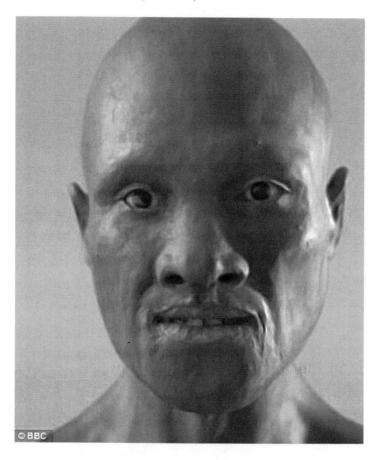

1. Reconstruction of early Upper Palaeolithic in Europe based on a cranium from Romania which is 40,000/35,000 years old. He is known as the "first European".

2. 26,000 year old ivory head from Europe. Notice brow ridges, heavy jaw and wider nose.

3. Reconstruction of Sunghir Man from an Upper Palaeolithic site in Russia about 190 km East of Moscow, dated to approximately 25,000 years BP.

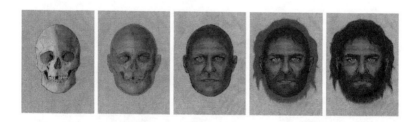

4. Reconstruction of Mesolithic hunter-gatherer, who is dated to 7,000 years ago and comes from La Braña-Arintero, Spain. Not known for certain whether eyes were blue; they know they were not brown, but possibly hazel or green. The skin is portrayed as brown.

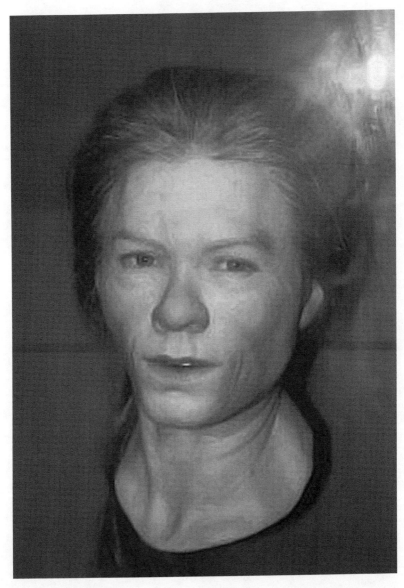

5. Reconstruction of the 'Bäckaskogswoman' from Skåne, Sweden. She died between 7010 and 6540 BC.

Media Reactions to the Discovery that Europeans Became White Recently

In essence, a narrative has been created to manipulate into thinking they are not the ancestral peoples of Europe. This has been achieved through claiming that the genes associated with white skin and traits such as the ability to digest milk as adults (and tallness!) were either brought to Europe by 'immigrants' who arrived relatively recently, or evolved much later than previously thought. Since the new research seems to say that the 'original Europeans' did not evolve lighter skin soon after leaving Africa and arriving in the colder climes of Europe starting around 45,000 years ago, but remained African-looking through most of the Upper Palaeolithic period, it would seem to follow that current Europeans are a later epiphenomenon preceded by true African founders.

This is the implied message of one of the most widely available articles in the web, with the title 'How Europeans Evolved White Skin'. It states in the opening paragraph: 'Most of us think of Europe as the ancestral home of white people. But a new study shows that pale skin, as well as other traits such as tallness and ability to digest milk as adults, arrived in most of the continent relatively recently.'[87] Apparently, not just North America, Australia, and New Zealand, but Europe too is not the homeland of whites. It was only after 7,000 years ago that white skin 'arrived' in Europe. Europeans have no right to complain about their demographic replacement thanks to immigration by Africans and Asians.

Before this scientific finding on the evolution of a white skin gene, it was assumed that lighter skin was a superficial trait that evolved gradually once Upper Paleolithic peoples spread in Europe, so that from the time they left Africa 50,000/60,000 years ago, to the time they colonized Europe, and steadily eliminated the Neanderthals, they evolved lighter skin some 40,000 years ago. Lighter skin, it was argued, was selected as a more efficient pigment for the synthesisation of vitamin D from the lower UV light environment in Europe. But recent analysis of the DNA of a

---

87   Ann Gibbons, 'How Europeans Evolved White Skin,' *Science News* (April 2, 2015).

skeleton from La Braña-Arintero, Spain, dated 7,000 years ago (as seen in Figure 4 above), shows a male who had blue eyes but dark skin. This finding led the mainstream media to report 'that for most of their evolutionary history, Europeans were not what many people today would call Caucasian.'[88]

In other words, the inhabitants of Europe were not white for most of their history; the prehistoric inhabitants of Britain and Scandinavia, as it was reported in another article, had a dark skin tone until about 5,500–5,200 years ago, but then as farming was adopted, their diet shifted from hunting and gathering wild plants to cultivating cereals, and this led to the rapid evolution of light skin.[89] The new grain diet from farming lacked vitamin D, and so lighter skin was selected as a more efficient way to synthesise vitamin D from the sun. These dietary changes were brought by the spread of a farming culture which originated in the Near East. Whiteness was brought from Near Eastern immigrants to an otherwise Negroid European population.

However, other articles were informing us that genes for light skin, blond hair, and blue eyes may have evolved already among hunter-gatherers in north Europe before Near Eastern farmers arrived. Thus, an archaeological site in Motala, Sweden, dated to 7,700 years ago contained skeletons with genes for light skin, blue eyes, and blond hair.[90] It was the inhabitants of central and southern Europe that remained dark until Neolithic farmers from the Near East with a white skin gene colonised these areas with their farming technologies. This white gene was selected in Europe as the lower vitamin D grain diet from the Near East spread.

All in all, the impression one takes away from reading these articles is that whites are but a blip in the annals of the genetic history of Europe, a

---

88   Tia Ghose, '7,000-Year-Old Human Bones Suggest New Date for Light-Skin Gene.' *Livescience* (January 26, 2014).

89   http://www.dailymail.co.uk/sciencetech/article-1210056/White-Europeans-evolved-5-500-years-ago-food-habits-changed.html#ixzz3iz15h2sI.

90   'Genetic Study offers Evidence of Recent Evolution in Europe' *Archeology* (April 6, 2015).

temporary, rather late phenomenon, in a continent that for the majority of its history has been inhabited by Negroids.

Was He Really the 'First European'?

Some critics of immigration reacted with disbelief at the African-like reconstruction of an early Upper Palaeolithic skull in Europe (see Figure 1 above, created by Dr Richard Neave), as a distortion of the actual profile of the 'first Europeans'. The late Lawrence Auster thus commented in Mathilda's Archeology Blog: 'Can you not think of a reason Neave made it so dark? Are you not aware of the overwhelming moral compulsion that people in our society have to put the black race at the center of things, even to go so far as to claim that the early Europeans were African blacks?'[91]

Mathilda equivocated without a clear response to Auster. There is no question the media used this reconstruction to put Africans at the centre of European ancestry, with the British anthropologist Dr. Alice Roberts gushing over the reconstruction, stating 'I look at that face and think I'm actually looking at the face of [my ancestors] from 40,000 years ago.' Inspired by her ancestors, she went to Africa to trace her roots for a BBC documentary called 'The Incredible Journey', which aired in 2009.[92]

Nevertheless, the fact that this early Upper Palaeolithic inhabitant of Europe was black, and that white skin was a later evolutionary acquisition, actually supports our side of the debate: there has been biological change in humans since Homo sapiens left Africa some 50,000 years ago. The cultural Marxist view that human genetic evolution somehow came to a halt after Homo sapiens migrated out of Africa, as Stephen Jay Gould and Richard Lewontin argued, and as the entire establishment today continues to insist, has been falsified. Moreover, if Europeans did evolve

---

91   https://mathildasanthropologyblog.wordpress.com/2009/05/05/reconstruction-of-an-early-european-skull/#comment-3538.

92   http://www.dailymail.co.uk/sciencetech/article-1177123/The-European-Created-fragments-fossil-face-forbears-35-000-years-ago.html.

in the continent of Europe, then they truly are the indigenous peoples of this continent, the ones selected by this environment, whereas the African-looking Homo sapiens who arrived 'first' were migrants before they started to evolve into Europeans born in this soil.

I need hardly say that we are only scratching the surface of knowledge at this point. We know little about when other racial traits and differences may have evolved in Europe, such as rate of physical maturation, gestation period, more details about body built, blood types, resistance and susceptibility to various diseases, and brain size. However, Hart, in *Understanding Human History*, offers a very useful hypothetical computer model estimating the evolution of IQ among humans in different regions after humans migrated out of Africa. The model assumes that the first Homo sapiens out of Africa had an averaged IQ of 70, in light of the fact that there are many groups living in sub-Sahara Africa today with such an average IQ. From this point, he offers a chronology of the evolution of IQ outside Africa, coming up with the following hypothetical numbers for south and north Europe, and Russia:

CHRONOLOGY OF IQ EVOLUTION					
Years ago	*30,000*	*25,000*	*20,000*	*15,000*	*10,000*
Southern Europe	81	84	87	89	92
Northern Europe	81	85	89	93	96
Russia	81	85	89	93	96

Now, Hart notes that, while rapid technological changes occurred from the beginning of the Upper Palaeolithic era (leading to sewing needles and cave paintings during the Aurignacian era and the bow and arrow in the Solutrean era), most of the innovations occurred during the Magdalenian era, lasting from 18,000 to 11,000 years ago, such as harpoons, fishhooks, spear throwers, and pottery, when the average IQ had risen above 90.[93] Were the Magdalenians the first Europeans?

'Mass Migration of Aryans from Russia Contributed a Lot to the Genetics of Europeans'

Even though recent research on this topic tells us that a mass migration 4,800 years ago of pastoralists from southern Russia contributed up to 50% of ancestry in some north Europeans, this finding has been framed so as to portray Europeans as a 'mixed' racial group consisting of not only Upper Palaeolithic Africans and Near Eastern farmers, but also of immigrants known as 'Yamnaya pastoralists' from the 'Asian' steppes. According to a BBC article, this 'third ancestral group' of Yamnaya people should be 'added to the melting pot' of ancient Europe.[94]

But if we were to concentrate on the actual science of these findings,[95] rather than pushing ideological agendas, we would see that this report of a mass migration from the steppes refers to a culture that is originally from southern Russia, the Yamnaya. The actual research also teaches us that the lineage of the Corded Ware people, located in north-central Europe around the 3rd millennium, were genetically close to the Yamnaya population. Roughly speaking, the genetic link between today's European population and the pastoral societies that migrated to Europe from southern Russia, or present-day Ukraine, is around 50% of the gene pool in Northern and Central Europe, and around 25% in the Iberian Peninsula.

93   Hart, *Understanding History*, pp. 133–136. Cochran and Harpending write of the great leap in innovations that marked the Upper Palaeolithic — cave paintings, jewellery, javelins, hearths, multi-barbed harpoons — but only in contrast to the Neanderthals displaced in Europe. In fact, for all their emphasis on biological change since Homo sapiens migrated out of Africa, they make very general references only about evolution during the Upper Palaeolithic, focussing instead on the contrast between this era and the preceding Neanderthal period, and on the new genetic traits that were selected as a result of changes in diet of the Neolithic era. The same is true of Wade.

94   'Genomes document ancient mass migration to Europe', http://www.bbc.com/news/science-environment-31695214.

95   'Genetic study revives debate on origin and expansion of Indo-European languages in Europe.' *Science Daily* (March 14, 2015).

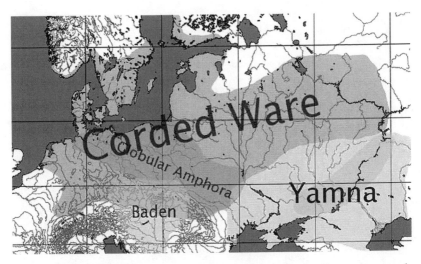

When we consider all the findings I have outlined above, this is the actual 'mixed' picture we get: the ancestors of Europeans consist of:

(1)   Upper Palaeolithic peoples in Europe who became white.

(2)   Near Eastern farmers who are racially classified as 'Caucasian' and brought a 'white gene' to Europe.

(3)   Yamnaya people (i.e. Indo-European speakers, the Aryans) who started coming to Europe 4800 years ago after they had evolved white traits.

But, as we saw in the first chapter in the case of the discipline of psychology, it is not just the mainstream media that engages in deception. Scientists tend now to frame findings in racial matters in politically correct terminology; thus *Nature*, an 'International Weekly Journal of Science', writes of Europe as a 'melting pot' in which Near Eastern farmers encountered blue eyed hunter gatherers 'who arrived from Africa more than 40,000 years ago', joined later by what it calls a 'more mysterious population' of 'Eurasians' (Yamnaya).[96]

---

96   Ellen Callaway, 'Ancient European genomes reveal jumbled ancestry' *Nature* (January 02, 2015).

Another article published in *Nature* in September 2014, a very techni-
cal paper authored by numerous scientists under the title 'Ancient Human
Genomes Suggest Three Ancestral Populations for Present-day Europeans',[97]
did not even used the term 'Indo-European' for this third ancestral population coming from Russia, but instead identified it as a population 'related
to Native Americans'. However, a more re-
cent study [98] is more definite in stating that
the 'Caucasian' genetic traits of the
Yamnaya population were original to the
steppes, belonging to the European continent and the European race, rather than
being of Near Eastern/Caucasian origin. This new study also distinguishes the
Yamnaya-Corded Ware people from other
European-derived populations from the
steppes, such as the Sintashta and
Andronovo, which migrated eastwards
and were gradually replaced by people of
East Asian ancestry or people who shared
ancestry with 'Native American'.

The Tocharians, a Caucasian
people that expanded out into
the Tarim basin, in Western
parts of China. They were an
Indo-European people, with
the standard fair skin and light
hair. The oldest mummy, called
the beauty of Loulan, dates at
about 4,000 years old.

Indo-Europeans were not 'immigrants'
and not a 'mysterious' people coming from
outside to join a European 'melting pot';
they were a people that evolved in the Pontic-Caspian steppes, which is
part of the European continent. There is evidence that the Indo-Europeans
who moved into the Asian side of the steppes, both as Iranian speakers
and as Tocharian speakers, into the Tarim Basin, were 'fair-skinned and
light-haired people', before they were replaced by Mongoloids.[99]

97   Iosif Lazaridis et. al., 'Ancient Human Genomes Suggest Three Ancestral Populations
      for Present-day Europeans.' *Nature* 513, Issue 7518 (September 18, 2014).
98   'Bronze Age population dynamics, selection, and the formation of Eurasian genetic
      structure', http://www.ebi.ac.uk/ena/data/view/PRJEB9021 (June 2015).
99   Mallory, J. P.; Mair, Victor H. The Tarim Mummies: Ancient China and the Mystery
      of the Earliest Peoples from the West. (London: Thames & Hudson, 2000).

'New Genetic Study of UK Shows 10,000 Years of Immigration'

This subheading is the title of an Associated Press article[100] on a recent study about the ancient genetic history of Britain,[101] but what the actual science says, again, is totally the opposite. The genetic makeup of Britain has barely changed in the last 1400 years, and that its ancestral people consists basically of different Celtic populations and Anglo-Saxons, with a bit of Viking blood. Yet, the first sentence of this article reads: 'Immigration might be a hot topic in the current general election campaign, but it's certainly not a recent trend.' When one reads the whole article it becomes transparent, however reluctant the wording is, that the new genetic study actually shows that the population of Britain consists of 'many distinct [Celtic] genetic clusters', Anglo-Saxons, and some Viking blood in Orkney. They could not lie outright about these findings, so they framed them within a pro-immigration agenda in order to dissuade any sense of ancestral identity among the British white population.

The Telegraph (a conservative newspaper) did accurately report the results of this scientific study. Geneticist Sir Walter Bodmer is cited therein: 'What it shows is the extraordinary stability of the British population. Britain hasn't changed much since 600 AD.' The genetic signature of the Viking invaders was restricted to Orkney, and there is also little Roman DNA in the British gene pool. The importance of this finding is that, in the case of Britain, it shows that once the peoples of Europe evolved into Europeans their genetic makeup remained very stable, with no genetic additions from non-Europeans. This is the concluding thought of Bryan Sykes' book, *Saxons, Vikings, and Celts: The Genetic Roots of Britain*: 'We are an ancient people, and though the Isles have been the target of invasion and opposed settlement from abroad ever since Julius Caesar first

---

100 Blathnaid Healy, 'New genetic study of UK shows 10,000 years of immigration and invasions' (March 19. 2015), http://mashable.com/2015/03/19/genetic-map-uk/.

101 Stephen Leslie, et. al.'The fine-scale genetic structure of the British population' *Nature* 509 (March 19, 2015).

stepped on to the shingle shores of Kent, these have barely scratched the topsoil of our deep-rooted ancestry.'[102] The strongest genetic signal, the substructure, is Celtic, followed by Anglo Saxon, with some Viking traces; Roman 'genes are very rare in the Isles'.

The Great Value and Limitations of Wade, Cochran and Harpending

Despite their being published before, in assessing these results the works of Hart, Wade, Cochran and Harpending have been of great use. This is because they are fully cognisant of the genetic changes that occurred in humans after Homo sapiens left Africa. Wade, Cochran and Harpending are really lucid in showing how some gene variants were favoured and gradually increased in frequency, as a result of new environmental pressures and new cultural practices. With their departure from Africa, the Homo sapiens' gene pool was split into different branches in Asia, Australia, Africa, Europe, and then the Americas. Through the process known as genetic drift, and in substantial isolation from each other, these different branches evolved into different races. Cochran and Harpending are very good in challenging the 'conventional wisdom' expressed most notoriously by Stephen Jay Gould and Richard Lewontin that 'there has been no biological change in humans in 40,000 or 50,000 years.'[103] According to this wisdom, all the changes we have witnessed in the past 50,000 years were the product of humans with the same brains changing their cultural artefacts. The development of new technologies and cultural ways, not biology, was responsible for all the changes we have seen in the last 50,000 years.

But Cochran and Harpending turn the tables, arguing that 'culture itself has been an increasingly important part of the human environment.'

---

102 Bryan Sykes, *Saxons, Vikings, and Celts: The Genetic Roots of Britain* (W.W. Norton, 2007), p. 287.

103 These words from Gould are cited in Cochran and Harpending, *The 10,000 Year Explosion*, p. 1.

Not just new habitats, but cultural innovation also resulted in new selective pressures on humans leading to biological change. For example, new techniques of food preparation, such as the use of fire, eventually resulted in humans with smaller teeth. Racial differences such as a prevalence of blue vs. brown eyes and dark vs. light skin, were the product of recent selection. Gene variants in the colour of eyes and skin increased in frequency in response to different environmental and cultural pressures, and this led to marked racial differences in human populations.

Unfortunately, Wade, Cochran and Harpending mainly contrast the behavioural innovations of modern Homo sapiens to the archaic humans of 100,000 years ago and to the Neanderthals in Europe. They do not say much about biological changes during the Upper Paleolithic era inside Europe. [104] They do explain how the culture (and diet) of farming increased the need for vitamin D among farmers living in regions with low levels of ultraviolet light, leading to the selection of light skin. Wade spends considerable time on the emergence of lactose tolerance among the people of the Funnel Beaker culture located in north central Europe, which lasted from 6,000 to 5,000 years ago, or, if I may date it more precisely, from about 4100 BC to 2900 BC. He explains that the Funnel Beaker people's heavy reliance on the herding of cattle and sheep eventually led to the evolution of a genetic trait known as lactose tolerance, or the ability to

---

104 The identification of Upper Palaeolithic Europeans as the 'first Europeans' is common as well in New Right circles, which is understandable since only now we are learning that the first Homo sapiens who arrived in Europe continued to evolve. See the seven-part article by Collin Cleary, 'The Stones Cry Out: Cave Art & the Origin of the Human Spirit' *Counter-Currents Publishing* (January 1–9, 2014). This otherwise very good article draws a distinction, just like Wade, Cochran and Harpending, between the 'behaviorally modern Homo sapiens' who arrived in Europe around 45,000 years ago and the preceding archaic sapiens and Neanderthals, without considering the changes that the first Homo sapiens experienced inside Europe during the Upper Palaeolithic era. Cleary writes that the 'Stone Age European art is simply on a far higher level than that of Africa or North America.' He is focussing mainly on the art of 30,000 thousand years ago, from the Aurignacian era, but it would have been more appropriate to designate this art not as 'European' point blank but as art by 'Europeans-in-the-making'.

digest milk in adulthood. In his view this is a powerful example of how culture (that of animal husbandry/dairy farming) causes genetic changes. I might add that, while the Funnel Beaker people are seen as non-Indo-European, they learned their culture of dairy farming and using wheeled vehicles from their more advanced Indo-European neighbour, the Late Cucuteni-Tripolye culture. The Funnel Beaker culture also made a relatively swift and smooth transition to the Indo-European Corded Ware culture roughly around 2900 BC. Speaking of which, Cochran and Harpending think that what gave Indo-Europeans an 'edge' in their ability to expand across Europe and into the more advanced cultures of Anatolia, Mesopotamia, Iran, and India, was the higher frequency of lactose tolerance among their population due to their culture of dairying pastoralism. Using cattle primarily for milk is more efficient than for raising cattle for slaughter; it 'produces five times more calories per acre,' which increases the ability to raise and feed more warriors per acre. Better nutrition also produced Indo-Europeans that were on average four inches taller than people relying on grain farming without dairy products. [105] Cochran and Harpending also play up Indo-Europeans as highly mobile pastoralists who relied on carts pulled by oxen and horse-riding, who were organised into warlike and patriarchal clans 'constantly raiding for cattle and revenge,' with individual men joining 'egalitarian warrior brotherhoods' dedicated to berserker warfare. All of this, together with their more nutritious diet, 'produced a far more aggressive culture' energising them across Eurasia.

This view fits with the argument I advance in *Uniqueness* about how the aristocratic culture of Indo-Europeans constituted the original foundation of the West's far more creative and dynamic path. I wonder whether this lifestyle left an imprint on the genetics of Indo-Europeans, producing personality traits, such as a greater willingness to take risks and to be aware of oneself as an individual rather than being completely submerged within one's group. Cochran and Harpending only offer general

---

105 Cochran and Harpending, pp. 181–183.

statements about how some populations are selected for submission to authority, but one can indeed envision the culture of Indo-Europeans as having selected for highly strung individuals with a strong sense of aristocratic pride and quick to take offence. This is an argument, however, that is far more difficult to prove scientifically than the emergence of lactose tolerance, and which requires further research.

Jean Manco's Ancestral Journeys

There is strong genetic evidence showing that once a European subrace emerged inside Europe, it did not experience any major genetic mixing from non-European races, aside from with Caucasoid Neolithic arrivals from the Near East (who spread across the Mediterranean from 7000 BC onwards through Sardinia, Corsica, Italy, Spain, Portugal, Greece, and into the Balkans from around 6200 BC). Farming would transform the way of life of most Europeans by 4000 BC, but in the northern regions the spread involved less a migration of peoples and more a movement of farming ideas. This is the message contained within the (thus far) most in-depth discussion on European genetic history; Jean Manco's *Ancestral Journeys: The Peopling of Europe from the First Venturers to the Vikings*. This book draws on the recent ability of geneticists to trace ancestry and human migrations by studying two types of DNA, mtDNA, which traces direct chains of descent from mother to maternal grandmother, and Y-DNA, which traces descent from father to paternal grandfather. Using this technique it investigates the 'peopling' of Europe from the 'first Europeans' all the way to the Viking era.

One would think, however, upon reading the opening two chapters that Manco gives credence to the view that Europe was a cauldron of race mixing since prehistoric times. She observes that an 'anti-migrationist' view prevailed from the 1960s until recently, in a political climate in which 'invasion and colonisation were no longer appealing concepts' and emphasis on 'indigenous cultures' was popular among academics in the

West.[106] But this idea, she informs us, has now lost its appeal with more and more studies offering a view in which mobility and migrations were the norm in European societies since the Stone Age. She writes:

> The continent was not barred to incomers after the arrival of the earliest human beings. On the contrary, the tracks of Neolithic arrivals from the Near East can be seen in DNA. Nor were the Neolithic waves of migration the last ones of importance. Movements in the ages of metal had a massive impact, as did those after the fall of Rome.[107]

She claims that waves of migrants moved across the boundary that separates Europe and Asia, the Ural Mountains, and across the Mediterranean. Yet, when one reads the rest of the book, most of the 'invaders' and 'migrants' she mentions actually came from within Europe's boundaries, and the ones coming from outside barely had any genetic impact on Europeans, except for the impact of Near Eastern Caucasians on certain regions of southern Europe. This is the reason for her claim that there is a 'high degree of genetic similarity among Europeans.'[108]

Manco avoids any discussion of race, the word does not even come up, but in a rather revealing passage in which she refers to the facial reconstruction (see Figure 1 above) by Richard Neave of the 40,000–35,000 old skull discovered in Romania, which portrayed the 'first European' as a 'mixture of modern western Eurasian, East Asian and sub-Saharan African,' she slips in the following scientific judgment: 'The continental differences we see today had yet to evolve.'[109] That is, the continental differences in racial features between the populations of the continents of Europe, Asia, and Africa had yet to evolve; the emergence of a unique European sub-race out of the Caucasoid race had yet to occur. But Manco does not discuss this evolution. Nevertheless, on the basis of Manco's observations on migration patterns, I can confidently assert that barely any

---

106 Manco, *Ancestral Journeys*, p. 15.

107 Ibid., p. 12.

108 Ibid., p. 13.

109 Ibid., p. 49.

race mixing took place in Europe other than the mixing occasioned in the south through the arrival of Near Eastern farmers. Let me outline Manco's observations.

Manco says there is no sign of Neanderthal blood in the 'few Paleolithic Europeans whose mtDNA has been retrieved or in people living today'.[110] From the time Paleolithic hunters first arrived in Europe some 45,000 years ago until the first farmers arrived after 7000 BC, Manco's only example of DNA from outside the continent of Europe interacting with Europeans comes by way of the speakers of Uralic languages, spread through Baltic Europe into Russia-Asia. After emphasising the mixture brought by Near Eastern farmers, particularly in some southern areas of Europe, she highlights the arrival of dairy farming into the Funnel Beaker culture (mentioned above) in the North European plain, by way of the Late Cucuteni-Tripolye culture, an Indo-European culture located near the Black Sea. In fact, everything Manco says about the Indo-Europeans is consistent with my thoughts and what I wrote in *Uniqueness* about the greater mobility of Indo-Europeans. She adds that Tocharians were the first Indo-European pastoralist culture to bring domesticated sheep and horses into the Altai, and that China 'gained domesticated sheep, horses and wheeled vehicles', starting as early as 2500 BC, 'via this trail across the steppe' from the Urals into what is now northwest China.[111] She refers to the Tocharian mummies discovered in the Tarim Basin as 'western-ers' in appearance.[112] She agrees with Cochran and Harpending that what allowed Indo-Europeans to spread was 'the genetic edge' gained from lactose tolerance.[113]

Manco not only emphasises the importance of the Yamnaya spread into Europe, but shows the intimate cultural, linguistic and genetic connections between the current white British and the Bell-Beakers people, who brought the Bronze Age into the British Isles and laid the

---

110   Ibid., p. 56.
111   Ibid., pp. 128–129.
112   Ibid.
113   Ibid., p. 157.

Celtic foundations of Britain. In other words, the Celtic ancestry of Britain is connected to the Indo-European movement out of the steppes, the Corded Ware and Yamnaya horizon, and directly to the Bell Beaker culture (2700–2000 BC), which spread over a large area of Europe, and is presumed to have spoken a Proto-Italo-Celtic language. The Bell-Beaker culture brought the Bronze Age to the Isles around 2400 BC, and there melded with the descendants of the hunter-gatherers who had come back to Britain after the last Ice Age 12,000 years ago. Likewise, Manco shows that the Angles and Saxons who colonised Britain around AD 400–600 came from the Proto-Germanic Corded Ware and Bell-Beaker cultures that had mixed during the Nordic Bronze Age (1730–760 BC) in Jutland, or what is present day Denmark, and the coasts of Norway and Sweden (where they had in turn melded with the descendants of the Funnel Beaker and Ertebolle cultures).

Having connected the Mycenaeans to the Indo-Europeans, she writes that the Classical Greeks 'came to think of themselves as European.'[114] She refers to Rome as a 'melting pot', but then adds that those contemporaneous Roman authors, in the first centuries AD, who 'railed against the level of immigration' for diluting the Roman character, were 'rather short-sighted' since the Italian-born, she estimates, made up about 95% of its inhabitants.[115] She writes about the 'great wandering' of the Germanic peoples who overran the Roman empire (the Goths, Gepids, Vandals, Burgundians, Angles and Saxons), as evidence of her 'migrationist' thesis. However, not only were these movements strictly intra-European affairs, but, as she observes, 'we should not expect much, if any, genetic distinction between these peoples. They were of the same stock.'[116]

She writes about the Slavic movements and expansions between 300–700 AD through what we today consider to be Slavic countries, yet goes on to emphasise 'the striking genetic similarity of Slavic speakers...Slavic

114 Ibid., p. 177.
115 Ibid., p. 199.
116 Ibid., p. 213.

populations are more similar across national boundaries than non-Slavic nations.'[117] She describes the movements of Bulgars and Magyars in the 7th century AD, two mobile peoples from the Asian side of the steppes, connected to the Turkic-Mongoloid in race. But she then informs us that, while the Bulgars gave their name to Bulgaria, the Bulgarians of today are genetically similar to Slavic speakers, with genes distinctive for Asian Turkic speakers occurring in only 1.5% of Bulgarians. While the Magyars gave their Ugric language to Hungary, 'modern Hungarians appear genetically much like their Slavic neighbors', for even though the Magyars imposed their rule upon a Slavic population, subsequent migrations from Slavs diluted the Magyar input to Hungary.[118]

Thus, for all the 'anti-migrationist' thinking Manco adheres to, in conformity with the expectations of the cultural world she operates within, the essential message we should take from her book is that Europeans have remained a very cohesive subrace through their entire history, apart from some Caucasoid input from the Near East. Manco's correct observation that Europeans were a restless people predisposed to mobility in no way supports any notion about 'waves of immigrants' coming into Europe from the outside. Rather, as we will see in chapter 4, the restlessness of Europeans was originally grounded in their dairy pastoralism, wheel-vehicle and horse-riding techniques, combined with their aristocratic spirit. Mass immigration into Europe is a phenomenon of post WWII promoted by our current traitorous elites. The elites in charge of our precious heritage have no qualms with lying and misusing science to promote white genocide. Europeans evolved in the course of time inside Europe and have remained European through almost their entire history.

Non-Western Civilisations are Easy

Now, having established that a European subrace evolved in Europe, remaining very stable genetically with minimal outside racial mixing, here

---

117   Ibid., p. 224.
118   Ibid., pp. 235–240.

is a revised answer to the question I brought up in chapter 1: where has the historical West been in the course of time as created by this subrace? This is not an easy question to answer for the simple reason that the West has been, by far, the most dynamic territorial civilisation, making it very difficult to trace geographically and to determine whether those areas governed by the West were really Western, considering that their peoples were not of the European subrace. By contrast, non-Western civilisations are relatively easy to locate on historical maps. Their borders and sizes may have changed over time, they may have disappeared altogether, but we can simply identify Mesopotamian civilisations, the ancient Sumerian city-states (3000–2340 BC), the Akkadian Empire (2340–2150 BC), the rise of the Sumerian city at Ur (2112–2000 BC), which witnessed a final flowering of Sumerian culture, or the Amorites/Old Babylonians, rulers of this region from 2000 to about 1550 BC, best known for the Code of Hammurabi (1700s). We can identify the cultures/civilisations of ancient Egypt, the Mayas, Aztecs, Incas, the empire of Ghana (900–1180 AD), the Songhai Kingdom in Africa (1450–1600 AD).

We can also identify the Shang dynasty (1766–1050 BC), known as the first Chinese civilisation, and all subsequent kingdoms up until the current territory of China.[119] The borders of China certainly changed over time. Sometimes it was unified under a stable dynastic order extended over a wide area, sometimes it was divided into two dynasties, sometimes occupied by external rulers (as was the case when the Mongols ruled, 1206–1368), and sometimes the country was characterised by intense competition between city-states each dominated by its own dynasty (as was the case during the Warring States period, 481–221 BC). But these changes occurred within a clearly identifiable geographic location. The overall tendency of China's history has been toward occupation and dispossession of non-Han ethnic peoples by the Han majority. From their original homeland along the Yellow River, the Han Chinese, through successive waves of immigration, demographic expansion, and bureaucratic

---

119   John Haywood, *Atlas of World History* (MetroBooks, 2000).

consolidation, dispossessed one ethnic group after another, from the tropical regions below the Yangtze River, from the jungles of the south-west regions known as Guangdong, Guangxi, Guizhou, and from Yunnan and Sichuan. During the 1700s, 'Outer China', a vast territory controlled by Mongols, Turkish and Tibetan-stock peoples, was taken over politically and demographically. During 1800s, Manchuria and Taiwan were forcibly colonised and the indigenous cultures liquidated. Tibet's inhabitants are currently experiencing displacement by masses of Chinese migrants.[120] Thus was born The People's Republic of China, a clearly identifiable civilisation with a clearly identifiable ethnic character. According to the 2010 census, 91.51% of the population in China is ethnic Han.

Throughout its entire history Japanese civilisation, except for its short lived empire in the 1930s and 40s, has generally remained located where Japan is today, with its own unique ethnicity even though it borrowed much from China (its writing system, the ideas of Confucianism and Buddhism, the bureaucratic methods of government, city-planning, road systems, artistic and architectural styles). The ethnic Japanese, which is often use in some contexts to refer to smaller sub-ethnic Japanese groups such as the Yamato, Ainu and Ryukyuan people, comprise 98.5% of the total population, with the rest consisting mostly of Koreans and Chinese. Today, as the world's third largest trading nation, Japan's economy is tightly enmeshed with the world's economy; yet Japan is still a separate place enjoying the same ethnic homogeneity of the past, unwilling to open its borders to immigration despite a fertility rate standing at 1.1 children per woman, coupled with the oldest population in the world. When we look at a historic map of Japan we are certain it is the land of the Japanese.[121]

Islamic civilisation is trickier to identify on a map. The terms 'Islamic' and 'Muslim' do not refer to a common racial, ethnic, or national group. Throughout much of history and still today they refer to a wide variety of cultures, ethnic groups and nation states, following Islam's expansion out

---

120　Caroline Blunden and Mark Elvin, *Cultural Atlas of China* (Stonehenge Press, 1992).
121　Albert M. Craig, *The Heritage of Japanese Civilization* (Prentice Hall, 2010).

of the Arabian peninsula in the 7th century. From its beginnings, it expanded into areas previously populated not just by other ethnic groups and cultures but by far more advanced civilisations. These civilisations were conquered by Arabic forces, including the lands of ancient Mesopotamia, Persia, Egypt, and former Roman lands. Although historians speak of the 'golden age of Islamic civilisation' under the Abbasid Dynasty, which ruled from the mid-8th century until the mid-13th century across the near East, north Africa, and Spain, this 'golden age' was a blending of Persian, Mesopotamian, Egyptian, and Greco-Roman achievements, mostly borrowed with some Muslim input in pharmaceutics, optics, and astronomy.

In the 1400s, the Turks, a people from the steppes who had converted to Islam, conquered much of Greece (widely seen as the birth place of Western civilisation), capturing Constantinople in 1453 and replacing Byzantium with the Ottoman Empire. The Ottomans would expand right to the 'gates of Vienna' in the 1500s. Earlier Muslims came to occupy most of the Visigoth Kingdom in Spain in 716 AD (with only the northern reaches of Spain remaining in Christian hands), although Islamic Spain was eventually reconquered by the Spaniards by the end of the 15th century. Today, all of North Africa, parts of sub-Sahara Africa and most of Eastern Africa is Muslim; as is Pakistan, huge parts of India, and Indonesia.[122]

Despite this geographical and cultural diversity, scholars readily identify these lands as part of the Muslim world. They do so in the degree to which they agree that the term 'Muslim world' is a religious term which refers to those who adhere to the teachings of Islam. While the Islamic world covers countries with varying ethnicities, religiously speaking Muslim places include locations where one can identify a community of Muslims (*Ummah*) living under the precepts of the Koran, a religious text which universalises the term 'Muslim' by applying it to the tribe writ large: the whole Muslim world envisioned as a single people. The Islamic world numbers between 1.2 and 1.6 billion people, roughly one-fifth of

---

122   Efraim Karsh, *Islamic Imperialism* (Yale University Press, 2007).

humanity, spread across many different sovereign states and ethnic groups but consisting almost entirely of non-Europeans and non-Orientals. The initial expansion during the Umayyad period (660–750) should be seen as an Arabic effort to wrest control away from Greco-Roman and Persian influences in the name of a Semitic Empire with its own Semitic religion. It is determined to govern the fates of men with the arbitrary despotism typical of an Eastern monarch.[123]

India is touted today as the most multicultural, ethnically diverse country in the world. This country is home to four major racial groups, which overlap due to racial admixture: Caucasoids, Australoids, Mongoloids and Negritos. With over two thousand ethnic groups, four major families of languages, and multiple religions (Hindus do comprise the vast majority at 80.5% with Islam at 13.4%), India, in the words of Coon, is 'the most complicated geographically, racially, and culturally'.[124] Yet all these racial groups are descendants of waves of invaders centuries ago; immigration is practically non-existent today, apart from a trickling of Bangladeshi, Pakistani, and Burmese migrants. With its endogamous rules, India has remained racially stable for centuries; its caste divisions have been historically deep, with limited gene flows across racial boundaries. The racial differences that exist can still be traced back to the migrations into India before Christ. The Indian racial populations can be well demarcated as separate from most of the other Asian populations, from the Persian Gulf, Arabia, Burma, China, Vietnamese and Malayan lands. It is not a complicated land to locate on a map; historically the country has always been located more or less in the same place.[125]

123 For this interpretation, see Christopher Dawson, *The Making of Europe* (Sheed & Ward, London, 1935), pp. 135–168.

124 *The Living Races of Man*, p. 191.

125 Herman Kulke and Dietmar Rothermund, *A History of India* (Routledge, 1990).

The West is Difficult

The European peoples, as the creators of Western civilisation, are the most difficult to identify geographically for two reasons:

(1) The West has been the most dynamic territorially, developing across many lands, while advancing to higher stages of knowledge and power in the course of which it experienced 'rises' and 'declines' in different territories

(2) The West is the only civilisation with a developmental pattern characterised by dramatic alternations in its philosophical outlooks and institutions.

All in all, the West has displayed far more territorial movements, cultural novelties, and revolutions in the sciences and arts. For this reason, answering 'where is the West?' requires one to ask 'what is the West?' with an awareness of the fact that both the 'what' and the 'where' have changed over time.[126] This civilisation, for example, is not simply 'Christian' in the way others are 'Confucian' or 'Hindu' in a more stable, less varying way. Its Christian character alone has been infused with a theological and institutional dynamic (flowing from its synthesis with Classical reason and Indo-European aristocratic expansionism) stimulating a multiplicity of monastic movements (i.e. Cluniacs, Cistercians, Franciscans, Dominicans etc.) and heterodox movements (Pelagians, Waldensians, Cathars etc.), not to mention Crusades and numerous Protestant denominations lacking elsewhere.[127] The West — depending on locality, time, and groups — has been

---

126 On the 'continuous creativity' of Europeans, see *Uniqueness*; reviewed by Kevin MacDonald, 'Going Against the Tide,' *The Occidental Quarterly*, 11, 3 (Fall 2011), 47–74.

127 Christopher Dawson argues in *Religion and the Rise of Western Culture* (1950), that the 'sharp dualism' between 'the war society' of the Germanic barbarians 'with its cult of heroism and aggression,' and 'the peace society of the Christian Church with its ideals of asceticism and renunciation and its high theological culture [...] is to be regarded as the principal source of that dynamic element which is of such decisive significance for Western culture' (p. 23). This view should be contrasted to the often mentioned view associated with Leo Strauss which highlights the 'dynamic tension'

Platonic, Aristotelian, Epicurean, Stoic, Cynic, Augustinian, Monarchist, Newtonian, Gothic, Anglican, Humanist, Republican, Machiavellian, Hegelian, Fascist, Marxist, Darwinian, Surrealist, Cubist, Romantic, Socialist, Liberal, and much more. By contrast, the intellectual traditions set down in ancient/medieval times in China, the Near East, India, and Japan would persist in their essentials until the impact of the West brought some novelties.

We must have a sense of the changing cultural character of the West when we ask where it is. The West in Roman times is not the same West in Classical Greece, and the West in Elizabethan England is not the same in Renaissance Italy. Parts of the Roman Empire ceased to be Western, and huge parts of the world previously not Western became Western, i.e. Australia and North America. Much of the Hellenistic world never became Western, and Classical Greece fell out of the West in Ottoman times. What I will do first is locate the West by way of a rough outline of the major epochs that shaped it.

The West originated and expanded:

(1) Through the spreading out of the aristocratic warlike cultures of the pre-historic Indo-Europeans out of the Pontic Steppes into Europe after the 4th millennium BC.

(2) Through the successful establishment in the Greek mainland of the Mycenaean civilisation, starting in the 2nd millennium until its eclipse in the 1100s.

(3) Through the flourishing of Hellenic Classical culture in the period between 800 and 300 BC.

(4) Through the Macedonian conquests of Alexander the Great and the creation of the Hellenistic World from 323 BC onwards.

---

between the Bible and Greek Philosophy, faith and reason, to the neglect of the aristocratic warrior ethos of Indo-Europeans, their will, passion, and heroic pursuit of glory. Strauss's view is intended to place the Hebrew Bible at the centre of the West, while ignoring altogether the Indo-Europeans and the Germanic peoples who conquered Rome and generated the Medieval Catholic flowering.

(5) Through the rise of Rome to its greatest extent in the 3rd century AD until its end around 500 AD.

(6) Through the Germanic invasions and the revival of the aristocratic Indo-European spirit.

(7) Through the rise of Christianity in fusion with Greco-Roman culture and its dynamic spread through the Mediterranean world and Europe.

(8) Through the medieval enlargement of Christendom's frontiers and the stretching of the West's boundaries into north and eastern Europe, solidifying the Catholic High Middle Ages.

(9) Through the rise of cities, the Renaissance, and the Discovery of the World in the 16th century.

(10) Through the rise of Modern Science and the spread of Industrialisation.

(11) Through the spread of Bourgeois Institutions and the Enlightenment.

(12) Finally through the pioneering migration of whites into North America and Australia leading to the creation of three massive new countries.

The Indo-Europeans

The above claims call for many questions in need of immediate answers. Firstly: who are the Indo-Europeans and why is their culture/geographical movements the first to be classified as Western? As we briefly saw above, Indo-Europeans were Homo sapiens who evolved into a European subrace within the continent of Europe in the Pontic steppes (not to be confused with the 'Asian' steppes located east of the Urals). They were a pastoral people who initiated the most mobile way of life in prehistoric times, starting with the riding of horses and the invention of wheeled vehicles in the 4th millennium BC, together with the efficient exploitation of the 'secondary products' of domestic animals (dairy products, textiles, harnessing of animals), large-scale herding, and the invention of chariots in the 2nd millennium. By the end of the 2nd millennium they had 'Indo-Europeanised' the continent of Europe culturally, with some intermixing with their racial compatriots in 'Old Europe' (i.e. Europe before their arrival) which initiated the Bronze Age. The Indo Europeans who came into Anatolia, Syria, Mesopotamia were eventually absorbed into the far more advanced and populated non-White civilisations of this region; these regions outside Europe were not Indo-Europeanised, except temporarily or marginally.

As explained in *Uniqueness* (and later in this book), the Indo-Europeans were uniquely ruled by a class of free aristocrats grouped into war-bands. These bands were contractual associations of men operating outside strictly blood ties, initiated by any powerful individual on the merits of his martial abilities. The relation between the chief and his followers was personal and based on mutual agreement: the followers would volunteer to be bound to the leader by oaths of loyalty wherein they would promise to assist him while the leader would promise to reward them from successful raids. This aristocratic culture was the primordial source of Western heroic individualism, originality, and Faustian expansion.

The Indo-Europeans colonised Europe. Starting from their homelands in present-day Ukraine, the Sredni Stog culture (4200–3400 BC) was followed and displaced by the Yamnaya culture (3400–2300), which spread across the Caspian region and moved into the Danube region. This was followed by the Corded Ware or Battle Axe culture, which spread across northern Europe from the Ukraine to Belgium after 3000 BC. Finally, the Bell-Beaker culture emerged, which grew within Europe and spread further westwards into Spain and northwards into England and Ireland between 2800–1800 BC.[128] The Indo-Europeans also spread eastwards across

---

128 The best book on the archeology of this subject is David Anthony's *The Horse, the Wheel, and Language: How Bronze-Age Riders from the Eurasian Steppes Shaped the Modern World* (Princeton, 2007).

the steppes as far as the Tarim Basin in present-day Xinjiang, China, but these groups were eventually Asianised.

European Connections

The second question one must ask is how to separate the West geographically from the Near East, Africa, and even Asia? Parts of Africa and the Near East were included into the Roman Empire and the Hellenistic world included Persia, Bactria, Sogdiana, even lands adjacent to the Indus River. The eastern boundaries of the European continent itself extend to the Ural Mountains, cutting Russia into European and Asian parts. While the Mediterranean Sea separates Europe from Asia and Africa, historically it has been the major source of Europe's connection to the Near East leading some historians to conclude that Ancient Greece, Rome, and Renaissance Italy are best identified as 'Mediterranean'. Cultural Marxists have exploited these connections to promote 'Mediterranean Studies' against the traditional Classic programs. Europe's very uniqueness, its dynamism, explorations, colonisation, and Westernisation, has obscured its identity and boundaries.

From a strictly geographical point, irrespective of historical connections, Europe *is* the most connected region of the planet. It is not even a clear continent on its own but a peninsula on the western end of Asia. With its deeply convoluted coasts and its scattered island fragments, the sheer length of Europe's interface between land and sea has been estimated to be 37,000 km, which is equivalent to the circumference of the earth. Europe is connected to more seas than any other place or civilisation, accessing the Black Sea, the North sea, the Baltic, the Atlantic Ocean, the Arctic Ocean, and the Mediterranean Sea, which is itself a collection of many conjoined 'sub-seas'.[129]

In contrast, China has been a relatively isolated civilisation, both geographically and historically. On the eastern side stands the vast Pacific

---

129   Michel Mollat du Jourdin, *Europe and the Sea* (Blackwell, 1995).

Ocean; to the south and the west, the impassable gorges of the Burma border and the inhospitable plateau of the Tibetan Himalayas, and to the northwest and north, the sparsely populated grasslands of Central Asia and the Gobi desert, the fifth largest desert in the world. Contact with other regions did occur, with India through the northwest corridor, with the Arab world by sea, and through the Silk Road along the steppes. But the salient point is that China has developed her own culture in a far less connected way than Europe.

Black African kingdoms have been very isolated: sub-Saharan Africa is surrounded by the Sahara Desert in the north, which hindered contact with the Mediterranean, and by the Kalahari Desert in the south, which partially disconnected the southern plateau and coastal regions from central Africa. On the western side, Africa is faced by the vast Atlantic Ocean that Portuguese navigators only managed to navigate southwards in the 16th century. To the north and south of the equator, Black Africa had to contest with dense rainforests which occupy a west-east band of territory from the southern coast of West Africa across to the Congo basin and all the way to the Kenya highlands. Moreover, with an average elevation of 660 meters, African cultures were limited by the presence of few natural harbours where ships can dock, and few navigable rivers. Of the Niger, the Congo, the Nile, the Zambezi, and the Orange Rivers, only the Nile has relatively long navigable areas.

The Hellenistic World

Europe's connectedness has created much confusion and opened the door for the imposition of a Trotskyite program claiming that Europe's history was dictated by developments occurring elsewhere. However, despite its many connections, external influences, internal changes and colonising, prior to the open borders policies Europe could be identified geographically and racially with a good degree of certainty.[130] Identifying

---

130 In addition to the sources cited below, this overview of the location of the West, as well as the location of the non-West, draws on key standard texts used in courses

the Mycenaeans and Classical Greece is easy enough, as these were European-centred polities. The difficulty starts with the Hellenistic world, a vast area testifying to the vigour of Europeans yet hardly 'Western' beyond the main cities. Western Civilisation textbooks always include a full chapter on the Hellenistic era to describe a period of about three centuries, roughly from 323 BC to 30 BC. During this time Greek culture, after the conquests of Alexander the Great, was spread over a remarkably large area, including Egypt and far into the Iranian plateau. The significance of the Hellenistic era, however, does not consist in the vast areas and diverse peoples it covered, but in the *high* cultural accomplishments this period saw in literature, art, science, medicine, and philosophy *led by ethnic Greek individuals*, particularly in the cities of Alexandria and Pergamum.[131] The new schools of philosophy (Epicureanism and Stoicism) were actually centred in Athens, including the characteristics of Hellenistic sculpture and literature, were all Greek. Moreover, it should be emphasised that this epoch produced the first true scientists in human history, as argued by Lucio Russo in *The Forgotten Revolution: How Science Was Born in 300 BC and Why it Had to Be Reborn*.[132] What Russo argues in great detail has long been known by Classicists. For example, Marshall Clagett, in *Greek Science in Antiquity* (1955), calls the Hellenistic period 'the great period of Greek science', correctly identifying the Presocratics as philosophers rather than scientists, and offering an overview of the original writings of Strato, Aristarchus, Eudoxos, Erastosthenes, Hipparchus, and Archimedes.[133] This Hellenistic accomplishment in science should

---

over the years, namely, *The Heritage of World Civilizations*, by Craig et al. (Prentice Hall, Sixth Ed., 2003); *Europe, A History*, by Norman Davies (Pimlico, 1996); Jackson Spielvogel, *Western Civilization, Volume A: to 1500* (Wadsworth, 2012).

131   Theodore Vrettos, *Alexandria. City of the Western Mind* (Free Press, 2001).

132   *The Forgotten Revolution: How Science Was Born in 300 BC and Why it Had to Be Reborn* (Springer-Verlag, 2000).

133   Marshall Clagett, *The Science of Mechanics in the Middle Ages* (Madison: University of Wisconsin Press, 1959). See also excellent readable account by David Lindberg, *The Beginnings of Western Science. The European Scientific Tradition in Philosophical, Religious, and Institutional Context, 600 BC to AD 1450* (The University of Chicago Press, 1992).

actually be extended beyond 31 BC to cover the ideas of Euclid, Ptolemy, and Galen in the first two centuries AD in mathematics, solid and fluid mechanics, optics, astronomy, and anatomy.

The four Hellenistic kingdoms which emerged as Alexander's successors (i.e. Macedonia, the Seleucid kingdom in Mesopotamia, the Ptolemy dynasty in Egypt and the Pergamum kingdom in western Asia Minor) involved a clash and fusion of different cultures and ethnic groups. However, the political elites and high culture of these kingdoms were thoroughly Greek. The Greek/Macedonian rulers of these kingdoms encouraged the spread of Greek colonists to the Near East, with the result that cities were created replicating the architecture and political institutions of the Hellenic homeland. These new urban centres were completely dominated by Greeks, while natives remained cut off from all civic institutions. One scholar describes the relationship between the Greek/Macedonian elite and the rest of the population in terms of 'ethnic segregation'.[134] In the Seleucid kingdom, which is the Hellenistic kingdom furthest to the east, only 2.5% of the people in authority were non-Greek, and most of these were in local military positions.[135] A small percentage of non-Greeks adopted Greek language, culture and identity, but barely outside the cities. Hellenistic cities are best described as islands of Greek culture in a sea of non-Greeks

Despite this lack of Greekness in the demography of the Hellenistic kingdoms, the important role of Hellenistic Greeks in the making of the West is unmistakable. The legacy of this epoch lies in the amplification of Greek culture, eventually absorbed by the Romans. Almost all the area occupied by the Greeks in the East would be reabsorbed culturally by its non-European inhabitants. By the 2nd century AD, the Indo-Iranian world would go on to revive and develop their traditional cultural forms. The Sassanid Empire (224–651 AD) drew on Hellenistic, Bactrian-Indian,

---

134 Azar Gat, *Nations: The Long History and Deep Roots of Political Ethnicity and Nationalism* (Cambridge University Press), pp. 118–119.

135 Jackson Spielvogel, *Western Civilization, Volume A: to 1500* (Wadsworth, 2012), p. 99.

and Roman influences, but they championed above all else Iranian legitimacy, claimed to be the rightful heirs of the Persian rulers before the conquest of Alexander, and institutionalised Zoroastrian ritual and theology as state orthodoxy. Under the age of the Guptas (320–550 AD), Indian culture evolved with little outside influences from the West until Muslim times; her contacts were with Southeast Asia and China and most of these were from India to the east rather than the other way around. But the legacy of the Hellenistic era, or more accurately, the Greeks at large, not only survived but mightily shaped the culture of the Romans.[136] Although the Romans conquered much of the Hellenistic world, they became, as the Roman poet Horace said, captives of its culture. They seriously cultivated the study of the Greek language, literature, philosophy, and the idea of an education in the humanities. By the last century of the Republic, with the Greek legacy copiously assimilated, the Romans were ready to produce their own towering literary figures in the names of Cicero, Lucretius, Virgil, Horace, Ovid, and Livy. While the Hellenistic scientific contribution was not developed theoretically to its full extent by the practical Romans, the post-Renaissance revolution of the 17th was due to the conscious recovery of the Hellenistic deductive/experimental method in mathematics, mechanics of solids and fluids, anatomy, medicine, and cognitive sciences.[137]

Rome

The Roman Empire was extended over many lands that were racially non-European, and in North Africa and the Near East these would fall out of the Western orbit with the decline of Roman rule. On the other hand, the Romans ruled over areas in Europe that would also break out of Roman rule, such as the territory of present day Germany and regions in northern

---

136 Arnold Toynbee, 'Rome's Reception of Hellenism,' in *Hellenism, The History of a Civilization* (Oxford University, 1959), pp. 143–162.

137 Lucio Russo, *The Forgotten Revolution: How Science Was Born in 300 BC and Why it Had to Be Reborn.*

and eastern Europe, which were European racially and would continue the Western tradition. Although this is a long discussion, there is a tendency among some scholars to identify Rome as a multiracial empire, but this is a mistake. As Azar Gat has observed in *Nations: The Long History and Deep Roots of Political Ethnicity and Nationalism*, ethnicity was no less an important component of the makeup of empires generally than domination by social elites over a tax paying peasantry or slave force. 'Almost universally they were either overtly or tacitly the empires of a particular people or ethnos.'[138] While Gat does not identify the Romans and Italians as a race, but writes of the Romans and Italians as ethnic groups with their own distinctive culture, it is worth noting first that the Etruscans were the only non-Indo-European people in the Italian peninsula, and secondly that as the Romans defeated all other ethnic groups in Italy they imposed a process of acculturation to Roman ways. This was achieved through elite connections, military service, and eventually the granting of citizenship. Citizenship was granted to all Italian residents after the so-called Social War of 91–88 BC. Gat writes that 'if ethnic differences in Italy were still noticeable at the beginning of the 1st century BC, they had practically disappeared by the end of that century. By the time of Augustus, the concepts of Roman and Italian had become virtually identical.'[139]

Now, it is true that as the process of Romanisation continued, in 212 AD the entire free population in the Empire, including members of other races, was given citizenship status. This means, however, that before this rather late date in Rome's history, the vast majority of those who held Roman citizenship were Italian. Moreover, historians agree that the only reason the Emperor Caracalla extended citizenship was to expand the Roman tax base. All in all, the acquisition of citizenship came in graduated levels with promises of further rights with increased assimilation; and, right until the end, not all citizens had the same rights, with Romans and Italians generally enjoying a higher status. Rome was a very Eurocentric

---

138 *Nations: The Long History and Deep Roots of Political Ethnicity and Nationalism* (Cambridge University Press, 2013), p. 111.

139 Ibid., p. 120.

empire. Beyond citizenship, Romanisation was largely successful in the Western half of the empire, i.e. Italy, Gaul, and Iberia, all of which were Indo-European in race. Meanwhile, the Eastern Empire retained its upper crust of Greekness, with a mass of Mesopotamian, Egyptian, Judaic, Persian, and Assyrian peoples following their ancient ways, virtually untouched by Roman culture. The process of Romanisation and expansion of citizenship was effective only in the Western (Indo-European) half of the Empire, where inhabitants were European in race; whereas in the East it had superficial effects apart from the Greek inhabitants.[140]

Byzantium

The Byzantine empire is also a case study that offers major difficulties to anyone trying to identify the historical geography of the West, for it is a culture all of its own in many ways and yet one that played a 'core' role in the making of the West culturally while being racially European in a very limited way. It is also a civilisation that fell out of the Western orbit for centuries, to be become an Islamic 'core' region under the Ottomans. Byzantium was born out of the 'Eastern' Roman Empire. The division of Rome into 'Eastern' and 'Western' parts may be traced to the period from Diocletian (c. 284–305) to Valentinian (c. 364–375), but what is worth noticing is that, despite later efforts to unify Rome again, and despite the continued influence of Greek culture in the Eastern side, these two halves of Rome would become increasingly separate and different, with the Eastern half becoming another civilisation called Byzantium, and the Western half becoming the basis of Catholic Europe proper.

Historians do not generally assign a date as to when Byzantium was born, but an important point is Emperor Constantine I's transfer in 324 AD of the capital of the Eastern Empire from Nicomedia (in Anatolia) to Byzantium on the Bosporus, which became Constantinople (sometimes

---

140 Bill Warwick writes in his book, *Rome in the East: The Transformation of an Empire* (Routledge, 2000), that Roman rule in the regions of Syria, Jordan, and northern Iraq was 'a story of the East more than of the West.'

called the 'New Rome.') In any case, the Eastern Roman Empire would eventually be distinguished from ancient Rome proper as a separate culture called Byzantium, as it became oriented towards Greek culture and Christianity became its official religion (in 394 AD), rather than Roman paganism, and Greek became its official language (around the 6th century) rather than Latin.

So, why would Greek and Christian Byzantium fall out of the orbit of the West? It should be noted that the Roman world was long coming under the influence of 'orientalising' motifs particularly in the eastern areas of the Empire, Syria, Jordan, and northern Iraq.[141] These areas were barely Romanised. A distinctly oriental flavour was evident from the very 'first' Byzantine ruler, Constantine (306–337), who was addressed as *dominus* ('lord') and his right to rule was no longer seen as derived from the Roman people but from God, in whose presence everyone had to prostrate themselves and kiss the hem of his robe. The provinces which lay nearest to the emperors' concern were not Gaul or Spain, but Egypt and Syria. By the 5th century the state had become a church-state, and the emperor a priest-king, earthly representative of the sovereignty of the Divine Word. The power of the monarch was no longer disguised under the constitutional forms of republicanism, but came to be surrounded with all the ceremonial pomp of oriental despotism; the court of the ruler was seen as the 'Sacred Palace,' his property as the 'Divine Household,' and his edicts as 'celestial commands'.[142]

Yet the cultural elite of Byzantium was Greek; and during the reign of Justinian (527–565 AD) there was a revival of Western influences as some of the former Roman regions in North Africa, Italy and Spain were re-conquered from barbarians. These lands were soon lost but Justinian's legal reforms would constitute a lasting contribution to the making of the West. He promoted the completion of the *Code of Justinian*, which simplified and organised the vast body of civil law accumulated over the

141 Ball Warwick, *Rome in the East*.

142 Kallistos Ware, 'Eastern Christendom,' in *The Oxford Illustrated History of Christianity*, ed., John McManners (Cambridge, 1990).

centuries, supported lawyers in the creation of a handbook called *Institutes* for the education of students, as well as a *Digest* which was an extremely valuable collection and summary of centuries of commentary on Roman law by legal experts. This codification of Roman law would serve as a basis for the Papal Revolution of the 11th century in Europe, leading to the first comprehensive systematisation of law, the definition and relationships between different kinds of law.[143]

But after the death of Justinian, during the 7th and 8th centuries, knowledge of Classical literature and science gradually disappeared from this civilisation, except for a tiny community in Constantinople. Looking at a map of the borders of the Byzantine Empire in 750 we see a small regional power struggling for survival under the pressure of constant Persian attacks in the south, combined with assaults from the north by the Avars and by a dynamic new enemy, the Muslims, who defeated the Persians, captured the Holy Land, North Africa, and Asia Minor, and almost conquered the city of Constantinople itself between 716 and 718. Nevertheless, Byzantium would go on to reassert itself through the 9th, 10th, and early 11th centuries, and while the Empire remained significantly smaller than it was during the reign of Justinian, it was also more integrated geographically, as well as politically and culturally. The cities expanded, population rose, and production increased. This political revival was accompanied by a 'revival' of Hellenistic culture, as ancient Greek texts were preserved and patiently re-copied, and Byzantine art flourished. While this revival was not characterised by originality as much as a return to some of the achievements of the Greco-Roman past, we should not underestimate the role Byzantium played in preserving for us today the great gifts of the Classical world, more so than the much talked-about role of Islamic civilisation. It has been estimated that of the 55,000 ancient Greek texts in existence today, some 40,000 were transmitted to us by Byzantine scribes. The Greek scholars who moved to Italy during the 15th century

---

143 Harold Berman, *Law and Revolution: The Formation of the Western Legal Tradition* (Harvard, 1984).

in response to Muslim aggression played a very significant role in spreading the Greek heritage to Italy, fuelling the Renaissance.[144] Another major legacy of Byzantium was the extension of its Orthodox Christianity into the Slavic world in the Balkans, Ukraine and Kievan Russia.

In 1071, the Seljuk Turks inflicted a major defeat on the Byzantine army; the Empire's heartland in Asia Minor was overturned, from which it never fully recovered; and, finally, in the 14th century the Ottoman Turks entered Europe and completely destroyed the last remnants of the Empire. Greece, seen as the 'birthplace' of Western civilisation, became a part of the Ottoman Empire from the 15th century until its declaration of independence in 1821. Yet, what is striking is the strong consensus regarding the European-ethno character of the nations that came into shape after the Balkan Wars (1912–1913) and the expulsion of the Turks from this Mediterranean and Indo-Europeanised region. Currently, apart from Albania, Kosovo, and Bosnia-Herzegovina, the region's principal religion is Christianity, and the ethnicity and demographics are Caucasian/European.[145] The evidence today generally supports Coon's view that the ancient and contemporary Greeks were (and still are) members of a Mediterranean-Alpine-Dinaric mix with a weak Nordic component.[146]

---

144   Lars Brownworth, *Lost to the West: The Forgotten Byzantine Empire That Rescued Western Civilization* (Random House, 2009). George Ostrogorsky concludes his canonical work, *History of the Byzantine State* (Rutgers University Press, 1969), with these words: '[T]he cultural contribution of Byzantine to the West is by no means negligible. The Byzantine state was the instrument by means of which Graeco-Roman antiquity survived through the ages, and for this reason Byzantium was the donor, the West the recipient. This was particularly true at the time of the renaissance, when there was such passionate interest in classical civilization and the West found that it could satisfy its longing to explore the treasures of antiquity from Byzantine sources. Byzantium had preserved the heritage of the ancient world and in so doing had fulfilled its mission in world history. It had saved from destruction Roman law, Greek literature, philosophy and learning, so that this priceless heritage could be passed on to the peoples of Western Europe who were now ready to receive it', p. 572.

145   The Wikipedia article 'Balkans' is particularly good on the ethnic demographics of this region.

146   http://ancientgreekdna.blogspot.ca/.

The Barbarian West

The most intriguing question of all is why the far less developed Western Roman Empire became the core of the West through the entire medieval and modern eras? The answer is that the Western Empire and the areas under Germanic rule were populated by Celtic-Germanic Europeans. We always hear about the importance of Classical culture and the spread of Christianity to the making of medieval Europe, but hardly a word about the more 'primordial' role of the barbarians who conquered Rome. Despite the eventual exhaustion of Classical Greece, the stagnation and 'orientalisation' of the Hellenistic kingdoms, and the aging despotism of Imperial Rome, the dynamic spirit of the West was sustained thanks to the infusion of new sources of aristocratic will to power brought on by fresh waves of barbarians. The first Europeans who founded the 'civilised' West were the Mycenaean warriors who comprised the background to Classical Athens.[147] The second were the Macedonians who rejuvenated the mar-

---

147 In *Uniqueness* I cited a handful of books specifically about the Myceaneans supporting the argument that they were uniquely aristocratic and intensively warlike. They borrowed civilisational tools from the older Near Eastern world while remaining strongly aristocratic. A book that further solidifies this view is Rodney Castleden's *Mycenaeans* (Routledge, 2005). If I may quote at length: 'The Mycenaeans left behind them a hard, militaristic tradition that would be held up by many later generations as a model for individual manliness and collective strength...Above all, the Mycenaeans gave us the heroic ideal—that notion that it is nobler than anything else imaginable to risk everything for glory. The Homeric picture of the Mycenaean Greeks is a picture of a quarrelsome people, quick to anger, quick to resort to arms. It is a picture of a warrior elite to whom personal honour meant everything. The Homeric heroes were brave to the point of foolhardiness...Athenians were inspired by the Homeric ideals evidenced by the Olympic Games, where anyone could compete and gain fame and glory; they overthrew Isagoras, recalled Cleisthenes and set up a democracy. Mycenaean values enshrined in Homer conditioned both aristocrats and ordinary citizens in Greece to behave in a particular way, conditioned them to pursue victory, fame and glory at any cost. This found echoes in several later cultures, including classical Greece, Rome, and the major revival aspects of those cultures in the Renaissance. The grand reckless gestures of the great Elizabethans, for example, owe much to the Mycenaean heroic tradition. The Mycenaeans' great wish was to be remembered for their heroic deeds, "and live in song for generations". It was Homer's epic poetry that made their dream come true. The still-grand ruins of their tombs show that Homer's heroic view was real. The warriors hoped to transcend death through the memory of the living—by leaving an everlasting tomb, by achieving fame in the flower of youth. The Mycenaean concept of beauty

tial virtues of Greece after the debilitating Peloponnesian War, and went on to conquer Persia and create the basis for the intellectual harvest of Alexandrian Greece.[148] The third were the early Romans who founded an aristocratic republic, preserved the legacy of Greece, and cultivated their own Latin tradition.[149] And the fourth were the Celtic-Germanic peoples who interacted for some centuries with the Romans, and then continued the Western legacy.[150]

I have barely addressed this here; suffice it to say that without the dynamics of an expansionary barbarian aristocracy the Latin West would have been unable to overcome the degeneration of Rome under the pervading influence of Eastern Despotism. It was the racial-make up, the aristocratic vigour and acquisitiveness of Germanic war-bands that kept the West alive. By the mid-8th century, these war-bands had managed to consolidate themselves into four kingdoms in the lands that had once formed the western side of the Roman Empire: the Lombard in Italy, the Visigoths in Spain, the Franks in Gaul, and the Anglo-Saxons in England.

---

in death has fed cultures for many generations since, an almost irresistibly heart-swelling — yet dangerous — idea' (pp. 235–236).

Another book depicting the entire Bronze Age of the whole of Europe as aristocratic is Katie Demakopoulou et al., *Gods and Heroes of the European Bronze Age* (Thames and Hudson, 1998). This richly illustrated book, with chapters authored by over 40 different experts, is an excellent source with titles such as 'Adventurers, Artisans, Travelers,' 'The Heroes and their Palaces,' 'The Heroes: Life and Death,' 'The Chieftain's Grave of Hagenau and Related Warrior Graves,' 'Horses in the Bronze Age.'

148 R. M. Errington, *A History of Macedonia.* University of California Press, 1990.

149 T. J. Cornell, *The Beginnings of Rome from the Bronze Age to the Punic Wars, 1000–264 BC* (Routledge, 1995).

150 Stephen Allen, *Lords of Battle. The World of the Celtic Warrior* (Osprey Publishing, 2007). Hans Delbruck, *The Barbarian Invasions* (Greenwood Press, 1990; orig. 1909 in German) likewise gives additional credence to the claim that the Germans were not passive actors compelled by demographic pressures to colonise Roman lands but 'moved into the Roman provinces as armies and not as farmers looking for land. As holders of the power, they created new political arrangements and established new political organizations in which they themselves represented the armed power. Their warriorhood was based on the strength of their warlike nature, which they brought with them from their barbarian origins, on the cohesiveness of the clans, and on the savage personal courage of the individual' (387).

The most successful geographically were the Franks who managed to reunify most of the western European territories into the Carolingian Empire. By the 10th century, the Carolingian unity was gone, and local aristocrats stepped back into power. Then the Vikings arrived, expanding and settling in England, Iceland, Ireland, Greenland, and Newfoundland, and also Russia, down the Dnieper and the Volga down to the Black Sea and the Caspian.[151]

Some have argued that feudalism emerged out of the chaos that ensued with the collapse of the Carolingian unity and with the onset of the Viking invasions. Feudalism was derived in its essentials from the early Indo-European society of war-bands. The feudal bond between lord and vassal was a contractually based relation entered into between two men who had an intrinsic sense of their noble status. The West of the 11th century was still an extremely disorderly world. The rise of feudalism brought on numerous conflicts over boundaries and jurisdictional rights, disputes which could not easily be resolved by appeal to the authority of public institutions. Nevertheless, by about this time, all pagans had been Christianised, and thus the violent Christianisation of pagans had ceased. It was in this context that the Church sought to promote the ideal of peace in a sincere effort to quell the violence between Christians. The Peace of God and the Truce of God, enacted between 990 and 1048, were ecclesiastical laws designed to counter the atrocities and depredations of quarrelling lords and vassals. The period after 1000, which witnessed the revival of city life and commerce, the proliferation of heterodox religious movements, the veneration of the Virgin Mary and the ideal of the loving mother, saw a new romantic portrayal of the aristocratic hero. The brave and loyal but rather vindictive and callous pagan hero came to

---

151 Jesse Byock's, *Viking Age Iceland* (2001) may well be the best book on the Viking expeditions (consistent with the aristocratic thesis of *Uniqueness*) in emphasising both the 'republican free state' relations formed by Vikings in their newly founded colonies, the self-governing community of settlers, and the heroic ethos of its chieftains, in which honor was tied to competition, to maintaining life, property and status, and exacting revenge. These were aristocratic cultures alright, but without intense class divisions and without kings.

be supplemented by a new ideal knight who was equally courageous in combat but lived up to a more refined standard of behaviour: a warrior who had acquired courtly manners, a taste for music and literature, had learned about ceremony and fine clothes.[152]

Still, the acquisitive and aggressive expansionism of the European aristocracy continued through the 11th to 13th centuries, with German knights moving all the way into Estonia on the Gulf of Finland, into Silesia along the Oder, and throughout Bohemia. This period also saw a few belligerent families of Franks establishing new kingdoms in Castile, Portugal, Cyprus, Jerusalem, and Sicily, as well as predatory missions into the Welsh and Irish frontiers.[153] The expansionist aggression of the West is an inescapable expression of its roots in aristocratic men who are free and therefore headstrong and ambitious, sure of themselves, easily offended, and unwilling to accept quiet subservience. The 'civilising processes' of this era brought under restraint the original ferocity of the barbarians. But the goal of the Church was to spiritualise the baser instincts of this class, not to extirpate and emasculate them. The highly-strung and obstinate aristocrat has been a fundamental source of destruction in Western history as well as the source of all that is good and inspiring. This expansionist period also saw the invention of the university, a scholastic commitment to dialogue based on logic and evidence, the rise of autonomous cities, Romanesque and Gothic architecture, a new polyphonic music, and more.

Russia

The West also includes areas which are seen today as partially Western. I am thinking (firstly) of Russia. There is much uncertainty about Russia's Europeanism. Perhaps of all the cultural factors which may classify Russia as Western none is more important than the bringing of Christianity

---

152   Jacques Le Goff's *The Birth of Europe* (Blackwell, 2005) is particularly good on this topic.

153   Robert Bartlett, *The Making of Europe: Conquest, Colonization and Cultural Change, 950–1350* (Princeton University, 1993).

to the Slavs by Byzantium scholars in the 10th century. With the end of Byzantium, the role of the emperor as a patron of Eastern Orthodoxy was certainly claimed by Ivan III (1440–1505), Grand Duke of Muscovy. Yet, the same Caesaropapism we saw in Byzantium developed in Russia leads some historians to question Russia's place in the West. The Russian allegiance to Orthodox Christianity, they argue, kept Russia outside of the Catholic scholastic culture, the Papal Revolution, rise of autonomies cities and universities. Russia was the most resistant to classical liberalism. While Tsar Alexander I (1801–1825) was raised in the ideas of the Enlightenment, and during the beginning of his reign relaxed censorship and reformed the educational system, he refused to grant a constitution and, after the defeat of Napoleon, he returned to strict and arbitrary censorship. In 1914 the Russian autocracy and its police were firmly in control. In March 1917, the Tsarist autocracy fell apart, and a provisional government led by the middle classes and liberal nobles passed reforms that provided universal suffrage, civil equality, and an eight-hour workday. However, in October 1917 a small militant faction toppled this liberal government and set out to transform Russia into a bureaucratically centralised state dominated by a single party.[154] The Soviets tried to destroy every institution and cultural lifestyle associated with Russia's Christian past in order to reconstitute society on the basis of an anti-Western doctrine called Marxism.[155] This regime collapsed in the 1990s, but the emerging state structures, it is argued, remained mired in autocratic customs and policies.

But perhaps the most important reason why Russia is not altogether seen as Western is that geographically it occupies a vast territory extending from Eastern Europe deep into Central Asia, Siberia, and into the Far East. Other historians address Russia's 'distinctive' Slavic culture, but what is invariably left out from all these accounts is that Russia has

---

154 James H. Billington, *The Icon and the Axe, An Interpretative History of Russian Culture* (Vintage Books, 1970), and Nicholas V. Riasanovsky's, *A History of Russia* (Oxford University, [1963] 1984).

155 Kevin MacDonald, 'Stalin's Willing Executioners: Jews as a Hostile Elite in the USSR,' *The Occidental Quarterly*, 5.3 (Fall 2005).

been predominantly a culture and a territory founded and nurtured by Europeans. The origin of the first Russian state, the state of Kiev, is a matter of much controversy. Its existence has been dated roughly from 800 AD to 1240, at which point it was thoroughly destroyed by the Mongols, and one of the contending arguments is that the founders of Kiev were Norsemen or Vikings. The name of *Rus*, from which the name 'Russians' was derived, has been variously ascribed to 'red-haired' Vikings. Now, Russia before the 'Russians,' it is true, included a number of ancient cultures within the many landscapes that came to be enclosed within its boundaries, including Scythians, Cimmerians, and Sarmatians, but many of these groups belonged to the Iranian and Thracian divisions of the Indo-European language families, and only some to an Asiatic, Mongol and Turkic-speaking background. The Proto-Indo-European homeland, after all, was located in the general region of the Pontic-Caspian steppe, which is in present day Ukraine. The Indo-Europeans, who remained in this region, after the migrations, are said to be speakers of Balto-Slavic.

Looking at the ethnic composition of the former Soviet Union (circa 1989)[156], we find that of a total population of 262.436 million, the Russians and Ukrainians alone numbered 187.307 million, not counting the Baltic peoples and other Europeans. After the Soviet Union broke up in the 1990s, the Slavs (Russians, Ukrainians, and Belarusians) came to account for about 85% of Russia's demography. Most of the non-Slavic peoples found themselves neatly grouped within the newly demarcated nation states of Azerbaijan, Kazakhstan, Kyrgyzstan, Turkmenistan, and Uzbekistan. The 'Asian' part of the former Soviet Union was thus cut off. The Turkic speaking peoples which remained inside Russia are now widely and sparsely distributed in the middle Volga, the southern Ural Mountains, the North Caucasus, and above the Arctic Circle. Russia is not only the largest country in the world but homeland to the most numerous European group in Europe and one of the largest in the world — notwithstanding its current low fertility rate.

---

156   http://en.wikipedia.org/wiki/Demography_of_the_Soviet_Union.

Philippe Nemo's claim that Russia is not really Western because under its Orthodox Christian order it did not experience the separation of church and state, and the rise of representative institutions, is wrong on racial grounds.[157] It is wrong on high cultural grounds as well: Russia has contributed one of the greatest literary traditions to the West, starting with Alexander Pushkin, the poetry of Mikhail Lermontov and Nikolay Nekrasov, dramas of Aleksandr Ostrovsky and Anton Chekhov, and the prose of Nikolai Gogol, Ivan Turgenev, Leo Tolstoy, Fyodor Dostoyevsky, and Ivan Goncharov. It is wrong on geopolitical grounds: Russia's relentless geographical expansion into Siberia, beginning in the late-1500s and reaching the Pacific by 1639, is as deserving of admiration as the achievements of other well-known European explorations. Russia has been a land of numerous great explorers associated with heroic expeditions from Siberia to the Arctic into Space; it launched the first Earth-orbiting artificial satellite, the first human spaceflight in 1961, the first spacewalk in 1965, the first space exploration rover, on the Moon in 1970, and the first space station in 1971.[158] Guillaume Faye's vision of a Euro-Siberia federation covering all European lands in between the Atlantic and the Pacific is a salutation to Russia's geographical achievement and possible impending role in the struggle with the Asian world for the survival of Western civilisation.[159]

Latin America

Another area of the world often classified as both Western and non-Western is Latin America. The countries comprising Latin America, one argument goes, inherited many of the feudal institutions of 17th and 18th century Spain and Portugal, which had long stagnated. In contrast one

---

157   *What is the West?* (Duquesne University Press, 2006).

158   Brian Bonhomme, *Russian Exploration, from Siberia to Space: A History* (McFarland Publishers, 2012).

159   Frances Alexander, 'Toward Euro-Siberia,' *Counter Currents Publishing* (August 2011).

sees North America, which was founded by a group of settlers representing the latest phase in the cultural progression of Europe, the principles of limited government, natural rights, religious tolerance, and individual enterprise. The North was gradually populated by enterprising families who brought with them the basis for the creation of "an institutional matrix" that committed the emerging state to set up a set of legal and political organisations, rules and enforcement of property rights, which ensured relative order and economic prosperity. Latin American culture however became rooted in the Iberian tradition of a privileged nobility and a medieval landholding system in which most of the land was owned by a small clique ruling over a mass of impoverished peasants lacking property rights and land. Historians also point to the persistence of a mercantilist disposition among Latin American rulers. From colonial times, the crown acted as the supreme economic patron, with the result that much commercial activities came to depend on special licenses, grants, monopolies, and trade privileges. The import-substitution policies adapted from the 1930s through to the 70s created economies dominated by bloated and inefficient state sectors that either managed the economy directly or burdened it with massive regulations.[160]

The message of this rather influential interpretation is that Latin America can be classified as Western in the degree to which it has adopted liberal democratic values and institutions. Mario Vargas Llosa, winner of the 2010 Nobel Prize in Literature and an avowed admirer of Margaret Thatcher, believes that there is already 'a Westernised Latin America that speaks Spanish, Portuguese and English (in the Caribbean and in Central America) and is Catholic, Protestant, atheist or agnostic.' There is another Latin America that remains authoritarian, hierarchical, corporatist, and patrimonial. But he is 'convinced' this Latin America will become, 'sooner rather than later,' Western thanks to further modernisation and democratisation. Latin American, he adds, has been bedevilled not only by a

---

160   Richard Morse, 'The Heritage of Latin America,' in Louis Hartz, ed., *The Founding of New Societies* (New York, 1964); Douglas North, *Institutions, Institutional Change and Economic Performance* (Cambridge 1990).

pre-liberal Hispanic political culture, but by an indigenous 'pre-Hispanic' presence particularly in countries like Mexico, Guatemala, Ecuador, Peru, and Bolivia. Once liberalism takes firm roots, *and* 'race-mixing' is extended 'in all directions,' then 'all Latin Americans' will join the Western world. Vargas Llosa opportunely announces that 'the distinctive identity of a mestizo continent' will make Latin America 'a model for the rest of the world.'[161] Latin America possesses some Western traits, this cannot be denied. The Spanish legacy, Christianity, and a high number of original writes (e.g. Jorge Luis Borges, known for his invention of the philosophical short story, Rubén Darío and the *modernismo* poetic movement, Alejo Carpentier, Miguel Ángel Asturias and Julio Cortázar, to name but a few). But Mario Vargas Llosa is correct to emphasise the overwhelming reality of *mestizaje* in this continent even if he wants to promote two incompatible things:

(1) The idea that Latin American is becoming liberal, transcending its ethnic identity and creating a culture 'possessed by individuals and not collectivities'.

(2) The idea that Latin America is becoming a place where a new race, the Mestizo, will emerge standing as a 'model' (a new and improved species?) for the rest of the world.

The implied logic of his argument is that Indians should willingly engage in miscegenation in the name of *La Raza Cósmica*.[162] He neglects altogether the wishes of the more than 2000 different Indian groups in Latin America to retain their racial makeup, shared habits, folkways, and

---

161 Mario Vargas Llosa, 'The Paradoxes of Latin America,' *The American Interest* (January/February 2009).

162 As the Wiki article explains: 'Published in 1925, *La Raza Cósmica* (The Cosmic Race) is an essay written by late Mexican philosopher, secretary of education, and 1929 presidential candidate, José Vasconcelos, to express the ideology of a future 'fifth race' in the Americas; an agglomeration of all the races in the world with no respect to color or number to erect a new civilization.'

collective rights to their ancestral lands.[163] The notion of the autonomous individual is not a cultural construct of Indians.

Mestizaje is also a denial of whiteness in Latin America. The ethnic composition of most Latin Americans is not European.[164] Nevertheless, some countries, certainly Uruguay, regions of Argentina and even Brazil, do exhibit a considerable European genetic heritage. There is debate, and acrimonious exchanges on this question, for example, about the exact whiteness of Argentineans, with some studies[165] questioning the commonly held view that Argentina is uniquely a European nation. Still, the bio-geographic ancestry of Argentineans has been shown to contain 'a large fraction of European genetic heritage in their Y-chromosomal (94.1%) and autosomal (78.5%) DNA, but their mitochondrial gene pool is mostly of Native American ancestry (53.7%)'.[166] While the mitochondrial or the maternal gene inheritance may seem low, many Argentines are the descendants of an exceptionally high rate of European immigration: between 1857 and 1950, 6,611,000 European immigrants arrived in Argentina. According to a 1914 Census, over 80% of the Argentine population were immigrants, their children, or grandchildren. [167] Uruguay, with about 88%

---

163 'Indigenous Latin Americans mobilize to defend their rights.' *Oxfam International* (29 May 2009).

164 As Octavio Paz observed, 'the core of Mexico is Indian. It is non-European,' cited in Huntington, *The Clash of Civilizations*, p. 149. Huntington is uncertain about Latin America's Western character: 'Latin America has a distinct identity which differentiates it from the West; [it] incorporates indigenous cultures, which did not exist in Europe, were effectively wiped out in North America' (p. 40). But its religion is Christian, and its elites were oriented towards Europe; it 'could be considered either a subcivilization within Western civilization or a separate civilization closely affiliated with the West and divided as to whether it belongs in the West' (p. 40).

165 Bobillo MC, et al., 'Amerindian mitochondrial DNA haplogroups predominate in the population of Argentina: towards a first nationwide forensic mitochondrial DNA sequence database,' *International Journal of Legal Medicine* 124(4) 2010, pp. 263–268.

166 Daniel Corach et al., 'Inferring Continental Ancestry of Argentineans from Autosomal, Y-Chromosomal and Mitochondrial DNA,' *Annals of Human Genetics* (2009). For an assessment of these findings, see http://blogs.discovermagazine.com/gnxp/2009/12/how-argentina-became-white/#.UPA4EuQr2xo.

167 See the Wikipedia article 'Ethnography of Argentina,' which also notes: 'Most Argentines are descendants of colonial-era settlers from the 15th to the 18th

of its population white and descended from Europeans, and only 4% black and 8% mestizo, is more European than the present United States.

Concluding Thought

The transformation of the vast pristine continents of North America and Australia into core members of Western civilisation is one of the supreme accomplishments of Europeans. The countries erected out of these continents, Canada, United States, Australia and New Zealand, were overwhelmingly white not long ago. This is no longer true. The headlines speak for themselves: 'For the first time in history, there were more minority children born in the United States than white, according to 2011 census data.' 'Australia's Asian population is soaring as immigrants from across the region — particularly China and India — enter the country, official data suggests.' To offer some statistics about Canada, where I reside, as late as 1971, when official multiculturalism was introduced, Eurocanadians still made up over 96% of the population. Projections by Statistics Canada (2010) now estimate that one-third of Canada's population will be a visible minority by 2031, 'whites will become the minority in Toronto and Vancouver over the course of the next three decades.'[168] South Asians, including Indians, Pakistanis and Sri Lankans, are expected to make up 28% of the population in these two cities, and the Chinese alone are estimated to constitute 21%. In the city of Vancouver, according to Daniel Hierbert, white residents in Vancouver will be reduced to 2 out of 5 residents by 2031. In Toronto, Europeans will number only 37% of the population. Statistics Canada defines 'visible minorities' as 'persons, other than aboriginal peoples, who are non-Caucasian in race or non-white in colour,' be it noted that, if we take aboriginals into account, the projections are that 'between 21% and 24% of the population of the province of

---

centuries, and of the 19th and 20th century immigrants from Europe, with about 90% of the population being of European descent.'

168 'Minorities to rise significantly by 2031: StatsCan,' *CBC News* (March 09, 2010).

Saskatchewan and between 18% and 21% of the population of the province of Manitoba' will have an Aboriginal identity in 2031.[169]

Europe is experiencing similar trends; the 'Africanisation' France is well underway.[170] Race mixing is being promoted by the media, universities, textbooks, and politicians. Where will the West be in the future? The difficulties we encountered identifying the historical West will pale in comparison to the immense struggles we will face recognizing this civilisation in a thoroughly mongrelised geography.

---

169 'Population Projections by Aboriginal Identity in Canada: 2006–2031,' http://www.statcan.gc.ca/pub/91-552-x/91-552-x2011001-eng.pdf.

170 Falko Baumgartner, 'The Africanization of France' *Alternative Right* (November 3, 2012).

3

Multicultural Historians: The Assault on Western Civilisation and Defilement of the Historical Profession

World history was conceived in part to counteract a Eurocentric perspective on the human past, deriving from several centuries of Western dominance on the world stage. This book seeks to embrace the experience of humankind in its vast diversity.

ROBERT STRAYER, *Ways of the World* (2010)

Mass Immigration and the Abolition of Western Civ courses

The Western Civ course was a standard curriculum offering 40 years ago, but according to a National Association of Scholars report issued in 2011, 'The Vanishing West: 1964–2010,' only 2% of colleges in the United States currently offer Western Civilisation as a course requirement.[171] The teaching of World History survey courses is now the norm across American and Canadian campuses. The standard argument offered to justify World History instead of Western Civ has been that the former course offers a more comprehensive and empirically truthful account of the historical

---

171 Glenn Ricketts, Peter Wood, Stephen Balch, and Ashley Thorne, *The Vanishing West: 1964-2010. The Disappearance of Western Civilization from the American Undergraduate Curriculum* (New York: National Association of Scholars, May 2011).

experience of the peoples of the world, including the peoples of Europe, because civilisations generally have been historically enmeshed within a wider world of connections, migration movements, commercial exchanges, religious and cultural influences, as well as environmental realities transcending civilisational borders. This is an argument flawed to its very core. It is driven far less by scholarly criteria than by the ideological imperative that white people have never belonged to a civilisation with its own unique dynamics, but have always been 'connected' to the rest of the world, progressing to the current reality of mass immigration and race mixing inside all Western countries.

The intention of this chapter is to exhibit the extent to which multicultural world historians have been willing to violate two basic principles of the historical profession — respect for the scholarly sources and reliability in the evaluation of the evidence — in order to downplay Western uniqueness, equalise the achievements of all races in world history, blame Europeans for the backwardness of other civilisations, while emphasising the connections of the West with the rest of the world in order to make non-European immigrants feel that they have contributed as much to the making of the West as Europeans. In this way, they wish to create a historical account that is suitable to a heterogeneous race-mixed Western culture consistent with the protocols of diversity enrichment.

In history departments across the West, Europe and Asia are now regularly portrayed as 'surprisingly similar' as late as 1750/1800 in their economic advances, standard of living, scientific knowhow and overall cultural achievements. Jack Goldstone has even argued that there 'were no cultural or institutional dynamics leading to a materially superior civilisation in the West' before 1850, except for the appearance in Britain, 'due to a host of locally contingent factors,' of an 'engineering culture.'[172] Indeed, this animus against the West has even led to the claim that Europeans

---

172 Jack Goldstone, 'Capitalist Origins, the Advent of Modernity, and Coherent Explanation' *Canadian Journal of Sociology* 33, no. 1 (Winter 2008): pp. 119–133. Goldstone has been making this argument for some years; now available in a student-oriented book, *Why Europe? The Rise of the West in World History, 1500–1850* (Boston: McGraw Hill, 2009).

were never a people unto themselves but members of a wider connected world, with Muslims as key creators of the West no less than Christians. Ian Morris, in his highly advertised book, *Why the West Rules — For Now*, brushed aside all prior identifications of the West with Europe, claiming that the Islamic world was central to the West's identity, celebrating the rise of Asians. He even told Westerners not to worry about their eventual demise since, after all, 'wherever you go, whatever you do, people are all much the same;' 'humanity's biological unity rules out race-based theories.'[173]

Multicultural historians are instructing their students that Europeans don't inhabit a continental homeland independently of Asia and Africa, that Europe's history can only be understood within the context of 'reciprocal connections' within the globe. 'The exceptional interconnectedness of Afroeurasia shaped the history of this world zone in profound ways,' wrote David Christian, author of *Maps of Time: An Introduction to Big History*.[174] Students are being indoctrinated to believe that Europeans were unique mostly in the 'windfall' profits they obtained from the Americas, the 'lucky' presence of coal in England, and the blood-stained manner they went about creating a new form of international slavery combined with 'scientific' racism.[175]

This state of affairs has been in the making for some decades now, as evident in the formation of numerous programs dedicated to ethnic minorities, the establishment of well-funded organisations, journals, and the continuous conferences taking place every week and month throughout the West promoting every multicultural idea and policy imaginable. The old experts on European history are divided, heedless, and confined to

---

173 *Why the West Rules — For Now*, p. 61.

174 David Christian, *Maps of Time: An Introduction to Big History* (Berkeley: University of California Press, 2005). The cited sentence comes from Christian's article 'Afroeurasia in Geological Time,' *World History Connected* 5, no. 2 (February 2008), http://worldhistoryconnected.press.illinois.edu/5.2/christian.html.
       Maps of Time landed Christian a Ted Talk: https://www.ted.com/talks/david_christian_big_history?language=en.

175 John M. Hobson, *The Eastern Origins of Western Civilization* (Cambridge: Cambridge University Press, 2004).

circumscribed fields lacking a coherent vision. No wonder the authors of recent Western Civ texts, pleading for survival, have been adopting a globalist approach. Brian Levack et al. thus write in *The West, Encounters & Transformations* (2007): 'we examine the West as a product of a series of cultural encounters both outside the West and within it.'[176] They also insist that the religion of Islam was one of the prominent cultural features of the West. Similarly, Clifford Backman, in his recently released textbook, *The Cultures of the West* (2013), traces the origins of the West to Iraq, Syria, Lebanon, and Israel. He then goes on to tell students that his book is different from previous texts in treating Islam as 'essentially a Western religion' and examining 'jointly' the history of Europe and the Middle Eastern world.[177]

World historians continually boast about their emphasis on 'connections' between regions and continents, emphasising the role of trade, migrations, and environmental events that transcend national boundaries. They also brag about their 'scientific' emphasis on the geographical, geological, climatic, economic, and demographic aspects of history, as contrasted to the parochial, cultural, Eurocentric biases of historians who write about the unique features of Western civilisation.[178] It would make

176   Brian Levack, Edward Muir, and Meredith Veldman, *The West, Encounters & Transformations, Volume I: To 1715*, 2nd ed. (Upper Saddle River, NJ: Pearson, 2007), p. xxx.

177   Clifford Backman, *The Cultures of the West* (New York: Oxford University Press, 2013), p. xxii. Writing about Western Civ texts from a globalist approach has been eagerly promoted as a new 'teaching' approach since the 1990s; Michael Doyle thus encourages teachers, in 'Hisperanto: Western Civilization in the Global Curriculum,' published in *Perspectives* (May 1998), a publication of the American Historical Association, 'to continue to incorporate a more inclusive approach to all cultures with which it [the West] came into contact.' 'Certainly Western Civ students should read parts of the Qur'an and understand the attitudes that produced Fanon's *The Wretched of the Earth*.' He refers to the Communist Eric Hobsbawm's widely read books on European history as a model to be emulated by students and teachers.

178   According to Patrick Manning's *Navigating World History: Historians Create a Global Past* (New York: Palgrave Macmillan, 2003), histories that do not treat Europe as an integrated part of the African, Asian, or American continents cannot be categorised as works of 'world history.' Only histories emphasising connections can be said to constitute 'world history,' even if such histories area about small local regions in Africa connected to other localities elsewhere. The history of cotton planters in the American South is world history in its connection to the Atlantic; the history of the

for an interesting essay showing the ways in which this 'scientific' emphasis is seriously impaired by the way multicultural historians envision the
geological, biological, and human history of the planet as a communal
affair wherein all natural things, cultures, and regions are seen as equal
partners marching in unison under the guidance of 'progressive' elites.
It would also make for an interesting paper explaining the ways in which
politically correct would-be scientific historians employ post-modernist
discourses as a means to confuse, detract from, or avoid facing up to
the overwhelming reality of the evidence standing in opposition to their
poorly supported claims. It would be very revealing to show how multicultural historians have suppressed the findings of Darwinian theory and
evolutionary psychology in their efforts to write of a common, generic
humanity without ethnic distinctions or group interests.

However, my aim here is to bring to light the flagrant manner in
which multicultural historians go about misusing sources, misreading
books, misinterpreting the evidence, concealing the facts, and overall
violating the principles of historical objectivity and respect for scholarship — all in the name of creating a consensus around the imagined merits
of a multiracial society inside European-created cultures. I will do this by
examining four recent articles which appeared separately:

(1) In the *Journal of Global History*, published by Cambridge
    University Press.

(2) In the flagship *Journal of World History*.

(3) In the distinguished *American Historical Review*.

(4) In the widely read leftist newspaper *The Guardian*.

Hundreds of other publications could have served as well to illustrate this
abuse of the historical profession. In *Uniqueness*, I elaborated on some of
the ways Kenneth Pomeranz, John Hobson, Bin Wong, Patrick Manning,
and others relied on dated sources, misread, and sometimes wilfully

---

rise of modern science in Europe is not world history, unless the rise of this science
is seen to be connected to some place in Africa, Asia, or the Americas.

misinterpreted authors. Examining these four articles will allow me to make my case in a detailed and in-depth way. What is going on here cannot be attributed to mere empirical incompleteness and understandable errors of judgment. Our students today may be said to be the targets of a deep-seated educational effort to impose a multicultural view of Europe's history, that is heavily infused with fabrications and the mistreatment of scholarly sources.

The Pathological Historiography of Patrick O'Brien on the Scientific Revolution

Patrick O'Brien, Professor of Global History at the London School of Economics and Political Science, proudly sent proof copies of the following title to a number of historians including myself: 'Historical Foundations for a Global Perspective on the Emergence of a Western European Regime for the Discovery, Development, and Diffusion of Useful and Reliable Knowledge.' Soon enough the essay appeared in *The Journal of Global History* (March 2013). The essay seemed fair enough in its concluding statement that 'historians of global economic development might wish to retain the "older" view of the Scientific Revolution.'[179]

The global historians O'Brien was referring to are Pomeranz, Wong, Goldstone, Prasannan Parthasarathi, Ian Morris, Felipe Fernández-Armesto, Andre Gunder Frank, Manning, Christian, and indeed almost the entire global history professoriate dominating our educational institutions. The research of these historians has been invariably about the so-called 'similarities' — economic and institutional — between Europe and Asia before the Industrial Revolution.

These academics have generally insisted that the rise of modern science and industry was a global phenomenon. For example, Frank has

---

179 Patrick O'Brien, 'Historical Foundations for a Global Perspective on the Emergence of a Western European Regime for the Discovery, Development, and Diffusion of Useful and Reliable Knowledge,' *The Journal of Global History* 8, no. 1 (March 2013): pp. 1–24, 15.

written that Newtonian science was not peculiar to Europe but 'existed and continued to develop elsewhere as well.'[180] Fernández-Armesto has shown no hesitation stating that the science and philosophy of Copernicus, Kepler, Laplace, Descartes and Bacon was no more original than the neo-Confucian 'scientific' revival of the 17th century—both were 'comparable in kind.'[181]Morris, in *Why the West Rules—For Now*, has said that an intellectual movement in 17th to 18th century China known as Kaozheng 'paralleled western Europe's scientific revolution in every way—except one: it did not develop a mechanical model of nature', a rather large difference given that nature can't be understood scientifically without such models.[182] Parthasarathi, in his recent book, *Why Europe Grew Rich and Asia Did Not: Global Economic Divergence, 1600–1850*, has rejected the 'older' claim that Europe possessed superior markets, rationality, science or institutions, tracing the divergence instead to different competitive and ecological pressures structured by global dynamics.[183]

Now, while O'Brien thinks that these historians have been 'successful' in their 'assault upon a triumphalist tradition of European global economic history,'[184] he guardedly questions their claim that the rise of modern science was a global phenomenon. The Scientific Revolution, he writes, was 'something less than a short, sharp discontinuity in the accumulation of scientific knowledge, and more a profound conjuncture *locatable for its time in the history of western Europe*.'[185] Yet, O'Brien accepts the idea that world history should be the study of 'connections in the human community,' the story of humanity's 'common experience,' an idea

---

180 Andre Gunder Frank, *Re-Orient: Global Economy in the Asian Age* (Berkeley: University of California Press, 1998), pp. 188–189.

181 Felipe Fernández-Armesto, *The World: A History* (Upper Saddle River, NJ: Pearson, 2007), p. 630.

182 Ian Morris, *Why the West Rules—For Now: The Patterns of History, and What They Reveal About the Future* (New York: Farrar, Straus and Giroux, 2010), p. 473.

183 Prasannan Parthasarathi, *Why Europe Grew Rich and Asia Did Not: Global Economic Divergence* (Cambridge: Cambridge University Press, 2011).

184 O'Brien, 'Historical Foundations,' p. 2.

185 Ibid., p. 23.

which precludes seeing historical transformation in terms of the 'internal logics' of nations or particular civilisations. The result is one of the most convoluted, awkward and poorly documented papers I have read.

This paper is part of a 'project funded by the European Research Council.' In an earlier 'Proposal to the European Research Council' (2009), O'Brien spoke of the need for 'an international alliance ... to respond to demands from a cosmopolitan generation of students now at university for greater engagement with big questions that are ... clearly relevant to the geopolitical and moral concerns of their (and our) times of accelerated globalisation.'[186] He mentioned the names of Montesquieu, Voltaire, Hume, Quesnay, Turgot, Miller, Hegel, and other Enlightenment thinkers known for their 'universal' approaches, but then summarily dismissed them for their 'superficial' discussions of economic matters, including in his indictment Spencer, Spengler, and Toynbee. He acknowledged the stimulating discussions occasioned by 'neo-Weberian explanations of the rise of the west' (by Eric Jones, Nathan Rosenberg, Douglas North, Joel Mokyr, David Landes, and Angus Maddison). But, again, he quickly brushed them off in favor of 'Wallerstein and his followers in the World Systems School of Historical Sociology.'

O'Brien further insisted that the 'divergence of European economies from Asia is explicable in terms of the gains the former made from the discovery and exploitation of the Americas and (as Marx asserted) by way of the systematic use of naval power and colonisation in Asia.' He told the European Council that Pomeranz, Wong, Goldstone, Harriet Zurndorfer, and Parthasarathi ('aided by that indefatigable polemicist Gunder Frank') had in effect refuted the old Eurocentric view on Western uniqueness. O'Brien articulated similar ideas in his inaugural essay for the *Journal of Global History*, 'Historiographical Traditions and Modern Imperatives for the Restoration of Global History,' published in 2006, where he emphasised the marginalised narratives of the non-Western world, their struggle

---

186 Patrick O'Brien, 'Proposal to the European Research Council' (2009). http://www.lse.ac.uk/economicHistory/Research/URKEW/Proposal%2ofor%2opublication%2o%28Apr%202009%29.pdf.

against 'the interests of the wealthy, the powerful and the West,' and the need for a new global history 'inclusive' of the diversity of the world, in resistance to the 'master narratives' of the West.[187] The Council agreed with O'Brien's proposal, and awarded him 'a large grant,' and so was born the project, 'Useful and Reliable Knowledge in Global Histories of Material Progress in the East and the West' (URKEW) at the London School of Economics, with O'Brien as 'principal investigator.'

The article we are examining here, O'Brien's 2013 article,[188] is the main product, thus far, to be generated by the leading researcher of this project. A close examination offers some revealing insights on the way world historians are rewriting the history of Europeans in accordance with the principles of cultural egalitarianism and racial inclusiveness. They face a major task: how to frame Europe's unparalleled revolutions and novelties within a global framework even if the existing research simply does not validate their perspective. The Scientific Revolution, O'Brien acknowledges in this paper, was 'locatable for its time in the history of western Europe.' Yet the purpose of the entire Global Economic History Network housing the URKEW project is to advance and demonstrate the veracity of the idea that 'a global perspective' is required because the major transformations of history have been occasioned and structured by world connections and 'two-way' cultural influences. He says in the opening pages that the questions of 'how, when, and why western Europe' witnessed a Scientific Revolution can only be answered by a 'programme of historical research' that emphasises 'reciprocal comparisons' transcending 'the myopias imposed by the frontiers and chronologies of continental, national, or local histories.'[189] But O'Brien never manages to find a solid source either refuting the old Eurocentric explanation or demonstrating that Asia nurtured anything close to Newtonian mechanics, apart from some generalities about 'reciprocal comparisons,' a reference to Arun Bala's unspecified

187 Patrick O'Brien, 'Historiographical Traditions and Modern Imperatives for the Restoration of Global History,' *Journal of Global History* 1, no. 1 (March 2006): p. 38.
188 O'Brien, 'Historical Foundations.'
189 Ibid., p. 3.

'dialogue of civilisations,' and citations from one unscholarly book and another refuted book.

We are thus privy to a very strange paper which boasts about the superiority of global history, promoting the perspective that 'much of the modern debate on the Scientific Revolution looks Eurocentric, provincial, and obsessed with local detail,'[190] but which relies almost entirely on Eurocentric sources. It is therefore obligated to conclude that the rise of modern science was a European-generated phenomenon, *but which nevertheless* still frames this revolution in global terms.

O'Brien's paper takes us through a historiographical journey of some key books published since roughly the 1990s. Nearly all these books were written by specialists in European history; they are not products of a globalist approach. World historians have yet to produce anything that can justify a global view of modern science; accordingly, O'Brien has no option — unless he foregoes the act of writing about this subject — but to rely on the very Eurocentric sources he otherwise derides. This startling contradiction results in one of the most tortuous, muddling, and diffident papers I have read. It is worth going over the details of this historiographical paper both to educate readers regarding the state of the research about a momentous revolution in the history of Europe, and to also alert them to the strategies globalists are employing in their quest to dissolve Europe's identity and sense of accomplishment.

The first notable trait is the use of the term 'useful and reliable Knowledge' in the title of the URKEW project, and the Global Economic Network generally. This means that contributions to natural science in the East and the West will be deemed part of this debate, so long as they can be shown to be concerned with useful applications for the material welfare of humanity. The ideas don't need to be associated with immediate applications, but they must be closely timed 'behind the emergence of contrasts in labor productivity and standards of living' in eastern and western regions. In essence, they must be closely arranged behind 'the

---

190 Ibid.

successful assault' on the traditional Eurocentric interpretation of the Industrial Revolution. The question of Western scientific uniqueness is thus framed in terms of the more important and 'useful' question of why, when, and how the societies of the world followed trajectories that led to divergent prospects for modern economic growth and technological change.

This way of thinking goes unquestioned among all the participants in this debate. Cultural traits are open to discussion only insofar as they can be shown to have influenced economic development. This is also true of 'critics' of global historians. Many who emphasise Europe's internal culture and institutions cannot avoid focusing on Europe's ascent to *global economic domination, in a Marxist oriented way.* Peer Vries criticises the Pomeranz/Wong focus on colonial windfalls, but differs from them only in his 'internalist' emphasis on the fiscal/administrative capacity of imperial Britain to impose itself economically on the world.[191] Similarly, Joseph Bryant vigorously questions the short-term perspective of Pomeranz, Goody, and Goldstone, and their reduction of the divergence to 'fortuitous accidents of geography,' in favour of long-term institutional changes in Europe. However, the issue for Bryant remains how to account for 'the causes that facilitated the European passage to colonial domination and capitalist modernity.'[192]

These sides have been debating each other heartily from conference to conference, grant to grant, invitation to invitation. This is what academia understands by intellectual diversity today. This faux diversity is further embellished with the presence of non Europeans such as Wong, Parthasarathi, and Sanjay Subrahmanyam. These three have assimilated the basic tenets of Western political correctness, Marxist political economy, and the idea of 'connected histories.' They particularly enjoy pointing

---

191 Peer Vries, 'Are Coal and Colonies Really Crucial? Kenneth Pomeranz and the Great Divergence,' *Journal of World History* 12, no. 2 (Fall 2001): pp. 407–446.

192 Joseph Bryant, 'The West and the Rest Revisited: Debating Capitalist Origins, European Colonialism, and the Advent of Modernity,' *Canadian Journal of Sociology* 31, no.4 (2006): p. 403.

to similarities in Eastern and Western economic development before Europe's industrial acceleration after 1800. This is not difficult, since societies like China and India with their historically massive populations inevitably generated higher levels of output, coupled with the fact that differences in average economic indicators can never be very large when we are dealing with pre-industrial societies living on the margins.

They pay attention only to those cultural factors that can be shown to have brought about an economic outcome. The Greek invention of philosophical reasoning and citizenship politics, the medieval invention of universities and the seven liberal arts, the Copernican Revolution and the Cartographic Revolution, do not qualify, on their own, as part of this debate. Books such as Charles Murray's *Human Accomplishment: The Pursuit of Excellence in the Arts and Sciences, 800 B.C. To 1950* (2003),[193] are of no interest to them. Never mind that this book systematically arranges 'data that meet scientific standards of reliability and validity' for the purpose of evaluating 'as facts' the accomplishments of individuals and countries across the world in the arts and sciences (this is achieved by calculating the amount of space allocated to these individuals in reference works, encyclopaedias, and dictionaries).[194] They could not care less about Murray's finding that 97% of accomplishment in science, whether measured in people or events, occurred in Europe and North America from 800 BC to 1950.[195] For O'Brien such cultural facts are 'Eurocentric, provincial, and obsessed with local detail,' or too focused on immaterial events without 'usefulness.'

This emphasis on 'divergence in quantifiable economic terms' allows O'Brien to evaluate Europe's contribution to science only in terms of its economic implications.[196] For all his condemnation of Eurocentrism, he shows no awareness that this abstraction of humans to economic

---

193 Charles Murray, *Human Accomplishment: The Pursuit of Excellence in the Arts and Sciences, 800 B.C. to 1950* (New York: HarperCollins, 2003).

194 Ibid., p. xvi.

195 Ibid., p. 252.

196 O'Brien, 'Historiographical Traditions,' p. 2.

agents alone is itself a modern European idea which cannot be projected backwards onto Europe's history or to all cultures. O'Brien is a Eurocentric egalitarian who has been thoroughly socialised *not* to permit himself any 'triumphalist' notion of heroism according to which his people produced a far higher number of explorers (95%), musical composers (100%), philosophers (about 95%), and scientists. To the contrary: just because Europe did, it must make amends by speaking of equal dialogues and by blaming itself for outperforming the rest of the world. The 'academic offensive' of the URKEW project against European national histories should be seen as a curricular effort to wheedle native European students into accepting the denial of their ethno-cultural identity in favour of a heterogeneous race-mixed society; one in which all the inhabitants are seen essentially as interchangeable economic agents.

O'Brien promises in the abstract that his paper will first suggest 'that the Scientific Revolution's remote antecedents might be traced back to Europe's particular transition from polytheism to monotheism.'[197] This is the focus of a few pages in this 24-page paper, and the most confounding set of pages I have read in a long time. After suggesting a link between monotheism and the maturation of a unified metaphysical cosmography, against the polytheistic and animistic views of pagans, he then tells us that pagan intellectuals in both the eastern and western sides of Eurasia had extended the cognitive capacities of humans long before monotheism through accurate observation and logical styles of argument. He does not tell us however that it was the Greeks who formulated laws of logical thinking, the law of non-contradiction, or that the history of logic is overwhelmingly European. Nevertheless, from a global perspective, even the magisterial eleven-volume work, *Handbook of the History of Logic* (2004–2012)[198] is lacking (despite containing four chapters in the first two volumes on Indian and Arabic logic), because it omits reciprocal connections for each volume. Instead, O'Brien goes on to criticise this pagan

---

197 Ibid., p. 3.
198 Dov M. Gabbay, ed., *Handbook of the History of Logic*, 11 vols. (Amsterdam: Elsevier, 2004–2012).

cosmography — 'all schools of classical philosophy' — by which he now means *Greek* pagan thinking. He says that Greek thinkers 'offered nothing approximating to proofs for their theoretical and logical speculations.'[199]

This is plainly wrong. Aristotle's logical works, which have been grouped under the name of *Organon*, deal precisely with the techniques and principles of proof. Aristotle is regarded as the inventor of the syllogism for his emphasis on logical operators such as 'if', 'then', and 'or' (which all retain the same meaning every time they are employed), and for his efforts in building propositions and arguments from combinations of such univocal terms. This was new in philosophy. What about Euclid's *Elements* (300 BC), a compilation of ancient geometric proofs over the centuries, carefully categorised and formalised? This work is purely theoretical in that it contains no useful applications. But 'it has had an enormous number of applications to practical questions in engineering, architecture, astronomy, physics,'[200] not least within Roman engineering, which 'reached the high point of geometric perfection' based on theoretical knowledge gained from Greece that was useful in resolving complications of measurement and calculation.[201]

O'Brien adds that Greek 'theories' (Epicureanism, Platonism, Stoicism, and Aristotelianism) 'never became highly regarded as economically useful,' or as 'effective prescriptions' for bodily health and the alleviation of 'humankind's eternal angst about life and death.'[202] Therefore, he concludes 'there is no reason to link the rise of modern science to Greek theories.' Let's forget about Hippocrates, the pursuit of the Greek 'good life,' Stoic tranquillity, or Epicurean happiness; how can one summarily disqualify the contributions of the Greeks to science simply because they were not aimed at the production of useful items? What is weird is that, in making

199 O'Brien, 'Historiographical Traditions,' p. 6.

200 Marvin Jay Greenberg, *Euclidean and Non-Euclidean Geometries: Development and History*, 4th ed. (New York: W. H. Freeman, 2008), p. 9.

201 Isaac Moreno Gallo, *Roman Surveying* (2004). http://www.traianvs.net/pdfs/surveying.pdf. First published as *Elementos de ingeniería romana* [Elements of Roman Engineering], *Proceedings of the European Congress* 3 (2004), pp. 25–68.

202 O'Brien, 'Historiographical Traditions,' p. 6.

these claims, O'Brien cites three books by G. E. R Lloyd, namely, *Cognitive Variations: Reflections on the Unity and the Diversity of the Human Mind* (2007);[203] *Adversaries and Authorities* (1996);[204] *Methods and Problems in Greek Science* (1991)[205] — all of which argue that the Greeks were unique in the degree of explicitness and self-consciousness of their inquiries, and in the cultivation of exact and explicit concepts of proof in theoretical knowledge.

In fact, through most of the first half of his paper there is an outlandish incongruity between what O'Brien writes and the sources he refers to. Many sentences are seemingly supported by excellent sources, but these rarely square in their content with what the sources say. Apparently, O'Brien had no sources to counter the Eurocentric view, which is why he eventually calls for 'successful' globalists to accept the old idea that modern science was a European affair; consequently, he is forced to rely on Eurocentric books. However, as he does this, he reinterprets them, or pulls ideas from them which contradict their intended meaning, as if to separate them from any notion of European uniqueness. Moreover, *at the same time* he writes that these sources 'suggest' that the Scientific Revolution may have had 'antecedents' in Europe's past.

But since he does not want to trace modern science to Greece, he goes back to Christian monotheism, starting with the confounding statement that Christian 'fundamentalists' 'suppressed' classical polytheism and all philosophies that had elevated reason above faith. 'Before' the renaissance of the 12th century, he writes, Christian authorities were not particularly willing to 'engage seriously with classical perceptions of nature.'[206] They rejected the classical notion that nature operated according to rational laws, in favour of a world operating according to God's will and unknowable

---

203 G. E. R Lloyd, *Cognitive Variations: Reflections on the Unity and the Diversity of the Human Mind* (New York: Oxford University Press, 2007).

204 G. E. R. Lloyd, *Adversaries and Authorities: Investigations into Ancient Greek and Chinese Science* (New York: Cambridge University Press, 1996).

205 G. E. R. Lloyd, *Methods and Problems in Greek Science* (New York: Cambridge University Press, 1991).

206 O'Brien, 'Historiographical Traditions,' p. 6.

intentions. Again, the sources he cites don't support O'Brien; rather, they point in an opposite direction. Let me begin with some highlights from Marcia Colish's *Medieval Foundations of the Western Intellectual Tradition, 400–1400* (1997):

> [The Latin Apologists of the first centuries A.D.] were convinced that classical thought could and should be used to clarify and defend the Christian message.[207]

> [For Augustine] the universe is subject to an orderly, rational law of nature in which nothing happens arbitrarily.... Classical science and philosophy [were the source of this Augustinian idea].[208]

In a chapter titled "Western European Thought in the *Tenth and Eleventh Centuries*" (my emphasis), Colish focuses on St. Anselm as a logician familiar with 'paronyms, modal propositions, hypothetical syllogisms, and negative formulations.'[209] These are not incidental highlights; Colish's entire book is dedicated to the idea that 'medieval Europe is the *only traditional society* to modernise itself from within, intellectually no less than economically and technologically.'[210]

The second book O'Brien footnotes is Edward Grant's *Science and Religion, 400 B.C.–A.D. 1550: From Aristotle to Copernicus* (2004).[211] The editorial description of this book reads:

> Historian Edward Grant illuminates how today's scientific culture originated with the religious thinkers of the Middle Ages. In the early centuries of Christianity, Christians studied science and natural philosophy only to the extent that these subjects proved useful for a better understanding of the Christian faith, not to acquire knowledge for its own sake. However, with the influx of Greco-Arabic science and natural philosophy into Western Europe during the twelfth and thirteenth centuries, the Christian attitude toward science changed

---

207 Marcia L. Colish, *Medieval Foundations of the Western Intellectual Tradition, 400–1400* (New Haven, CT: Yale University Press, 1997), p. 10.

208 Ibid., p. 30.

209 Ibid., p. 167.

210 Ibid., p. x.

211 Edward Grant, *Science and Religion, 400 B.C.–A.D. 1550: From Aristotle to Copernicus* (Baltimore: Johns Hopkins University Press, 2004).

dramatically. Despite some tensions in the thirteenth century, the Church and its theologians became favorably disposed toward science and natural philosophy and used them extensively in their theological deliberations.[212]

Grant does emphasise changes during and after the 12th century, but he also brings up the ways in which early Christians eagerly assimilated the classical heritage, setting the ground for the breakthrough in the 12th century. In another book, *God and Reason in the Middle Ages* (2001), Grant distinctly states that the 'self-conscious use of reason and the emphasis on rationality go back to the classical Greeks,' and that 'despite' some difficulties in the transmission and spread of this heritage during the centuries after the fall of Rome and the coming of the Germanic peoples and Vikings, 'natural philosophy was welcomed within Western Christendom.' The following passage is worth citing:

> With perhaps few exceptions, philosophers, scientists and natural philosophers in the ancient and medieval periods believed unequivocally in the existence of a unique, and objective world that, with the exception of miracles, was regarded as intelligible, lawful, and essentially knowable.[213]

Grant specifically says that from the 1st century AD onward 'Christianity adopted the idea of using philosophy and science ... for comprehending revealed theology,' providing as well a section on the 'Early Stirrings [in reason and logic] in the Ninth to Eleventh Centuries.'[214]

The third book O'Brien mentions is David Lindberg's edited volume, *Science in the Middle Ages* (2008), which also happens to be about the enormous contribution medieval thinking made to scientific knowledge and the origins of the Scientific Revolution. In his *The Beginnings of Western Science: The European Scientific Tradition in Philosophical, Religious, and Institutional Context, 600 B.C. to A.D. 1450* (1992), which

---

212 http://www.barnesandnoble.com/w/science-and-religion-400-b-c-to-a-d-1550-edward grant/1101796402?ean=9780801884016.

213 Edward Grant, *God and Reason in the Middle Ages* (Cambridge: Cambridge University Press, 2001), pp. 11–13.

214 Ibid., pp. 33–48.

O'Brien references later, Lindberg limits the heyday of Islamic creativity to the period between 800 and 1100, and he notes that, by 1200, Europe had recovered much of the Greek scientific and philosophical legacies maintained by Muslims.

Despite these sources, O'Brien's next move consists in fostering the misleading impression that the Roman Catholic Church was mostly intent on "suppressing" or "evading" "the Eastern-cum-classical [sic] heritage of the West," until eventually the Church "found it expedient" to make concessions to it. After a truly unreadable paragraph, he tries to imply that it was Islam's "advanced economies" that suggested to Christians "that the forces of nature could be manipulated technologically to improve the … material welfare of the faithful, and thus promoted their case for their systematic study."[215] Here, in footnotes 25 and 26, every single book he references refutes his reasoning, and overwhelmingly supports the standard Eurocentric account. These sources are:

Michael Allen Gillespie, *The Theological Origins of Modernity.*[216]

Toby E. Huff, *The Rise of Early Modern Science: Islam, China and the West.*[217]

David C. Lindberg, ed., *The Beginnings of Western Science: The European Scientific Tradition in Philosophical, Religious, and Institutional Context, 600 B.C. to A.D. 1450.*[218]

David Levine, *At the Dawn of Modernity: Biology, Culture, and Material Life in Europe after the Year 1000.*[219]

---

215 O'Brien, 'Historiographical Traditions,' p. 7.

216 Michael Allen Gillespie, *The Theological Origins of Modernity* (Chicago: University of Chicago Press, 2008).

217 Toby E. Huff, *The Rise of Early Modern Science: Islam, China and the West* (Cambridge: Cambridge University Press, 1993).

218 David C. Lindberg, ed., *The Beginnings of Western Science: The European Scientific Tradition in Philosophical, Religious, and Institutional Context, 600 B.C. to A.D. 1450* (Chicago: University of Chicago Press, 2007).

219 David Levine, *At the Dawn of Modernity: Biology, Culture, and Material Life in Europe after the Year 1000* (Berkeley: University of California Press, 2001).

Marshall Clagett, *The Science of Mechanics in the Middle Ages.*[220]

S. R. Epstein and Maarten R. Prak, eds., *Guilds, Innovation and the European Economy, 1400–1800.*[221]

Bert S. Hall and Delno C. West, eds., *On Pre-modern Technology and Science: A Volume of Studies in Honor of Lynn White, Jr.*[222]

Frances Gies and Joseph Gies, *Cathedral, Forge, and Waterwheel: Technology and Invention in the Middle Ages.*[223]

None of these books are discussed and none of them support O'Brien. He then writes that 'by the twelfth century,' the medieval Church finally decided to 'encourage the introduction' ('under strictly regulated rules and conditions') of natural philosophy based on Greek Classical sources. Attached to this statement is this source: Stephen Gaukroger, *The Emergence of a Scientific Culture: Science and the Shaping of Modernity, 1210–1685.*[224] Again, this book refutes his efforts to portray Christianity as a reluctant endorser of Classical philosophy. More than this, Gaukroger argues that Christianity 'set the agenda' for science all the way into the Revolution in a way that no other religion in the world ever had:

> A distinctive feature *of the Scientific Revolution* is that, *unlike* earlier scientific programmes and cultures, it is driven, often explicitly, by religious considerations. Christianity *set the agenda* for natural philosophy in many respects and projected it forward in a way *quite different from that of any other scientific culture.*[225] (My emphasis).

---

220 Marshall Clagett, *The Science of Mechanics in the Middle Ages* (Madison: University of Wisconsin Press, 1959).

221 S. R. Epstein and Maarten R. Prak, eds., *Guilds, Innovation and the European Economy, 1400–1800* (Cambridge: Cambridge University Press, 2008).

222 Bert S. Hall and Delno C. West, eds., *On Pre-modern Technology and Science: A Volume of Studies in Honor of Lynn White, Jr.* (Malibu, CA: Undena Publications, 1976).

223 Frances Gies and Joseph Gies, *Cathedral, Forge, and Waterwheel: Technology and In- vention in the Middle Ages* (New York: HarperCollins, 1994).

224 Stephen Gaukroger, *The Emergence of a Scientific Culture: Science and the Shaping of Modernity, 1210–1685* (Oxford: Oxford University Press, 2006).

225 Ibid., p. 3.

Incredibly, O'Brien goes on to stress that in the four centuries preceding Copernicus (1150 to 1550), pagan texts coming from Byzantium and, 'in elaborated form, from Islamdom,' flowed in successive waves into Europe, with Christian authorities doing their best to 'resist' and 'suppress' them, particularly 'those texts which contradicted core tenets of Christianity' such as the idea that God controlled everything in the world through divine interventions.[226] But, to be fair, O'Brien finally uses sources that square with his claim regarding Islamic transmission. Unfortunately, both these sources happen to be seriously flawed:

John Freely, *Aladdin's Lamp: How Greek Science Came to Europe Through the Islamic World* (New York: Knopf/Doubleday, 2009).

George Saliba, *Islamic Science and the Making of the European Renaissance* (Cambridge, MA: MIT Press, 2007).

O'Brien relies on these books to support the idea that Islamic scholars were teachers of Europeans up until Copernicus and through the entire High Middle Ages in the face of Christian opposition. *Aladdin's Lamp*, however, is a popular account which ignores the books we have been citing, and makes the sweeping claim, without scholarly documentation, that Greek science *tout court* came to Europe through the Islamic world. Saliba's book is more scholarly but its image of a highly creative Islamic tradition lasting well into the 16th century, thereby producing the Italian Renaissance, has been refuted by Huff's argument that Saliba's thesis is based on the supposition that the mere presence of literate men in Muslim lands bespeaks of scientists engaging in outstanding work.[227] The consensus quite firmly supports the view that by the 12th century Europe was in possession of the Islamic contribution and about to move well beyond it.

The two sources O'Brien uses to back the claim that Christians were ambivalent towards the spread of Islamic texts, for fear that these would challenge the idea of God's divine interventions in nature, are: Michael

---

226 O'Brien, 'Historiographical Traditions,' p. 8.

227 Huff, *The Rise of Early Modern Science*.

Allen Gillespie, *The Theological Origins of the Rise of Early Modernity*;[228] and Michael Horace Barnes, *Stages of Thought: The Co-evolution of Religious Thought and Science.*[229] Gillespie makes the opposite argument about the theological 'origins' of modernity, and the book by Barnes has nothing to do with Christianity's relationship to science in medieval Europe; rather, it is authored by a contemporary religious person brought into the debate by O'Brien to confuse and misdirect attention from the issues at hand.

O'Brien keeps pressing the point about how scholastic theologians welcomed investigations of nature while 'resolutely' insisting 'upon the sovereignty of revelation.'[230] 'Most' natural philosophers, 'as true believers ... before, during, and after the Scientific Revolution,' refrained from questioning Christianity's foundational beliefs; 'they operated within authoritarian regimes.' Fortunately, some Christians 'courageously ... referred for support and guidance to Averroes, Avicenna, and other Muslim commentators'. As a result, Christians finally began to deploy 'classical modes of logical reasoning to persuade ecclesiastical and secular elites in the West that God had created and designed a natural world to operate on intelligible principles.'[231]

Every single one of the sources he cites stands against these claims. The title of James Hannam's *God's Philosophers: How the Medieval World Laid the Foundations of Modern Science,*[232] speaks for itself. Richard Olson's *Science and Religion, 1450–1900: From Copernicus to Darwin* [233] is about the profound influence Christianity had on the lives and work of

---

228 Michael Allen Gillespie, *The Theological Origins of Modernity* (Chicago: University of Chicago Press, 2008).

229 Michael Horace Barnes, *Stages of Thought: The Co-evolution of Religious Thought and Science* (New York: Oxford University Press, 2000).

230 O'Brien, "Historiographical Traditions," p.9.

231 Ibid.

232 James Hannam, *God's Philosophers: How the Medieval World Laid the Foundations of Modern Science* (London: Icon Books, 2009).

233 Richard Olson, *Science and Religion, 1450–1900* (Baltimore: Johns Hopkins University Press, 2003).

Galileo, Newton, and Darwin. Edward Grant's *Planets, Stars and Orbs: The Medieval Cosmos, 1200–1687* argues that medieval cosmology was a fusion of pagan Greek ideas and biblical descriptions of the world.[234] The same applies to three other sources he uses.

What is all the more perplexing is the continuous effort by O'Brien to paint Islam as the religion that gave Christian Europe the intellectual sources to think of natural phenomena in terms of natural laws explainable by reason, when it was the other way around. The idea that emerges out of Christian Europe early on is that God is conterminous with reason, whereas in Islam the idea that Allah has limits to his own arbitrary wilfulness remains unthinkable to this day. As Robert Reilly argues in *The Closing of the Muslim Mind: How Intellectual Suicide Created the Modern Islamist Crisis*, Islam was at first engaged with Aristotle but eventually rejected his reasoning when Abu Hamid al-Ghazali established a theology in which Allah came to be portrayed as the personal and immediate director of the movement of every molecule in the universe through his sheer incomprehensible wilfulness.[235] In contrast, starting with St. Anselm's (1033–1109) effort to logically demonstrate the existence of God and continuing with Aquinas and others, Christianity went on to conceptualise the movement of material bodies in terms of natural laws.[236]

O'Brien eventually starts to acknowledge the contribution of medieval Christianity to a 'deeper intelligibility about the natural world,' though he cannot help inserting phrases about 'Islamic discoveries' and how Christians were 'deeply indebted' to Islamic thinking,[237] even though he only has two faulty sources (Saliba[238] and Freely[239]) backing him.

---

234 Edward Grant, *Planets, Stars and Orbs: The Medieval Cosmos, 1200–1687* (New York: Cambridge University Press, 1994).

235 Robert Reilly, *The Closing of the Muslim Mind: How Intellectual Suicide Created the Modern Islamist Crisis* (Wilmington, DE: Intercollegiate Studies Institute, 2010).

236 Hannam, *God's Philosophers*.

237 O'Brien, 'Historiographical Traditions,' p. 11.

238 Saliba, *Islamic Science and the Making of the European Renaissance*.

239 Freely, *Aladdin's Lamp*.

One really has to wonder why O'Brien would misuse text after text; some may want to think this is a sign of his willingness to engage sources that contradict his thesis. But this is not reasonable; the standard practice is, in the first instance, to use sources to support one's arguments. One must refer to countering sources but then try to show what the weaknesses and failures of these sources are. If one is unsure, or the debate is quite undecided, one should acknowledge the opposing sources with statements such as 'for a different view, see a, b, and c,' or, 'for a serious challenge to the ideas presented here, consult x, y, and z,' and the like.

When O'Brien writes about the Scientific Revolution proper, and admits that this revolution occurred inside Europe with antecedents in the medieval era, the sources he uses begin to square with his arguments. My view is that O'Brien, a specialist in quantitative economic history, was unprepared for the true state of scholarship on the question of medieval science, but was still determined to persist with a 'global perspective.' He had a hard time digesting this Eurocentric literature, so he decided to misconstrue one book after another (wording their arguments as closely as possible to his own way of thinking).

Nevertheless, O'Brien's paper will go unquestioned and become part of the 'conversation,' in a growing body of 'scholarly literature' on European history offering a 'new,' 'exciting,' and 'liberating' global perspective. Historians preoccupied with Europe's history lack the metapolitical language to counter the globalists. They are seen as archaic, myopic, and narrow-minded. And the fact is that many of the remaining Eurocentric scholars are 'quiet' academics who debate specialised topics only with their peers without thinking — never mind promoting — a cohesive view of Western civilisation. They are generally liberal minded, sympathetic to the idea of inclusive universities, multiculturalism, and diversity. Some are apolitical or uninvolved with broader political and cultural questions, completely unaware of the dramatic ethnic alteration their own societies are experiencing.

Meanwhile, in contrast to these reserved or 'moderate' academics, O'Brien is part of an activist group of academics who have no qualms forcing their ideological expectations upon the sources. Even though he concludes that global historians 'may sensibly retain the Scientific Revolution as a venerable and heuristic label,'[240] he still presents it as a 'conjuncture in global history,'[241] as a 'fortuitous re-ordering of western Europe's cosmography,'[242] with both Eastern and Western antecedents. By 'conjuncture' he means that it was something that happened in Europe due to the 'fortuitous' dynamics of global forces, which could have happened elsewhere. There was nothing really unique about Europe; modern science, after all, is about engendering instruments 'for the accumulation of useful and reliable knowledge' for humanity.

O'Brien did not offer one original thought. He condemned the 'myopias imposed' by national histories of this revolution, but relied almost entirely on such histories; and, without any sources of his own, enforced the globalist approach on the literature, twisting it beyond the author's intentions. This is the strategy academic globalists are employing to dilute European identity, destroy European cultural pride and confidence, promote globalisation, and create a new economic man.

Meta-empirical Presuppositions in Multicultural History

Next I will examine a review of Toby Huff's *Intellectual Curiosity and the Scientific Revolution: A Global Perspective*[243] by Ting Xu and Khodadad Rezakhani in the *Journal of World History*, a leading journal in the field.[244] Both authors completed their PhDs in Western universities, respectively

---

240 O'Brien, 'Historiographical Traditions,' p. 13.

241 Ibid., p. 22.

242 Ibid., p. 15.

243 Toby Huff, *Intellectual Curiosity and the Scientific Revolution: A Global Perspective* (New York: Cambridge University Press, 2010).

244 Ting Xu and Khodadad Rezakhani, 'Reorienting the Discovery Machine: Perspectives from China and Islamdom,' *Journal of World History* 23, no. 2 (June 2012): pp. 401–412.

at the London School of Economics (LSE), and UCLA; both have been closely associated with the Global Economic History Network (GEHN) headed by Professor O'Brien. Both came to England as international students (Rezakhani first coming to obtain a master's degree at the LSE), and both appear to be citizens or permanent residents in Western countries. Xu is currently teaching at Queen's Law School, Belfast, and Rezakhani is Alexander von Humboldt Research Fellow at Freie Universität Berlin.

The GEHN is the product of cooperation across five partner institutions (LSE, the University of California–Irvine, UCLA, Leiden University, and Osaka University). It promotes England to the world and to potential international students as an ideal cosmopolitan place for the mixing of cultures and races against the 'parochial' identity of the British past. In operation since 2003, it has some 49 international academics on its roster, and is backed by numerous grants. Its mission statement distinctly states that this network 'seeks to broaden and deepen people's understanding of themselves, their cultures and their states by *extending the geographical spaces* and lengthening the chronologies that most historians normally take into their narratives and analyses' (emphasis added).[245] It further states, and this passage is worth quoting and clarifying:

> Aspirations to *transcend the confines of personal, local, national and European history* go back to Herodotus and were certainly present in histories published in the medieval era of Christendom. They blossomed in secular form during the Enlightenment, *almost disappeared during the centuries which witnessed the Rise of the West, but have revived again during recent decades of intensified globalisation and multiculturalism.* (Emphasis added.)

The claim is that Europeans were generally seeking to 'transcend' their national parochialism from ancient times through to the Enlightenment era. But then they became too flattered with their dominion over the world during the 19th century ('the Rise of the West') and, consequently, they lost interest in overcoming their ethnocentric biases. However, with

245 GEHN, 'Mission Statement.' http://www.lse.ac.uk/economicHistory/Research/GEHN/network/GEHNMission.aspx.

the intensification of globalisation and multiculturalism, there has been a revival of this transcendence, so that Europeans are escaping their confining nationalisms. Never mind that the Greeks only granted citizenship to ethnic members of the *polis* and that during the 19th century Europeans were exceptionally curious (anthropologically) about other cultures, eagerly writing the histories of non-Europeans in a scholarly manner.

The point to note is that the professors working or hired into this program, including the students, are expected to accept this political mission. Multiculturalism is accepted without definition, without analysis, and without debate about its costs to Europeans. The research publications of the members of GHEN are consistent, in varying ways, with the mission statement. The central premise of multiculturalism — that all cultures are equal in achievements and merit — is accepted *ab initio*. GEHN takes it for granted that England's (and Europe's) intensified globalisation ought to come with multiculturalism (and mass immigration), without making it a subject of research. Nor is there any interest in asking whether Asian nations, too, should be experiencing globalisation while undermining their own national identities and inviting their countries to be flooded by immigrants.

The history mandated by GHEN cannot possibly be seen in neutral, purely empirical terms, but instead as an ideological mission to promote an interpretation of Europe's history that suits the increasingly multiracial character of Western nations and is consistent with cultural egalitarianism. This does not mean that there are no debates over various factual matters and comparative assessments of the regions of the world. However, the overall tenor and objective of the program is geared toward the internationalisation of European culture from a pro-immigrant, multicultural perspective.

Maxine Berg, a major GEHN member and Director of the Global History and Culture Centre (GHCC) at the University of Warwick, eloquently expresses the same aim: a 'global approach to historical questions and research.'[246] The mission is not to encourage a global history because it is a more empirically in tune with the evidence, but to promote a 'global culture,' and a new way of writing the history of Europe by 'going beyond borders and pursuing wider concepts of connectedness and cosmopolitanism.' Included among her many appointments and fellowships are European Research Council Fellow (2010–2014), and Director of the European Research Council Fellowship project, 'Europe's Asian Centuries: Trading Eurasia 1600–1830.' Regarding the latter, Berg writes triumphantly that 'the 21st Century has witnessed a new Asian ascendancy over the West. Europe has lost the manufacturing catalyst of textiles, ceramics and metal goods back to India and China.'

Don't expect to find a similar expression about the ascendancy of Europe 'over Asia' after 1500. To the contrary, any talk of 'ascendancy' by the West has been suppressed unless it is about imperialism and unfair trade advantages; England may have experience the 'first' industrial revolution but this can only be explained in terms of 'Chinese, Indian, and African antecedents.'[247]

The Marxist orientation of the GHCC's teaching and research is apparent in a booklet celebrating its fifth anniversary:

> Focal points developed based on the specialism of Centre members, including the material culture of global connections, post- colonial theory, comparisons in technology, frameworks of local and regional histories, Chinese cities in global context, Caribbean and Spanish American trade and slavery, African decolonization, Indian Ocean diasporas, and South and East Asian health and medicine.[248]

The 'Selected Publications' from its members are overwhelmingly about Europe's slave colonies, and Asia's and Africa's liberation and

---

246 Maxine Berg, ed., *Writing the History of the Global: Challenges for the 21st Century* (Oxford: Oxford University Press/British Academy, 2013).

247 Patrick O'Brien, 'Provincializing the First Industrial Revolution,' Working Papers of the Global Economic History Network (GEHN) No. 17/06 (2006). http://www.lse. ac.uk/economicHistory/Research/GEHN/GEHNPDF/WorkingPaper17-POB.pdf.

248 *Global History and Centre at the University of Warwick: 2007–2012 5th Anniversary.* http://www2.warwick.ac.uk/fac/arts/history/ghcc/140197_ghcc_a5_7th_proof.pdf.

beautiful cultural tapestries — thus ignoring: (1) the slavery that was endemic throughout the non-Western world, and (2) the unique role Europeans played in abolishing slavery for moral reasons.[249]

The review of Huff's *Intellectual Curiosity and the Scientific Revolution* by Xu and Rezakhani cannot be adequately evaluated without an awareness of these meta-empirical objectives. Both Xu and Rezakhani are leftist in their politics, believers in multiculturalism and mass immigration, and well-trained in the prevailing academic orthodoxies. Rezakhani can be easily classified as an Iranian nationalist thoroughly committed to Marxist or world-systems theory, steeped in the anti-Western writings of Immanuel Wallerstein, Janet Abu Lughod, James Blaut, and Andre Gunder Frank. He is an enthusiastic advocate of 'an alternative, non-Eurocentric, and truly global history.' Xu is quieter; her parents survived Mao's Cultural Revolution, but she has embraced Western cultural Marxism, though she likely has no idea what this term means; either way, she lists Kenneth Pomeranz's Marxist text, *The Great Divergence*,[250] as one of the 'seminal' books in her education, along with Karl Polanyi's *The Great Transformation*[251] and other books which condemn Western neoliberal imperialism.

In using the term 'meta-empirical,' I am drawing loosely on Ludwig Wittgenstein's argument that all discursive claims are ultimately framed by language games, which the proponents of particular discourses do not subject to probing questions, but accept for moral or politically motivated reasons. I would not thereby conclude that the evidence a discourse marshals in support of its claims is subsidiary or incidental to its normative goals, or that it is all a matter of language games contesting for rhetorical and political influence. Different discourses generate different types of

---

249 Kevin MacDonald, 'Empathy and Moral Universalism as Components of White Pathology: The Movement to Abolish Slavery in England,' *The Occidental Quarterly* 13, no. 2 (Summer 2013): pp. 39–63.

250 Kenneth Pomeranz, *The Great Divergence: China, Europe, and the Making of the Modern World Economy* (Princeton, NJ: Princeton University Press, 2000).

251 Karl Polanyi, *The Great Transformation: The Political and Economic Origins of Our Time* (Boston: Beacon Press, 1944).

evidential support, and some discourses have a keener appreciation and commitment to the evidence available than others. But Wittgenstein is correct to alert us to the presence in all discourses of language games or metapolitical norms which stand independently of the evidence and are generally taken for granted.

The meta-empirical norms of multicultural historians are not explicitly stated in their arguments, but the promotion of diversity and immigrant racial mixing is certainly a key norm driving their historical interpretations. In the review-essay under examination these norms are understated, neutralised, and normalised, as if they were purely methodological in character; accordingly, their advocates don't feel obligated to offer justifications for them. Xu and Rezakhani thus write gently in their conclusion:

> His [i.e., Huff's] comparative study could have been more persuasive if he had adopted a framework of 'two-way comparisons.' Instead of asking 'why not' questions, such reciprocal comparisons establish what was similar about Chinese/Islamic and European proto-science before examining what was different. Instead of asking simply 'Why Europe?' and 'Why not China or the Islamic world?' historians need to observe and elaborate upon similarities while appreciating contrasts.

Xu and Rezakhani cite Pomeranz's *The Great Divergence* and Bin Wong's *China Transformed* as exemplary examples of this 'two-way' comparative 'method'.[252] It should be called 'attitude' rather than 'method.' From this 'two-way,' 'reciprocal' perspective, Pomeranz and Wong concluded that Europe and Asia were 'surprisingly similar' in their institutions and economic development as late as 1800. The Industrial Revolution was a late occurrence arising from a series of fortunate accidents and 'conjunctural' tendencies within the 'capitalist international economy.' It is not that Pomeranz and Wong did not collect any evidence; actually, they were both quite astute in gathering evidence. But their evidence was framed

---

252 Bin Wong, *China Transformed: Historical Change and the Limits of European Experience* (Ithaca, NY: Cornell University Press, 2000).

according to an attitude in which the industrial revolution had to be seen as equally probable in both Europe and Asia. With this method, there can never be a prognosis, a fore-seeing, an examination of extrapolative indicators, in such a way that one region is given priority (or not) in the search for indicators. Rather, the investigator is precluded from 'assuming' that one region or country *did* (or *did not*) experience an industrial revolution first.

Huff, however, is an old-school historian, who goes for evidence where he thinks it is likely to be, searching as well for contrary evidence and contradicting arguments. When he started *Intellectual Curiosity and the Scientific Revolution*, he was not guessing or 'supposing' that Europe invented the telescope and microscope; the evidence was already irrefutable that it *did*, and that Asia *did not*. But for Xu and Rezakhani, this is not a 'two-way' approach; Huff is not being 'reciprocal', that is, mutual and equivalent in his suppositions. He made the mistake of posing the 'binary' question: why *did* Europe embrace the invention of telescopes and microscopes? And, conversely: why did China, Mughal India, and the Ottoman Empire *not* show curiosity for these quintessential instruments of scientific discovery? These instruments were actually brought to China and India, but their elites showed little enthusiasm for them.

The second instance in which Xu and Rezakhani silently exhibit this multicultural normative evaluation of the evidence comes in the contrast they draw between Huff's 'clash of civilisations' approach, and their 'dialogue of civilisations' approach. The word 'clash' is defined in dictionaries as: 'To collide with a loud, harsh, usually metallic noise; to create an unpleasant visual impression when placed together; a conflict, as between opposing or irreconcilable ideas; an encounter between hostile forces.' The word 'dialogue' is defined in reverse terms: 'conversation between two or more persons; an exchange of ideas or opinions, especially a political or religious issue, with a view to reaching an amicable agreement or settlement.' Clearly, the message is that Huff does not have the right attitude. Whereas Xu and Rezakhani are frankly trying to debate in a good-natured, give-and-take manner, Huff is setting Europe above Asia. This they infer creates an unpleasant impression among Chinese and Iranian students who may feel left out, and nurtures an aggressive, strident attitude among European natives, who may exhibit vain pride.

The Greeks were the first to nurture the idea that truth is best attained through a dialogue rather than commandments imposed from above, as was the norm in the East. This dialogical style was adopted by Islamic scholars early in the 9th century, but as a way of determining Islamic orthodoxy through consensus. The scholastics of medieval Europe developed this method in a more intricate direction, along the lines of the following schema:

(1)   Thesis and counter-thesis.

(2)   Arguments for the thesis.

(3)   Objections to the argument.

(4)   Replies to the objections.

(5)   Pseudo-arguments for the counter-thesis.

(6)   Replies in refutation of the pseudo-arguments.[253]

Catholic scholastics would engage major works by renowned authors, read them thoroughly and then compare the book's theories to other sources, and through a series of dialogues they would ascertain the respective merits and demerits of these sources.

This did not imply that any argument expressed by anyone was taken to be on an equal footing and therefore deserving to be considered along with currently accepted ideas. Today, world historians are misusing this dialectical method to push through the notion that the ideas the West achieved through this method are incomplete unless they are integrated with the claims of other civilisations. Some are even pushing

---

253   George Makdisi, 'The Scholastic Method in Medieval Education: An Inquiry into Its Origins in Law and Theology,' *Speculum* 49, no. 4 (October 1974): pp. 640–661.

the absurd and destructive concept of 'Euroislam'[254] or 'Islamo-Christian Civilization'[255] as a way to create a more dialogical culture in Europe.

Xu and Rezakhani thus reference Arun Bala's book, *The Dialogue of Civilizations in the Birth of Modern Science*, for its ability to portray the rise of Newtonian mechanics as a friendly conversation involving Chinese mechanical inventions and cosmological views, Indian computing techniques and atomic hypotheses, Arabic planetary and optical theories, and Greek ideas.[256] Bala's dialogical explanation can be summed up in one sentence: Europe's overseas explorations opened the intellectual corridors of communication and exchange of ideas providing the impetus for the Renaissance and the birth of modern science and philosophy in Europe.[257] H. Floris Cohen demolished this pseudo-argument in one effective paragraph:

> Bala's point of departure is that in the history of science a 'dialogue of civilizations' is a priori plausible and is *not* in any given case in indispensable need of empirical evidence. He gives body to the point by means of the following criterion, meant to be more strict than Needham's apparent "everything goes" in this regard: "If, shortly after a new corridor of communication opens between a culture A and a culture B, and great interest [is] shown by A to understand B, a theme becomes dominant in A similar to a dominant theme in B, then we can presume that the development of the theme in A was due to the influence of B, even if the new theme had existed as a recessive theme in A prior to contact between the cultures." In practice Bala has now given himself sufficient leeway

---

254 Bassam Tibi, 'Europeanizing Islam or the Islamization of Europe,' in *Religion in an Expanding Europe*, ed. Peter Katzenstein (Cambridge: Cambridge University Press, 2006).

255 Richard Bulliet, *The Case for Islamo-Christian Civilization* (New York: Columbia University Press, 2004).

256 Arun Bala, *The Dialogue of Civilizations in the Birth of Modern Science* (New York: Palgrave Macmillan, 2006).

257 *Dialogue of Civilizations* propelled Bala, from Singapore, into the international academic scene with visiting professorships at University of Toronto, Dalhousie University, and the University of Western Ontario, including conference presentations at the prestigious GEHN, with approving references by leading researcher, Patrick O'Brien. He is now seen, according to *Wikipedia*, as a foremost contributor to the 'continuity thesis,' and a major voice in the exhaustive debate on Thomas Kuhn's conception of the structure of scientific revolutions.

for what he goes on to do in the remainder of his book. Without a shred of empirical evidence he allows critiques of Ptolemy in the Arabic world to affect Copernicus' thinking, or fifteenth/sixteenth century Indian mathematicians to contribute to Newton's discovery of the calculus, or Shen Kua's late-eleventh century discovery of magnetic declination to culminate in Kepler's laws.

This passage comes from Cohen's review essay, 'From West to East, from East to West? Early Science between Civilizations.'[258] In this essay, he addresses other similarly argued books, as well as 'Eurocentric' books, including Huff's, which he also criticises. Cohen reproaches Huff for portraying Asians as a people lacking in intellectual curiosity; Huff should have investigated the reasons why Asians were not as enthusiastic for these scientific instruments. In Cohen's view, Huff failed to appreciate the rather different 'cultural context' of Asians. It is Eurocentric to presume that the Asians should have exhibited the same curiosity in respect to these instruments. Besides, adds Cohen, Huff underestimates the resistance to science in Christian Europe proper.

Xu and Rezakhani offer a slightly more elaborate version of this same argument. They say that Huff 'failed' to identify the cosmographical or world views of the Chinese; a cultural context, which included the particular ways in which Chinese scholars thought about astronomy, mathematics, mechanics, and so on, which 'was strictly controlled by the state and was traditionally conceived in terms of 'correlations between man and the universe' or between the emperor and the heavens rather than an inquiry into the laws of motion and physics of some remote celestial sphere.'[259] It was not that the Chinese lacked curiosity, but that they inhabited a different cultural horizon.

This criticism actually reinforces the argument that Europeans were peculiarly scientific in a way that Asians (or the Chinese) were not *in profoundly cultural ways*. Cohen has done extensive research on the question at hand: why was there a scientific revolution in Europe and

258 H. Floris Cohen, 'From West to East, from East to West? Early Science between Civilizations,' *Early Science & Medicine* 17, no. 3 (June 2012): pp. 339–350.

259 Xu and Rezakhani, 'Reorienting the Discovery Machine,' p. 408.

not elsewhere? What is the point of looking for scientific evidence in a non-European context and then, at the moment one finds out that this context lacked a scientific mentality, concluding that it is unfair to look for scientific motivations in that context? This way of thinking (which Cohen has assimilated from multiculturalists, leading him to believe that Eurocentrism 'still' dominates academia and must be moderated by his middle-of-the-road attitude) is plainly characterised by a 'heads I win, tails you lose' style. Tails: 'Don't be so Eurocentric in believing that Asians were not equally important to the rise of modern science.' Heads: 'Don't be so Eurocentric in assuming that Asians should have been as curious in the use of scientific instruments.'

The focus of Xu and Rezakhani's review is to highlight the way Asians were the possessors of a legacy as important to science as that of the Europeans up until about 1500. They say that Huff ignores Islamic interest in the study of the vacuum and optics, citing an article from 1964 on the suction pump and a book on Islamic science from 1993. Actually, the vacuum was studied empirically only in the 17th century when Evangelista Torricelli produced the first laboratory vacuum in 1643. They attempt to dispute Huff's argument that only Europeans created universities with the institutional quality and autonomy to pursue rationally based knowledge by briefly referring to some alleged Muslim 'private foundations generating research comparable in range and quality to the medieval universities of the West.' But the only source they use to back this claim is an Iranian paper three pages long.

They rebuke Huff for relying heavily on *The Rise of Colleges*, a 1981 book by George Makdisi.[260] But what is revealing here is that Makdisi is the author of an article published in 1974, 'The Scholastic Method in Medieval Education: An Inquiry into Its Origins in Law and Theology'[261] (also cited above), which begins by referencing European scholars who long ago seriously acknowledged the extent of influence of Islamic scholarly culture

---

260 George Makdisi, *The Rise of Colleges* (Edinburgh: University of Edinburgh Press, 1981).

261 Makdisi, 'The Scholastic Method in Medieval Education.'

on the West. Since ancient times, Europeans have acknowledged their debts to others. Throughout the 20th century countless books and articles have been written by them on the history and accomplishments of other civilisations, and their influence on the West.

What multicultural world historians are doing today is something altogether dissimilar. The research has *never shown* that the sources of modern science were *not* primarily due to Europe's internal culture and institutions. Instead, all the evidence has shown that Europeans were progenitors of multiple novelties and revolutions (if you read beyond one epoch and contrary to Cohen's assumption that Western uniqueness is predicated on the 17th century): the inventors of universities, 95% of all the explorers in history,[262] the cartographic revolution of the 16th century,[263] the 'long' military revolution from 1350 onward, successive industrial revolutions, the Enlightenment, the Greek 'discovery' of the mind, politics, geometry, tragedy, and historical writing. One could also mention the astounding (but until recently underestimated) Roman contribution to technology,[264] besides their much celebrated anticipation of 'modern' legal principles; the singular European legacy in classical music;[265] the printing revolution,[266] mechanical clocks, changing styles in clothing, architecture, poetry, and literature.

Because of the dearth of data supporting their views, world historians have tacitly decided to frame the debate within a rather pleasant-sounding view that calls for the tolerance and inclusiveness of alternative viewpoints,

262 Ricardo Duchesne, 'A Civilization of Explorers,' *Academic Questions* 25, no. 1 (March 2012): pp. 65–93.

263 David Buisseret, *The Cartographic Revolution: Mapmaking in Western Europe, 1400–1800* (New York: Oxford University Press, 2003).

264 Unfortunately the prevailing view is still the one voiced by Moses Finley that Roman economy was 'underdeveloped and underachieving.' Moses Finley, *The Ancient Economy* (Berkeley: University of California Press, 1973). But the research no longer supports this view; see David Mattingly, 'The Imperial Economy,' in *A Companion to the Roman Empire*, ed. David Potter (London: Wiley-Blackwell, 2009), pp. 283–297.

265 Harold C. Schonberg, *The Lives of the Great Composers* (Preston, UK: Abacus Press, 2006).

266 Elizabeth Eisenstein, *The Printing Revolution as an Agent of Change* (Cambridge: Cambridge University Press, 1980).

notwithstanding the weight of the evidence. Actually, Xu and Rezakhani don't even try to find evidence against Huff's research on telescopes and microscopes. They simply think that his research 'runs contrary to a useful, multilinear study of scientific inquiry and diffusion in pre-modern world history.' Most of the counterpoints they bring are in the manner of 'he says, she says.' For example, they question Huff's observation that institutions of learning outside Europe did not enjoy an autonomous status, claiming that there were private academies in Asia that 'resembled their European counterparts in other respects.' But then they use other sources showing that 'studies of the natural world in China became marginal to a concentration on moral and ethical philosophy — especially after Neo-Confucianism became the state orthodoxy from the Yuan dynasty (1279–1368) onward.'

What a great conversation! Huff says that madrasas were pious centres of learning, unlike the curriculum at European universities which, in the words of Edward Grant, 'was overwhelmingly analytical and rational.'[267] But this is too one-sided, so Xu and Rezakhani counter that 'many of Europe's medieval universities were also pious, indeed monastic, foundations with closer ties to ecclesiastical and secular hierarchies than many madrasas of the post 13th century Islamic world.' The scholarship prodigiously favours Huff's and Grant's position, but that's not the point. As long as the other side can come up with a source that creates an impression of 'balance' and multicultural interconnections, the argument is taken seriously.

This debate is no longer about scholarly comparisons, but about which views fit the creation of a diverse curriculum consistent with mass immigration into Western lands. European historical memory *and* truthful historical scholarship must not be allowed to stand in the way of this meta-empirical goal.

---

267 Edward Grant, *God and Reason in the Middle Ages* (Cambridge: Cambridge University Press, 2001), p. 102.

The Absurd Globalisation of the Enlightenment

The Enlightenment has always been viewed as a European phenomenon, and is respected in academia for its call upon 'humanity' to subject all authority to critical reflection. However, it too is enduring a fundamental revision, as a movement that was global in origins and character. This is the view expressed in a recent article, 'Enlightenment in Global History: A Historiographical Critique,' authored by Sebastian Conrad, who holds the Chair of Modern History at Freie University, Berlin.[268] This is a 'historiographical' assessment based on current trends in the global history of the Enlightenment, not an isolated paper. It was published in *The American Historical Review*, the official publication of the American Historical Association, and a pre-eminent journal for the historical profession in the United States since 1895.

Conrad calls upon historians to move 'beyond the obsession' and the 'European mythology' that the Enlightenment was original to Europe:

> The assumption that the Enlightenment was a specifically European phenomenon remains one of the foundational premises of Western modernity.... The Enlightenment appears as an original and autonomous product of Europe, deeply embedded in the cultural traditions of the Occident.... This interpretation is no longer tenable.

Conrad's critique is vacuous, absurd, and unscholarly—a demonstration of the irrational lengths otherwise intelligent Europeans will go to in their efforts to promote egalitarianism and affirmative action on a global scale. It is important for defenders of the West to see with clear eyes the extremely weak scholarship standing behind the prestigious titles and 'first class' journals where these ideas are disseminated. Conrad's claims could have been taken seriously only within an academic environment bordering on pathological wishful thinking (he gratefully acknowledges nine established academic readers plus 'the anonymous reviewers' working for the *AHR*). The intended goal of Conrad's paper is not truth but

---

268 Sebastian Conrad, 'Enlightenment in Global History: A Historiographical Critique,' *The American Historical Review* 117, no. 4 (October 2012): pp. 999–1027.

the dissolution of Europe's intellectual identity within a mishmash of intercultural connections.

It should be noted, again, that Conrad and the *AHR* are operating within a normative context dedicated to diversity. The ploy to rob Europeans of their heritage is not an affair restricted to squabbling academics looking for promotion; it is now an established reality in every high school in the West. This can be partly ascertained from a reading of the 2011 AP World History Standard,[269] as mandated by the College Board. Created in 1900 to expand access to higher education, it has a current membership of 5,900 of the world's leading educational institutions. This Board is very clear in its mandate that the courses developed for advanced placement in world history (for students to pursue college-level studies while in high school) should 'allow students to make crucial *connections* … across geographical regions.' The overwhelming emphasis of the 'curriculum framework' is on 'interactions,' 'connected hemispheres,' 'exchange and communication networks,' 'interconnection of the Eastern and Western hemispheres,' and so on. For all the seemingly neutral talk about regional connections, the salient feature of this mandate is on how developments *inside Europe* were necessarily shaped by developments occurring in neighbouring regions or even the whole world. One rarely encounters an emphasis on how developments in Asia were determined by developments in Europe — unless, of course, they point to the destructive effects of European aggression.

Thus, the Board mandates the teaching of topics such as how 'the European colonisation of the Americas led to the spread of diseases,' how 'the introduction of European settlements practices in the Americas often affected the physical environment through deforestation and soil depletion,' how 'the creation of European empires in the Americas quickly fostered a new Atlantic trade system that included the trans-Atlantic slave trade,' and so on. The curriculum is thoroughly Marxist in its accent on class relations, coerced labour, 'modes of production,' imperialism, gender,

---

269 http://apcentral.collegeboard.com/apc/public/repository/AP_WorldHistoryCED_
Effective_Fall_2011.pdf.

race relations, demographic changes, and rebellions. Europe's contributions to painting, architecture, history writing, philosophy, and science are never highlighted except when they can be interpreted as 'ideologies' of the ruling (European) classes.

It is not that the curriculum ignores the obvious formation of non-Western empires, but the weight is always on how, for example, the rise of 'new racial ideologies, especially Social Darwinism, facilitated and justified imperialism.' Even the overwhelming reality of Europe's contribution to science and technology in the 19th and 20th century is framed as a global phenomenon in which all the regions were equal participants.

Conrad's article will be seen as normal and readily accepted by future generations accustomed to this 'scholarship.' Conrad was most likely a student of diversity in Germany. His article seeks to show that recent research has proven false the 'standard' Eurocentric interpretation of the Enlightenment. Conrad views this standard interpretation as the 'master' narrative today, which continues to exist in the face of mounting evidence against it.

It is true that the Enlightenment is still viewed as uniquely European by a number of well-respected scholars such as Margaret Jacob, Gertrude Himmelfarb, and Roy Porter. In fact, it is the most often referenced Western legacy used by right-wing liberals (or neoconservatives) against the multicultural emphasis on the equality of cultures. These days, defending the West has come down to defending the 'universal' values of the Enlightenment — gender equality, freedom of thought, and individual rights — against the 'intolerant' particularism of other cultures. The late Christopher Hitchens, Ayaan Hirsi Ali, Niall Ferguson, and Pascal Bruckner are some of the most notorious advocates of these values as universal norms that represent all human aspirations. The immigration of non-Europeans in the West poses no menace to them as long as they are transformed into happy consuming liberals.

I have no interest celebrating the West from this cosmopolitan standpoint. It is commonly believed (including by members of the European

New Right) that the global interpretation Conrad delineates against a European-centred Enlightenment is itself rooted in the *philosophes'* exaltation of 'mankind.' Conrad knows this; in the last two paragraphs he justifies his postmodern reading of history by arguing that the Enlightenment 'language of universal claim and worldwide validity' requires that its origins *not* be 'restricted' to Europe. The Enlightenment, if it is to fulfil its universal promises, must be seen as the actual child of peoples across the world.

This is all the more reason why Conrad's arguments must be exposed. Not only are they historically false, but they provide us with an opportunity to suggest that the values of the Enlightenment are peculiarly European, rooted in this continent's history, and not universally true and applicable to humanity. For one thing, these values are inconsistent with Conrad's style of research. Honest reflection based on reason and open inquiry shows that the Enlightenment was exclusively European. The great thinkers of the Enlightenment were aristocratic representatives of their people with a sense of rooted history and lineage. They did not believe (except for a rare few) that all the peoples of the earth were members of a race-less humanity in equal possession of reason. When they wrote of 'mankind' they meant 'European-kind.' When they wrote about equality they meant that Europeans have an innate a priori capacity to reason. When they said that 'only a true cosmopolitan can be a good citizen,' they meant that European nationals should enlarge their focus and consider Europe 'as a great republic.'

What concerns Conrad, however, is the promotion of a history in which the diverse cultures of the world can be seen as equal participants in the making of the Enlightenment. Conrad wants to carry to its logical conclusion the allegedly 'universal' ideals of the Enlightenment, hoping to persuade Westerners that the equality and the brotherhood of mankind require the promotion of a Global Enlightenment. But Conrad blunders right from the start when he references Toby Huff's book, *Intellectual Curiosity and the Scientific Revolution*, as an example of the 'no longer tenable' 'standard reading' of the Enlightenment. First, this book is about the uniquely 'modern scientific mentality' witnessed in 17th century Europe, not about the 18th century Enlightenment. It is also a study written, as the subtitle says, from 'a Global Perspective.' Rather than brushing off this book in one sentence, Conrad should have addressed its main argument, published in 2010 and based on the latest research, showing that European efforts to encourage interest in the telescope in China, the Ottoman Empire, and Mughal India 'did not bear much fruit.' 'The telescope that set Europeans on fire with enthusiasm and curiosity, failed to ignite the same spark elsewhere. That led to a great divergence that was to last all the way to the end of the 20th century.'[270]

The diffusion of the microscope was met with the same lack of curiosity. Why would Asia experience an Enlightenment culture together with Europe if it only started to embrace modern science with advanced research centres in the 20th century? This simple question does not cross Conrad's mind; he merely cites an innocuous sentence from Huff's book which contains the word 'Enlightenment' and then, without challenging Huff's argument, concludes that 'this interpretation is no longer tenable.'

Conrad then repeats phrases to the effect that the Enlightenment needs to be seen originally as 'the work of historical actors around the world.' But as he cannot come up with a single Enlightenment thinker from the 18th century outside Europe, he immediately introduces postmodernist lingo about 'how malleable the concept' of Enlightenment was from its inception, from which point he calls for a more flexible and inclusive definition, so that he can designate as part of the Enlightenment any name or idea he encounters in the world which carries some semblance of learning. He also calls for an extension of the period of Enlightenment beyond the 18th century all the way into the 20th century. The earlier 'narrow definitions of the term' must be replaced by open-minded and tolerant definitions which reflect the 'ambivalences and the multiplicity of Enlightenment views' across the world.

---

270 Huff, *Intellectual Curiosity and the Scientific Revolution*, p. 5.

From this vantage point, he attacks the 'fixed' standard view of the Enlightenment. Early on, besides Huff's book, Conrad footnotes Peter Gay's *The Enlightenment: An Interpretation* (1966–1969),[271] Dorinda Outram's *The Enlightenment* (1995),[272] Hugh Trevor-Roper's *History and the Enlightenment* (2010),[273] as well as *The Blackwell Companion to the Enlightenment* (1991).[274] Of these, I would say that Gay is the only author who can be said to have offered a synthesis that came to be widely held, but only from about the mid-1960s to the mid-1970s. In the first page of his book, Gay distinctly states that 'the Enlightenment was united on a vastly ambitious program, a program of secularism, humanity, cosmopolitanism, and freedom.'[275] In the case of Outram's book, it is quite odd that Conrad would include it as a standard account since the back cover alone says it will view the Enlightenment 'as a global phenomenon' characterised by contradictory trends. The book's focus is on the role of coffee houses, religion, science, gender, and government from a cross-cultural perspective. In fact, a few footnotes later, Conrad cites this same book as part of new research pointing to the 'heterogeneity' and 'fragmented' character of the Enlightenment. However, the book makes no claims that the Enlightenment originated in multiple places in the world, and this is clearly the reason Conrad has labelled it as part of the 'standard' view.

Conrad has no sources to back his claim that there is currently a 'dominant' and uniform view. Gay, Outram, Trevor-Roper,[276] and other

---

271 Peter Gay, *The Enlightenment: An Interpretation*, 2 vols. (New York: W. W. Norton, 1966–1969).

272 Dorinda Outram, *The Enlightenment* (New York: Cambridge University Press, 1995).

273 Hugh Trevor-Roper, *History and the Enlightenment* (New Haven, CT: Yale University Press, 2010).

274 John Yolton, Pat Rogers, Roy Porter, and Barbara Stafford, eds., *The Blackwell Companion to the Enlightenment* (London: Wiley-Blackwell, 1991).

275 Gay, *The Enlightenment*, pp. 1–3.

276 Designating Trevor-Roper's *History and the Enlightenment* as a 'standard' account seems out of place. Trevor-Roper died in 2003, and when his book was published (which consisted mainly of old essays), reviewers seemed more interested in Trevor-Roper the person than the authority on the Enlightenment. *The New Republic* (March 2011) review barely touches his views on the Enlightenment, concentrating on Trevor-Roper's lifetime achievements as a historian and man of letters. Anthony T. Grafton,

sources he cites later (to be addressed below), are not dominant, but show instead what Outram noticed in her book (first published in 1995): 'the Enlightenment has been interpreted in many different ways.'[277] This is why Conrad soon admits that 'at present, only a small — if vociferous — minority of historians maintain the unity of the Enlightenment project.' Since Gay died in 2006, Conrad then comes up with two names, Jonathan Israel and John Robertson, who apparently hold today a unified view. Yet, he then concedes in a footnote that these two authors have 'a very different Enlightenment view: for Israel the 'real' Enlightenment is over by the 1740s, while for Robertson it only begins then.' In other words, on the question of timing, they have diametrically different views.

'Historiographical' studies are meant to clarify the state of the literature in a given historical subject, the trends, schools of thought, and competing interpretations. Conrad instead misreads, confounds, and muddles up authors and books. The reason Conrad relies on Outram, and other authors, both as 'dominant' and as pleasingly diverse, is that European scholars have long recognised the complexity and conflicting currents within the Enlightenment at the same time that they have continued to view it as 'European' with certain common themes. We thus find Outram

---

'Learning and Pleasure,' *The New Republic*, March 3, 2011. http://www.newrepublic.com/article/books-and-arts/magazine/84508/hugh-trevor-roper-oxford-review.

The *Washington Post* (June 2010) correctly notes that Trevor-Roper was an 'essayist by inclination,' interested in the details and idiosyncrasies of the characters he wrote about, without postulating a unified vision (Michael Dirda, 'Book Review of Hugh Trevor-Roper's "History and the Enlightenment,"' *Washington Post*, June 24, 2010. http://www.washingtonpost.com/wp-dyn/content/article/2010/06/23/AR2010062305093.html.

The *Blackwell Companion to the Enlightenment* is a reference source encompassing many subjects from philosophy to art history, from science to music, with numerous topics (not demonstrative of a unifying/dominant view) ranging from absolutism to universities and witchcraft, publishing, language, art, music, and the theater, including several hundred biographical entries of diverse personalities. Better examples of a dominant discourse would have been Ernst Cassirer's *The Philosophy of the Enlightenment* (Princeton, NJ: Princeton University Press, 1932) or Norman Hampson's *The Enlightenment* (New York: Penguin, 1968). Mind you, Cassirer's book was published in the 1930s and Hampson's survey in 1968. The views of neither author are now seen as 'dominant.'

277 Outram, *The Enlightenment*, p. 8.

appreciating the variety of views espoused during the Enlightenment while recognising certain unifying themes, such as the importance of reason, 'non-traditional ways of defining and legitimating power,' natural law, and cosmopolitanism.[278]

Conrad needs to use the proponents of Enlightenment heterogeneity to make his case that the historiography on this subject has been moving in the non-Western direction (i.e. the one he has been nudging his readers into believing). But he knows that current experts on the *European* Enlightenment have not identified an Enlightenment movement across the globe from the 18th to the 20th century, so he must also designate them (albeit through insinuation) as members of a still dominant Eurocentric group.

In the end, the sources Conrad relies on to advance his globalist view are *not* experts of the European Enlightenment, but world historians (or actually, historians of India, China, or the Middle East) determined to unseat Europe from its privileged intellectual position. Right after stating that there are hardly any current proponents of the dominant view, and that 'most authors stress its plural and contested character,' Conrad reverts back to the claim that there is a standard view insomuch as most scholars still see the 'birth of the Enlightenment' as 'entirely and exclusively a European affair' which 'only when it was fully fledged was it then diffused around the globe.' Here Conrad finally footnotes a number of books exhibiting an old-fashioned admiration for the Enlightenment as a movement characterised by certain common concerns, though he never explains why these books are mistaken in delimiting the Enlightenment to Europe.

One thing is certain: these works go beyond Gay's thesis. Gertrude Himmelfarb's *The Roads to Modernity: The British, French, and American Enlightenments* (2005) challenges the older focus on France, its anti- clericalism and radical rejection of traditional ways, by arguing that there were English as well as American 'Enlightenments' that were quite moderate in

---

278 Ibid., p. 140.

their assessments of what human reason could do to improve the human condition, whilst remaining respectful of age-old customs, prejudices, and religious beliefs.[279] John Headley's *The Europeanization of the World* (2008) is not about the Enlightenment but the long Renaissance.[280]

Tzvetan Todorov's *In Defence of the Enlightenment* (2009), with its argument against current 'adversaries of the Enlightenment, obscurantism, arbitrary authority and fanaticism,' can be effectively used against Conrad's own unfounded and capricious efforts.[281] The same is true of Stephen Bronner's *Reclaiming the Enlightenment* (2004), with its criticism of activists on the Left for spreading confusion and attacking the Enlightenment as a form of cultural imperialism.[282] These two books are a summons to the Left not to abandon the critical principles inherent in the Enlightenment. Robert Louden's *The World We Want: How and Why the Ideals of the Enlightenment Still Eludes Us* (2007), ascertains the degree to which the ideals of the Enlightenment have been successfully actualised in the world, both in Europe and outside, by examining the spread of education, tolerance, rule of law, free trade, international justice, and democratic rights.[283] His conclusion, as the title indicates, is that the Enlightenment remains more an ideal than a fulfilled program.

What Conrad might have asked of these works is: why did they take for granted the universal validity of ideals rooted in the soils of particular European nations? Why did they all ignore the intense interest Enlightenment thinkers showed in the division of humanity into races? Why did all these books abandon the Enlightenment's own call for uninhibited critical thinking by ignoring the vivid preoccupation of

---

279 Gertrude Himmelfarb, *The Roads to Modernity: The British, French, and American Enlightenments* (New York: Vintage, 2005).

280 John Headley, *The Europeanization of the World: On the Origins of Human Rights and Democracy* (Princeton, NJ: Princeton University Press, 2008).

281 Tzvetan Todorov, *In Defence of the Enlightenment* (London: Atlantic Books, 2009).

282 Stephen Bronner, *Reclaiming the Enlightenment: Toward a Politics of Radical Enlightenment* (New York: Columbia University Press, 2004).

283 Robert Louden, *The World We Want: How and Why the Ideals of the Enlightenment Still Eludes Us* (New York: Oxford University Press, 2007).

Enlightenment thinkers with the differences, racial and cultural, between the peoples of the earth? Why did they accept (without question) the notion that the same Kant who observed that 'so fundamental is the difference between these two races of man [i.e., Black and White] ... as great in regard to mental capacities as in color,' was thinking about 'mankind' rather than about Europeans, when he defined the Enlightenment as 'mankind's exit from its self-incurred immaturity' through the courage to use [one's own understanding] without the guidance of another'?

Contrary to what defenders of the 'emancipatory project of the Enlightenment' would have us believe, these observations were not incidental but reflections expressed in multiple publications and debated extensively. What were the differences among the peoples of different climes and regions? The general consensus among Enlightenment thinkers (in response to this question) was that animals as well as humans could be arranged in systematic hierarchies. Carl Linnaeus, for example, considered Europeans, Asians, American Indians, and Africans to be different varieties of humanity.[284]

However, my purpose here is to assess Conrad's global approach, not to invalidate the generally accepted view of the Enlightenment as a project for 'humanity.' It is the case that Conrad wants to universalise the Enlightenment *even more* by seeing it as a movement emerging in different regions of the earth. The implicit message is that the ideals of this movement can be actualised if only we imagine its origins to have been global. But since none of the experts will grant him this favour, as they continue to believe it 'originated only in Europe,' notwithstanding the variety and tension they have detected *within* this European movement,

---

284 Emmanuel Chukwudi Eze, ed., *Race and the Enlightenment: A Reader* (Oxford: Blackwell, 1997). See also Aaron Garrett, 'Human Nature,' in *The Cambridge History of Eighteenth-Century Philosophy*, ed. Knud Haakonsen (Cambridge: Cambridge University Press, 2006), pp. 1:160–233. There is a section in this chapter dealing with 'race and natural character'; it is short, 20 pages in a 1,400-page work, but it is nevertheless well researched with close to 80 footnotes of mostly primary sources. One learns from these few pages that 'in text after text' Enlightenment thinkers proposed a hierarchical view of the races.

Conrad decides to designate these scholars, past and present, as members of a 'dominant' or 'master' narrative. He plays around with the language of postcolonial critiques — the 'brutal diffusion' of Western values, 'highly asymmetrical relations of power,' 'paternalistic civilizing mission' — the more to condemn the Enlightenment for its unfulfilled promises, and then criticises these scholars, too, for taking 'the Enlightenment's European origins for granted.'

Who, then, are the 'many authors' who have discovered that the Enlightenment was a worldwide creation? This is the motivating question behind Conrad's historiographical essay. He writes: 'in recent years ... the European claim to originality, to exclusive authorship of the Enlightenment, has been called into question.' He starts with a number of sources which have challenged 'the image of non-Western societies as stagnating and immobile': publications by Peter Gran on Egypt's 18th century 'cultural revival'; by Mark Elvin on China's 18th century 'trend towards seeing fewer dragons and miracles, not unlike the disenchantment that began to spread across Europe during the Enlightenment'; and includes Joel Mokyr's observation that 'some developments that we associate with Europe's Enlightenment resemble events in China remarkably.'

This is pure chicanery. First, Gran's *Islamic Roots of Capitalism: Egypt, 1760–1840* (1979) has little to do with the Enlightenment, and much to do with the bare beginnings of modernisation in Egypt. In short, this consists of the spread of monetary relations, the gradual appearance of 'modern products,' the adoption of European naval and military technology, the cultivation of a bit of modern science and medicine, the introduction (finally) of Aristotelian inductive and deductive logic into Islamic jurisprudence.[285] Gran's thesis is simply that Egyptians were not 'passive' assimilators of Western ways, but did so within the framework of Egyptian beliefs and institutions.

---

285 Peter Gran, *Islamic Roots of Capitalism: Egypt, 1760–1840* (Austin: University of Texas Press, 1979).

Mokyr's essay, 'The Great Synergy: The European Enlightenment as a Factor in Modern Economic Growth,' argues the exact opposite as the phrase cited by Conrad would have us believe.[286] Mokyr's contribution to the rise of the West debate has been precisely that there was an 'industrial' Enlightenment in the 18th century, which should be seen as the 'missing link' between the 17th century world of Galileo, Bacon, and Newton and the 19th century world of steam engines and factories. He emphasises the rise of numerous societies in England, the creation of information networks among engineers, natural philosophers, and businessmen, the opening of artillery schools, mining schools, informal scientific societies, numerous micro-inventions that turned scientific insights into successful business propositions, including a wide range of institutional changes that affected economic behaviour, resource allocation, savings, and invest-ment. There was no such Enlightenment in China, where an industrial revolution only started in the mid 20th century.

His citation of Elvin's observation that the Chinese were seeing fewer dragons in the 18th century cannot be taken seriously as indicating a Chinese Enlightenment, and neither can vague phrases about 'strange parallels' between widely separated areas of the world. Without much analysis but through constant repetition of globalist catchphrases, Conrad cites works by Sanjay Subrahmanyam, Arif Dirlik, Victor Lieberman, and Jack Goody. None of these works have anything to say about the Enlightenment. Some of them simply argue that capitalist development was occurring in Asia prior to European colonisation. Conrad deliber-ately confounds the Enlightenment with capitalism, globalisation, or modernisation. He makes reference to a section in Jack Goody's book *The Theft of History* with the subheading 'Cultural Similarities in East and West,' but this section is about (broad) similarities in family patterns, culinary practices, floriculture, and commodity exchanges in the major

---

286 Joel Mokyr, 'The Great Synergy: The European Enlightenment as a Factor in Modern Economic Growth,' Society for Economic Dynamics Meeting Papers (April 2005). http://faculty.wcas.northwestern.edu/~jmokyr/Dolfsma.PDF.

post-Bronze Age societies of Eurasia.[287] There is not a single word about the Enlightenment! He cites Arif Dirlik's book, *Glob- al Modernity in the Age of Global Capitalism* (2009), but this book is about globalisation.[288]

Conrad's historiographical study is a travesty intended to dissolve European specificity by way of sophomoric use of sources. He says that the Enlightenment was 'the work of many authors in different parts of the world.' What he offers instead are incessant strings of similarly worded phrases in every paragraph about the 'global context,' 'the conditions of globality,' 'cross-border circulations,' 'structurally embedded in larger global contexts'. To be sure, these are required phrases in academic grant applications assessed by adjudicators who can't distinguish enlightening thoughts from madrasa learning based on drill repetition and chanting.

A claim that there were similar Enlightenments around the world needs to come up with some authors and books comparable in their novelty and themes. The number of Enlightenment works during the 18th century numbered, roughly speaking, about 1,500.[289] Conrad does not come up with a single book from the rest of the world for the same period. Halfway through his paper of 20 plus pages he finally mentions a name from India, Tipu Sultan (1750–1799), the ruler of Mysore 'who fashioned himself an enlightened monarch.' Conrad has very little to say about his thoughts. From *Wikipedia* one gets the impression that he was a reasonably good leader, who introduced a new calendar, new coinage, seven new government departments, and who made military innovations in the use of rocketry. But he was an imitator of the Europeans; as a young man he was instructed in military tactics by French officers in the employment of his father. This should be designated as imitation, not invention.

---

287 Jack Goody, *The Theft of History* (New York: Cambridge University Press, 2006), pp. 118–122.

288 Arif Dirlik, *Global Modernity in the Age of Global Capitalism* (Boulder, CO: Paradigm Publishers, 2009).

289 This is an approximate number obtained by counting the compilation of primary works cited in *The Cambridge History of Eighteenth-Century Philosophy*, Vol. 2: pp. 1237–1293.

Conrad also mentions the slave revolt in Haiti led by Toussaint L'Ouverture, as an example of the 'hybridisation' of the Enlightenment. He says that Toussaint had been influenced by European critiques of colonialism, and that his 'source of inspiration' also came from slaves who had 'been born in Africa and came from diverse political, social and religious backgrounds.' Haitian slaves were presumably comparable to such Enlightenment thinkers as Burke, Helvétius, d'Alembert, Galiani, Lessing, Burke, Gibbon, and Laplace. But no, the point is that Haitians made their own original contributions; they employed 'religious practices such as voodoo for the formation of revolutionary communities.' Strange parallels indeed!

He extends the period of the Enlightenment into the 1930s and 1940s hoping to find 'vibrant and heated contestations of Enlightenment in the rest of the world.' He includes names from Japan, China, India, and the Ottoman Empire, but, like Tipu Sultan, what they all did was to simply introduce elements of the European Enlightenment into their countries. He rehearses the view that these countries offered their own versions of modernity. Then he cites the following words from Liang Qichao, the most influential Chinese thinker at the beginning of the 20th century, reflecting on his encounter with Western literature: 'Books like I have never seen before dazzle my eyes. Ideas like I have never encountered before baffle my brain. It is like seeing the sun after being confined in a dark room.' Without noticing that these words refute his argument that Asians were co-participants in the Enlightenment, Conrad recklessly takes these words as proof that 'the Enlightenment of the 18th century was not the intellectual monopoly of Europeans.' It does not occur to him that after the 18th century Europe moved beyond the Enlightenment, exhibiting a dizzying display of intellectual, artistic, and scientific movements: romanticism, impressionism, surrealism, positivism, Marxism, existentialism, relativism, phenomenology, nationalism, fascism, realism, and countless other 'isms'.

In the last paragraphs, as if aware that his argument was mostly make-believe, Conrad writes that 'an assessment of the Enlightenment in global history should not be concerned with origins, either geographically or temporarily.' The study of origins, one of the central concerns of the historical profession, is thusly dismissed in one sentence. Perhaps he means that the 'capitalist integration of the globe in an age of imperialism' precludes seeing any autonomous origins in any area of the world. World historians, apparently, have solved the problem of origins across all epochs and regions: it is always the global context. But why is it that Europe almost always happens to be the progenitor of the cultural novelties of modernity? One unfortunate result of this effort to see Enlightenments everywhere is the devaluation of the actual Enlightenment. If there were Enlightenments everywhere, why should students pay any special attention to Europe's great thinkers? It should come as no surprise that students are coming out with PhDs incapable of making distinctions between high and average achievements.

The originality of the Enlightenment stands like an irritating thorn in the march toward equality and the creation of European nations inhabited by rootless cosmopolitan citizens without ethnic and nationalist roots. Regardless of what the actual evidence says, the achievements of Europeans must be erased from memory, replaced by a new history in which every racial group feels equally validated *inside* the Western world. In the meantime, the rise of Asians *as Asians* continues unabated and is celebrated in Western academia.

Hybrid Fabrications Versus Greek Originality

Another recent example of the way history is being written and taught today is quite visible in a review in *The Guardian* of a book edited by Tim Whitmarsh, *The Romance Between Greece and the East*.[290] This book was

---

290 Charlotte Higgins, 'Ancient Greece, the Middle East, and an Ancient Cultural Internet,' *The Guardian*, July 11, 2013. http://www.theguardian.com/education/2013/jul/11/ancient-greece-cultural- hybridisation-theory.

portrayed as a major breakthrough in scholarship recasting the ancient Greek world 'from an isolated entity to one of many hybrid cultures in Africa and in the East.' Strictly speaking, there is little original about Whitmarsh's book; it is framed along the same lines as Martin Bernal's earlier attempt in *Black Athena* (1987) to place the origins of Greece in Africa and the Semitic Near East.[291] Whitmarsh calls the argument that the Greeks owed their brilliance to themselves, their own ethnicity as Indo-Europeans, a 'massive cultural deception.'

In our Western world of immigrant multiculturalism any idea attributing to Europeans any achievement — without including as co-partners the Muslims, Africans, and Orientals — is designated as a massive deception. The scholarship promoted by our current elites demands a view in which Europeans don't exist except as hybrids, borrowers, and imitators. But the historical and archaeological evidence used by Whitmarsh and multiculturalists in general never goes beyond showing that there were connections between the Greeks (or Europeans generally) and their neighbours. They have an easy time showing what many have shown before, that the Greek mainland was connected to the Mediterranean world via trade, travelling, colonising activities, and the residence of some Greeks outside Greece.

They also repeat as new discoveries what European scholars had already started showing in the 18th century; for instance, that ancient Greece was preceded by Mesopotamian and Egyptian civilisations and that the Indo-Europeans who arrived in the Greek mainland and established the Mycenaean civilisation in the early 2nd millennium borrowed some basic civilisational tools from these older civilisations, including some mythological motifs and the alphabet from the Phoenicians. They do not care to understand the unique world from which the Mycenaeans came, a world originating in the steppes, characterised by horse riding, chariot fighting, aristocratic liberalism and an ethos of heroism so vividly captured in the Homeric epics of the 8th century BC; one entirely

---

291 Martin Bernal, *Black Athena: The Afroasiatic Roots of Classical Civilization* (New Brunswick, NJ: Rutgers University Press, 1987).

absent in the Mesopotamian *Epic of Gilgamesh*. Rather, these 'multicultics' rush to conclude that the achievements of the archaic and Classical Greeks — such as Pindar, Sophocles, Thucydides, Aeschylus, Anaxagoras, Anaximander, Euripides, Thales, Heraclitus, Parmenides, Socrates, Plato, and Aristotle — were "hybrid" achievements.

In order to persuade their audience that there is more to these obvious connections (which older scholars never denied), Whitmarsh et al. then wrap their plain facts in a postmodernist package, complete with flashing neon signs screaming 'dialogue', 'intertwining', 'multivoiced conversations', 'polyglossia', 'the arts of cultural mediation', 'deep intercultural understanding'. How could a student deny such 'profound' words and phrases; indeed, how can anyone be so harsh as to disagree with such a peaceful image of Greeks conversing with Africans and Semites and thereby creating a culture by and for humanity? Whitmarsh admits as much: 'In a way, what we are saying is modish, it's multicultural, it's a model almost resembling the internet projected back on to the ancient world.' He adds:

> There is a strongly political dimension to the kind of claim I am making, and you would probably find that most people who were pushing for a very hybridised vision of the Greek world would ... be naturally more left-leaning and have their own idealised view of the ancient world as a place of opportunity and hybridisation.

Whitmarsh insists that this multicultic vision projected onto the past fits with 'the archaeological data.' Although I have not read his edited book, there is nothing in this review, not an iota of evidence or even logic that substantiates his thesis. The review mentions, as an example of Greek hybridity and borrowing, the fact that Herodotus was born in Asia Minor in a city named Halicarnassus — 'a city that during the Persian wars was part of the Persian Achaemenid empire, ruled by Queen Artemisia, herself half Halicarnassian and half Cretan.' From this trite observation about a hybrid ruler of a city, we are then asked to conclude that the 'father of history' was a hybrid himself! As if unsure of his footing, Whitmarsh begs the question: 'Herodotus's *The Histories* is a predominantly Greek-voiced text, but that doesn't mean that we should quieten all the other voices that can be detected within it.'

This is pure posturing, manipulation, and fraud. The importance of Herodotus is not only that he was the first to write a historical account based on the orderly collection of sources available at the time, but that he produced the first ethnographical account of the customs, lifestyles, and myths of other peoples. Here we have a Greek showing objectivity, interest, and real appreciation of non-Greeks. Rather than mention these virtues, the multicultics have nothing to say beyond interpreting his work as hybrid and borrowed. The fact that he exhibited an ethnographic interest is interpreted by them as an indication that he is a hybrid, rather than as an example of a uniquely Greek trait. Then they have the nerve to accuse the admirers of Herodotus of being promoters of a self-contained view of the Greeks! It is in fact the other way around: we admire him because he was unique both as a historian and as an ethnographer. This duplicitous manner of reasoning is being inflicted on our students across the West at the highest levels of academia, with the support of governments and the media!

The review mentions 'another culturally hybrid work ... a story that recasts the Macedonian conqueror [i.e., Alexander the Great] as secretly Egyptian, so the story of his annexation of Egypt becomes one not of conquest but of the return of pharaonic rule.' Whitmarsh says that this story 'is forged in a very distinctive culture in which there are Greeks and Egyptians working together. And it tells the story of Alexander the Great in Egyptian-friendly terms.'

In this context Whitmarsh asks, 'What if what we think of as the classical world has been falsely invented as European?' In other words, what if we think that Alexander was an Egyptian and that his conquest of Egypt was a friendly return by a native to his original homeland? After all, the older view that he was a Greek Macedonian was 'invented.' Therefore we go beyond the 'what if' scenario and actually argue that the 'archaeological record' actually supports this view of Alexander as more correct and more suitable to the transformation of England into an immigrant nation.

It was precisely this type of mythological thinking about history that Herodotus and Thucydides sought to rectify!

Whitmarsh is quite open that 'in this story of interconnectedness and hybridity ... there lie enormous intellectual and humanist opportunities.'

> There are three million Muslims in Britain, many of them learning an ancient language already. There's no reason why, in 50 years' time, undergraduate courses shouldn't be packed with people studying Arabic and Greek culture side by side. Of course, this already exists in a limited way, but it's not a cultural phenomenon at the moment and these worlds mostly exist entirely separately, but it seems to me there's nothing natural in that.

The Greeks cannot be seen separately from the Near East because that view does not fit an England filled with Muslims 'studying Arabic and Greek culture side by side.' Because of this contemporary political agenda, the ancient Greek world must be seen as having emerged together with the Near East 'side by side.'

One of the discursive strategies Whitmarsh and all multicultics employ in advancing this idea of interconnections is to create a false polarity according to which those who believe in Greek originality are automatically designated as holding view as of an ancient Greece that was 'hermetically sealed from outside influence.' This is a deceitful straw man — a wilful attempt to mislead students and the public at large. Classical scholars have never written that Greece owed nothing to the Near East. Burckhardt, like many others since, was plainly aware of the material tradition that the Greeks inherited from outside. '[The Greeks] themselves,' he wrote, 'did not generally begrudge other nations their inventions and discoveries.'[292] Western civilisation textbooks have always started with Mesopotamia and Egypt, just to teach students that Greece was not a self-made civilisation.

What, then, is the bone of contention? It is that multicultic historians want to go beyond claims of borrowings to argue that Greece was not original at all? They refuse to let their brains contemplate the thought that Greek originality does not preclude acknowledgment of debts to earlier

---

292 Jacob Burckhardt, *The Greeks and Greek Civilization* (New York: St. Martin's Press, 1958 [1898]), 136.

civilisations. What troubles Whitmarsh et al. is the undeniable reality of Greek originality, far above anything ever seen in the East to this day. How can this originality be squared with the multicultural egalitarianism which is now mandated, under penalty of censure and ostracism, in all public institutions in Britain? The only solution is to trample upon the historical record, confound the issues, and misinform the students in order to stay within the dictates of immigrant multiculturalism.

Whitmarsh et al. are so caught up inside the complacent blind box of diversity = egalitarianism that they cannot even fathom a simple question: If Greece was connected to the East and presumably the East was connected to Greece, why did all the achievements happen in Greece rather than throughout the Mediterranean? Beyond the Greeks, if Europeans were 'connected', as other historians now say about every creative epoch in Europe's history, then why do all these achievements always happen in Europe? Why are Eastern cultures and multicultics always piggybacking on Europe's achievements rather than those of the East in order to show that it was all about connections?

Don't expect them to pose these questions. Whitmarsh's book is part of a decades-old effort to create an academic culture in which European students are thoroughly acculturated to forget the accomplishments of their ancestors while being readied to remember the amorphous make-believe achievements of a hybridised humanity imposed from above by corporations seeking cheap docile workers and by liberals seeking docile students accustomed to Orwellian doublespeak.

4

The Faustian Soul of the West and the Indo-Europeans

MEPHISTOPHELES [the skeptical mind who does not understand FAUST's aspiration]:

Who could divine toward what you aspire?
It must have been sublimely bold, in truth,
Toward the moon you'd soar and ever higher;
Did your mad quest allure you there forsooth?
Faust [with self-confidence]:
By no means! For this earthly sphere
Affords a place for great deeds ever.
Astounding things shall happen here,
I feel the strength for bold endeavor.
Mephistopheles [still jeering and skeptical]
So you'd earn glory? One can see
You've been in heroines' company.
Faust: Lordship, possession, are my aim and thought![293]

Spengler's Contribution

I dedicated two long chapters in *Uniqueness* to the ideas of Max Weber and G.W.F Hegel for offering some of the most profound insights on the peculiar nature of Western Civilisation. I paid considerable attention to Nietzsche and many contemporary scholars who have addressed 'the rise

---

293 *Faust* in *Great Books of the Western World*, Vol. 47, *Goethe* (Chicago: Encyclopedia Britannica, 1952, pp. 247–248.

of the West'. But only a few pages were concentrated on Spengler, with other relevant comments spread out in the book in a disconnected way. This chapter will argue that Spengler's idea that the West was driven by a creative and expansive psyche is indispensable to the understanding of European history. The word 'Faustian' captures the multifaceted character of Western creativity in all the spheres of life better than such commonly used terms as 'individualism', 'liberty', 'rationalism', 'separation of church and state' or 'representative democracy'.

This chapter will also argue that the Indo-Europeans were the original Faustian men and the most historically significant nomads of the steppes. Tracing the origins of the West's Faustian spirit back to them will allow us to offer a materially rooted description of a concept that has otherwise remained rather elusive and overtly metaphysical, in both the writings of Spengler and his admirers. The other nomadic peoples from the steppes, such as the Scythians, Sogdians, Turks, and Huns, never came close to the deep and lasting changes associated with the 'Indo-Europeanisation' of the Occident. While Indo-Europeans were not the only people of the steppes organised as war bands and bound together by oaths of aristocratic loyalty and fraternity, they thoroughly colonised Europe with their *original* pastoral package of wheel vehicles, horse-riding, and chariots, combined with the 'secondary-products revolution.' In contrast, the relationship between the non-Indo-European nomads with their more advanced sedentary neighbours was one of symbiosis, trade, and conquest, rather than dominion and cultural colonisation. The non-Indo-European nomads were absorbed by the more advanced and anti-aristocratic cultures of the Orient, whereas only the Indo-Europeans were able to maintain their aristocratic spirit.

'Faustian' is the word Spengler used to designate the 'soul' of the West. He believed that Western civilisation was driven by an unusually dynamic and expansive psyche. The 'prime-symbol' of this Faustian soul was 'pure and limitless space.' This soul had a 'tendency towards the infinite', a tendency most acutely expressed in modern mathematics. The 'infinite continuum,' the exponential logarithm and 'its dissociation from all connexion with magnitude' and transference to a 'transcendent relational world' were some of the phrases Spengler used to describe Western mathematics. But he also wrote of the 'bodiless music' of the Western composer, 'in which harmony and polyphony bring him to images of utter 'beyondness' that transcend all possibilities of visual definition,' and, before the modern era, of the Gothic 'form-feeling' of 'pure, imperceptible, unlimited space.'[294]

This soul type was first visible, according to Spengler, in medieval Europe, starting with Romanesque art. It was however in the 'spaciousness of Gothic cathedrals', 'the heroes of the Grail and Arthurian and Siegfried sagas, ever roaming in the infinite... ...and the Crusades' that this Faustian soul type was particularly apparent. He lists 'the Hohenstaufen in Siciliy, the Hansa in the Baltic, the Teutonic Knights in the Slavonic East, [and later] the Spaniards in America, [and] the Portugese in the East Indies' as examples. Spengler thus viewed the West as a strikingly vibrant culture driven by a personality overflowing with expansive impulses, the 'intellectual will-to-power.' 'Fighting,' 'progressing,' 'overcoming of resistances,' battling 'against what is near, tangible and easy' —these were some of the terms Spengler used to describe this soul.[295]

The current academic consensus has reduced the uniqueness of the West to when this civilisation 'first' became industrial. This consensus believes that the West 'diverged' from other agrarian civilisations only when it developed steam engines capable of using inorganic sources of energy. Prior to the Industrial Revolution, we are led to believe, there were 'surprising similarities' between Europe and Asia. Both multiculturalist and Eurocentric historians tend to frame the 'the rise of the West' or the 'great divergence' in these economic and technological terms. David S. Landes, Kenneth Pomeranz, R. Bin Wong, Joel Mokyr, Jack Goldstone, E. L. Jones, and Peer Vries all single out the Industrial Revolution of 1750–1830 as

---

294 Oswald Spengler, *The Decline of the West, Volume I: Form and Actuality*. Translated by Charles Francis Atkinson (New York: Alfred Knopf, 1988 [1923]), pp. 53–90.
295 Ibid., pp. 183–216.

the transformation that signalled a whole new pattern of evolution for the West (or England in the first instance). It matters little how far back in time these academics trace this revolution, or how much weight they assign to preceding developments such as the Scientific Revolution or the slave trade, their emphasis is on the 'divergence' generated by the arrival of mechanised industry and self- sustained increases in productivity sometime after 1750.

But I believe that the Industrial Revolution, including developments leading to this revolution, barely capture what was unique about Western culture. While other cultures were unique in their own customs, languages, beliefs, and historical experiences, the West was uniquely exceptional in exhibiting in a continuous way the greatest degree of creativity, novelty, and expansionary dynamics. I trace the uniqueness of the West back to the aristocratic warlike culture of Indo-European speakers as early as the 4th millennium BC. Their aristocratic libertarian culture was already unique and quite innovative in initiating the most mobile way of life in prehistoric times, starting with the domestication and riding of horses and the invention of chariot warfare. So were the ancient Greeks in their discovery of *logos* and its link with the order of the world, dialectical reason, the invention of prose, tragedy, citizen politics, and face-to-face infantry battle.

The Roman creation of a secular system of republican governance anchored on autonomous principles of judicial reasoning was in and of itself unique. The incessant wars and conquests of the Roman legions, together with their many military innovations and engineering skills, were one of the most vital illustrations of spatial expansionism in history. The fusion of Christianity and the Greco-Roman intellectual and administrative heritage, coupled with the cultivation of Catholicism (the first rational theology in history), was a unique phenomenon. The medieval invention of universities — in which a secular education could flourish and even articles of faith were open to criticism and rational analysis, in an effort to arrive at the truth — was exceptional. The list of epoch-making transformation in Europe is endless: the Renaissance, the Age of Discovery, the Scientific Revolution(s), the Military Revolution(s), the Cartographic Revolution, the Spanish Golden Age, the Printing Revolution, the Enlightenment, the Romantic Era, the German Philosophical Revolutions from Kant to Hegel to Nietzsche to Heidegger.

One major limitation of current works on the rise of the West is that none of them address these transformations together. The norm has been for specialists in one period or transformation to write about (or insist upon) the 'radical' or 'revolutionary' significance of the period or theme they happen to be experts on. Missing is an understanding of the unparalleled degree to which the entire history of the West was filled with individuals persistently seeking, in Spengler's words, 'to transcend every optical limitation.'[296] In comparative contrast to the history of India, China, Japan, Egypt and the Americas, where artistic styles, political institutions, and philosophical outlooks lasted for centuries, there stands the 'dynamic fertility of the Faustian with its ceaseless creation of new types and domains of form.'[297] I can think of only three individuals, two philosophers of history and one historical sociologist, who have written in a wide-ranging way of:

(1)   The 'infinite drive', the 'irresistable thrust' of the Occident.

(2)   The 'energetic, imperativistic, and dynamic' soul of the West.

(3)   The 'rational restlessness' of the West. These three men are Hegel, Spengler and Weber, respectively.

Spengler overcomes in a keener way another flaw in the current works that emphasise Western achievement: his account of European distinctiveness is not limited to the intellectual and artistic spheres, 'great books' and 'great ideas', but includes as well conquerors, adventurers, colonisers, military leaders. Indeed, Spengler's identification of the West as 'Faustian' provides

---

296 Spengler, *The Decline of the West*, p. 198.
297 Ibid., p. 205.

us with the best framework for overcoming the current naïve separation between a cultured/peaceable West and an uncivilised/antagonistic West. His image of a strikingly vibrant culture driven by a type of Faustian personality overflowing with expansive, disruptive, and imaginative impulses is a more accurate rendition of the West's immense creativity and restless soul. For Spengler, the Faustian spirit was not restricted to the arts and sciences, but was present in the culture of the West at large. Spengler thus spoke of the '*morphological relationship* that inwardly binds together the expression-forms of all branches of a Culture.'[298] Such things as Rococo art, differential calculus, the Crusades and the Spanish conquest of the Americas were all expressions of the same soul.

The great men of Europe were artists driven by a desire for unmatched deeds. The 'great ideas' — Archimedes' 'Give me a place to stand and with a lever I will move the whole world,' or Hume's 'love of literary fame, my ruling passion'[299]—were associated with aristocratic traits, defiant dispositions no less than Cortés's immense ambition for honour and glory, 'to die worthily than to live dishonoured.'[300]

In contrast to Weber, for whom the West 'exhibited an unrivalled aptitude for rationalisation,' Spengler saw in this Faustian soul a primeval-irrational will to power. It was not a calm, disinterested, rationalistic ethos that was at the heart of Western particularity; it was a highly energetic, goal-oriented desire to break through the unknown, supersede the norm, and achieve mastery. The West was governed by an intense urge to transcend the limits of existence by a restless, fateful being, an 'adamantine will to overcome and break all resistances of the visible.'[301]

There was something Faustian about all the great men of Europe, both real and fictional: in Hamlet, Richard III, Gauss, Newton, Nicolas

---

298 Ibid., p. 6 (italics in original).

299 David Hume, "My Own Life," in An Enquiry Concerning Human Understanding, ed. with introduction by Charles Hendel (New York: Library of Liberal Arts, 1955), p. 10.

300 Buddy Levy, Conquistador: Hernán Cortés, King Montezuma, and the Last Stand of the Aztecs (New York: Bantam Books, 2009), p. 156.

301 Spengler, *The Decline of the West*, pp. 185–186.

Cusanus, Don Quixote, Goethe's Werther, Gregory VII, Michelangelo, Paracelsus, Dante, Descartes, Don Juan, Bach, Wagner's Parsifal, Haydn, Leibniz's Monads, Giordano Bruno, Frederick the Great, Ibsen's Hedda Gabler. In Spengler's words:

> The Faustian soul — whose being consists in the overcoming of presence, whose feeling is loneliness and whose yearning is infinity — puts its need of solitude, distance and abstraction into all its actualities, into its public life, its spiritual and its artistic form-worlds alike.[302]

For Spengler, Christianity, too, became a thoroughly Faustian moral ethic. 'It was not Christianity that transformed Faustian man, but Faustian man who transformed Christianity — and he not only made it a new religion but also gave it a new moral direction': will-to-power in ethics.[303] This 'Faustian-Christian morale' produced:

> Christians of the great style ... Innocent III and Calvin, Loyola and Savonarola, Pascal and St. Theresa ... the great Saxon, Franconia and Hohenstaufen emperors ... giant-men like Henry the Lion and Gregory VII ... the men of the Renaissance, of the struggle of the two Roses, of the Huguenot Wars, the Spanish Conquistadores, the Prussian electors and kings, Napoleon, Bismarck, Rhodes.[304]

The Faustian Personality

But what exactly is a Faustian soul? How do we connect it in a concrete way to Europe's creativity? To what original source or starting place did Spengler attribute this yearning for infinity? To start answering these questions we should first remind ourselves of Spengler's other central idea, his cyclical view of history, according to which:

(1)   Each culture contains a unique spirit of its own.

---

302 Ibid., p. 386.
303 Ibid., p. 344.
304 Ibid., pp. 348–349.

(2)   All cultures undergo an organic process of birth, growth and
decay.

In other words, for Spengler, all cultures exhibit a period of dynamic,
youthful creativity; each culture experiences 'its childhood, youth, manhood and old age.' 'Each culture has its own new possibilities of self-ex-
pression which arise, ripen, decay and never return.'[305] Spengler thus drew
a distinction between the earlier vital stages of a culture (*Kultur*) and the
later stages, when the life forces were nearly spent until all that remained
was a *Zivilisation* populated by individuals preoccupied with preserving
the memories of past glories, while drudging through the unexciting affairs of their everyday lives.

However, notwithstanding this emphasis on the youthful energies of
all cultures, Spengler viewed the West as the most strikingly dynamic culture driven by a soul overflowing with expansive energies and 'intellectual
will-to-power.' By 'youthful' he meant the actualisation of the specific soul
of each culture, 'the full sum of its possibilities in the shape of peoples,
languages, dogmas, arts, states, sciences.' Only in Europe did he see 'di-
rectional energy,' marching music, painters revelling in the use of blue
and green, 'transcendent, spiritual, non-sensuous colours,' 'colours of the
heavens, the sea, the fruitful plain, the shadow of the Southern moon,
the evening, the remote mountains.'[306] John Farrenkopf is right when he
argues that Spengler's appreciation for non-Western cultures as worthy
subjects of comparative inquiry always came together with an 'exaltation'
of the greater creative energy of the West.[307]

But what do we make of Spengler's insistence that ancient Greece and
Rome were not Faustian? Although Spengler is persuasive that in certain
respects the Greco-Roman soul was oriented toward the present rather
than the future, and that its architecture, geometry, and finite mathematics were bounded spatially, restrained, and perceptible, he overstates his

---

305   Ibid., pp. 18–24, 106–107.

306   Ibid., pp. 245–246.

307   John Farrenkopf, *Prophet of Decline: Spengler on World History and Politics* (Baton
Rouge: Louisiana State University Press, 2001), p. 35.

argument about the lack of an expansionist spirit and will to power. He downplays the incredible creative energies of Greeks and Romans, their individual heroism and urge for the unknown. Farrenkopf thinks that the later Spengler came to view the Greeks and Romans as more individualistic and dynamic. I agree with Jacob Burckhardt that the Classical Greeks were singularly agonal and individualistic, and with Nietzsche's insight that all that was civilised and rational among the Greeks would have been impossible without this agonal culture. The ancient Greeks who established colonies throughout the Mediterranean, the Macedonians who marched to 'the ends of the world,' and the Romans who created the greatest empire in history, were similarly driven, to use Spengler's term, by an 'irrepressible urge to distance,' as were the Germanic peoples who brought down the Roman Empire, the Vikings who crossed the Atlantic, the Crusaders who wreaked havoc on the Near East, and the Portuguese who pushed themselves with their gunned ships upon the previously tranquil world of the Indian Ocean. Spengler's efforts to downplay this Faustian side of the Greeks and Romans are not persuasive.[308]

---

308 The first volume of *Decline* is full of expressions denying the presence of a territorial dynamic and worldly spirit to the Greeks and Romans: 'What the Greek called Kosmos was the image of a world that is not continuous but complete' (p. 9); 'That the Romans did *not* conquer the world is certain; they merely took possession of a booty that lay open to everyone' (p. 36); 'The Greeks refuse to venture out of the Mediterranean along sea-paths long before dared by the Phoenicians and the Egyptians' (p. 65); 'Western man is in a high degree historically disposed, Classical man far from being so' (p. 97); 'The Greek willed nothing and dared nothing, but he found a stirring beauty in *enduring*' (p. 203). But, as the next chapter will show, the Greeks did establish far more colonies along the Mediterranean than the Phoenicians and Egyptians, as well as around the Black Sea; they also produced some great explorers. While the idea of progress was barely developed by the Greeks and Romans, these two cultures witnessed the first historical works with a serious concern for objectivity and accurate narrative of events, and the Romans produced a high number of great historians with a keen sense of the place of Rome's comparative place in the annals of empire-making. See Michael Grant, *The Ancient Historians* (London: Weidenfeld and Nicolson, 1970). Greek and Roman literature is full of vibrant, identifiable personalities; and from the pre-Socratics on, philosophers contested with each other pushing novel ideas in their irresistible quest for the truth. At a conference where I presented parts of this chapter, I was criticised by the German expert on Spengler, David Engels, professor at the Université Libre de Bruxelles, for speaking of Greek and Roman warfare in Faustian terms, on the grounds that there was nothing unique about their war-making activities *per se*; the

What was the ultimate original ground of the West's Faustian soul? There are statements in Spengler which make references to 'a Nordic world stretching from England to Japan' and a 'harder-struggling' people, and a more individualistic and heroic spirit 'in the old, genuine parts of the Mahabharata ... in Homer, Pindar, and Aeschylus, in the Germanic epic poetry and in Shakespeare, in many songs of the Chinese Shuking, and in circles of the Japanese samurai.'[309] Spengler makes reference to the common location of these peoples in the 'Nordic' steppes. He does not make any specific reference to the Caucasian steppes but he clearly has in mind the 'Aryan Indian' peoples who came out of the steppes and conquered India and wrote the Mahabharata. He calls the Greco-Roman, Aryan Indian, and Chinese high cultures 'half Nordic.'

In *Man and Technics*, he writes of how the Nordic climate forged a man filled with vitality:

> Through the hardness of the conditions of life, the cold, the constant adversity, into a tough race, with an intellect sharpened to the most extreme degree, with the cold fervor of an irrepressible passion for struggling, daring, driving forward.[310]

Assyrians, Egyptians, Chinese, and numerous other cultures, also engaged in warfare and territorial expansion. But, then, if Engels would have only asked himself: what criteria does Spengler use to identify medieval and modern Western warfare as 'Faustian'? Clearly, Spengler was aware that medieval and modern Europeans were not uniquely militaristic and imperialistic; that is not the point of his argument; it is that they were more intensively militaristic and expansionist as well more innovative and obsessive about improving the techniques, organisation, tactics and strategies of warfare. The Greeks introduced a wholly new type of warrior, heavily-armed foot soldiers known as hoplites; they also improved on a style of battle, leading to the Macedonian phalanx, which made possible the conquest of the Persian Empire, and so on to the Roman legions and the knights and long bowmen of the Middle Ages. Engels, it seems to me, has a dogmatic understanding of Spengler's ideas; in addition to which, he wants a Spengler that fits the politically correct expectations of academic promotion.

309 Farrenkopf, *Prophet of Decline*, p. 227.

310 Oswald Spengler, *Man and Technics: A Contribution to a Philosophy of Life*, trans. Charles Francis Atkinson (Westport, CT: Greenwood Press, 1976 [1932]), pp. 19–41.

Principally, he mentions the barbarian peoples of northern Europe, whose world he contrasts to 'the languid world-feeling of the South'.[311] Spengler does not deny the role of the environment, but rather than focussing on economic resources and their 'critical' role in the industrialisation process, he draws attention to the profound impact environments had in the formation of distinctive psychological orientations amongst the cultures of the world. He thinks that the Faustian form of spirituality came out of the 'harder struggling' climes of the North. The Nordic character was less passive, less languorous, more energetic, individualistic, and more preoccupied with status and heroic deeds than the characters of other climes. He was a human biological being to be sure, but one animated with the spirit of a 'proud beast of prey,' like that of an 'eagle, lion, [or] tiger.' For this 'Nordic' individual, 'the concerns of life, the deed, became more important than mere physical existence.'[312]

This deed-oriented man is not satisfied with a Darwinian struggle for existence or a Marxist struggle for economic equality. He wants to climb high, soar upward, and reach ever-higher levels of existential intensity. He is not preoccupied with mere adaptation, reproduction, and conservation. He wants to storm into the heavens and shape the world. But who exactly is this character? Is he the Hegelian master who fights to the death for the sake of prestige? Spengler paraphrases Nietzsche when he writes that the primordial forces of Western culture reflect the 'primary emotions of an energetic human existence, the cruelty, the joy in excitement, danger, the violent act, victory, crime, the thrill of a conqueror and destroyer.' Nietzsche too wrote of the 'aristocratic' warrior who longed for the 'proud, exalted states of the soul,' as experienced intimately through 'combat, adventure, the chase, the dance, war games.'[313] Who are these characters? Are their 'primary emotions' any different from humans in other cultures?

---

311   Farrenkopf, *Prophet of Decline*, p. 222.

312   Spengler, *Man and Technics*, pp. 19–41.

313   Friedrich Nietzsche, *The Birth of Tragedy and The Genealogy of Morals*, trans. Francis Golffing (New York: Anchor Books, 1956), p. 167.

Kant and the 'Unsocial Sociability' of Humans

A good way to start answering this question is to compare Spengler's Faustian man with what Immanuel Kant says about the 'unsocial sociability' of humans generally. In his essay, 'Idea for a Universal History from a Cosmopolitan Point of View', Kant seemed somewhat puzzled but nevertheless attuned to the way progress in history had been driven by the fiercer, self-centred side of human nature. Looking at the wide span of history, he concluded that without the vain desire for honour, property, and status, humans would have never developed beyond a primitive Arcadian existence of self-sufficiency and mutual love:

> All human talents would remain hidden forever in a dormant state, and men, as good-natured as the sheep they tended, would scarcely render their existence more valuable than that of their animals.... The end for which they were created, their rational nature, would be an unfulfilled void.[314]

There can no development of the human faculties, no high culture, without conflict, aggression, and pride. It is these asocial traits — 'vainglory', 'lust for power', 'avarice' — that awaken the otherwise dormant talents of humans and 'drive them to new exertions of their forces and thus to the manifold development of their capacities.' Nature in her wisdom, 'not the hand of an evil spirit', created 'the unsocial sociability of humans.'[315] But Kant never asked, in this context, why Europeans were responsible, in his own estimation, for most of the moral and rational progression in history. Separately in other writings Kant did observe major differences in the psychological and moral character of humans as exhibited in different places on earth, ranking human races accordingly, with Europeans at the

---

314 Immanuel Kant, "Idea for a Universal History from a Cosmopolitan Point of View," in *Kant: On History*, ed. Lewis White Beck (New York: Macmillan/Library of Liberals Arts, 1963), pp. 15–16.

315 Before Kant, there were varying versions of the 'unsocial sociability' of humans expressed by Turgot, Vico, and others, and then later by Hegel. Clare Ellis examines additional versions in 'The Agonistic Ethos of Western Man,' MA Thesis (Saint John, New Brunswick: University of New Brunswick, 2011).

top in 'natural traits.'[316] Still, Kant never connected his anthropology of racial differences with his principle of asocial qualities.

Did 'Nature' foster these asocial qualities evenly among the cultures of the world? These 'vices' — as we have learned today from evolutionary psychology — are genetically based traits that evolved in response to long periods of adaptive selective pressures associated with the maximisation of human survival. However, there is no reason to assume that the form and degree of these traits evolved evenly or equally among all the human races and cultures. It is my view that the asocial qualities of Europeans were different, more intense, strident, individuated. And that these traits have their origins in the unique lifestyle of the Indo-Europeans.

Indo-Europeans were the Most Historically Significant Nomads of the Steppes

In *Uniqueness* I traced the original Faustian men back to the aristocratic warlike culture of prehistoric Indo-Europeans. I would like to elaborate more on this question by way of a response to a criticism Martin Hewson made in his long review of *Uniqueness*, 'Multicultural vs. Post-Multicultural World History: A Review Essay.'[317] Hewson wondered about the exceptionality of Indo-Europeans vis-à-vis other pastoral peoples from the steppes. He also wondered whether my emphasis on the aristocratic 'soul' of Europeans abjured 'a materialist conception of history.'

Readers would benefit from reading the long chapter I wrote on the Indo-Europeans in *Uniqueness*. By 'Indo-Europeans' I understand a pastoral people from the Pontic-Caspian steppes who initiated the most mobile way of life in prehistoric times. This started with the riding of horses and the invention of wheeled vehicles in the 4th millennium BC, together with the efficient exploitation of the 'secondary products' of domestic animals

---

316 See forthcoming paper by Domitius Corbulo. "The Enlightenment from a New Right Perspective" in *North American New Right*, Vol. 2.

317 Martin Hewson, 'Multicultural vs. Post-Multicultural World History: A Review Essay.' *Cliodynamics* 3.2 (2012), pp. 1–19.

(dairy products, textiles, harnessing of animals), large-scale herding, and the invention of chariots in the 2nd millennium. By the end of the 2nd millennium, these nomads had 'Indo- Europeanised' the Occident, but the Indo-Europeans who came into Anatolia, Syria, Mesopotamia were eventually absorbed into the more advanced and populated civilisations of this region. In Neolithic Europe, the Indo-Europeans imposed themselves as the dominant cultural group, displacing the native languages. In Europe, they developed 'individualising chiefdoms' (to be contrasted to the group-oriented chiefdoms of the East) in which the status of the chiefs was linked with the pursuit of personal status in warfare and the control of exchange networks dealing with prestige goods.

Indo-Europeans were uniquely ruled by a class of free aristocrats, grouped into war bands that were egalitarian rather than ruled by autocrats. A state is 'aristocratic' if the ruler, the king, or the commander-in-chief is *not* an autocrat who treats the upper classes as unequal servants, but is a 'peer' who exists in a spirit of equality, as another warrior of noble birth, *primus inter pares*. This is not to say that leaders did not get to enjoy extra powers and advantages, or that leaders were not tempted to act in tyrannical ways. It is to say that in aristocratic cultures, for all the intense rivalries between families and individuals seeking their own renown, there was a strong ethos of aristocratic egalitarianism against despotic rule. A true aristocrat deserving respect from his peers could not be submissive; his dignity and honour as a man were intimately linked to his capacity for self-determination.

Different levels of social organisation characterised Indo-European society. The lowest level, and the smallest unit of society, consisted of families residing in farmsteads and small hamlets, practicing mixed farming with livestock representing the predominant form of wealth. The next tier consisted of a clan of about five families with a common ancestor. The third level consisted of several clans — or a tribe — sharing the same. Those members of the tribe who owned livestock were considered to be free in the eyes of the tribe, with the right to bear arms and participate in the tribal assembly.

The scale of complexity in Indo-European societies changed considerably with the passage of time, and the Celtic tribal confederations that were in close contact with Caesar's Rome during the 1st century BC, for example, were characterised by a high concentration of economic and political power. However these confederations were still ruled by a class of free aristocrats. In classic Celtic society, real power within and outside the tribal assembly was wielded by the most powerful members of the nobility, as measured by the size of their clientage and their ability to bestow patronage. Patronage could be extended to members of other tribes and to free individuals who were lower in status and were thus tempted to surrender some of their independence in favour of protection and patronage.

Indo-European nobles were also grouped into war bands. These bands were freely constituted associations of men operating independently from tribal or kinship ties. They could be initiated by any powerful individual on the merits of his martial abilities. The relation between the chief and his followers was personal and contractual: the followers would volunteer to be bound to the leader by oaths of loyalty, wherein they would promise to assist him while the leader would promise to reward them from successful raids. The sovereignty of each member was thus recognised even though there was a recognised leader. These 'groups of comrades,' to use Indo-European vocabulary, were singularly dedicated to predatory behaviour and to 'wolf-like' living by hunting and raiding, and to the performance of superior, even super-human deeds. The members were generally young, unmarried men, thirsting for adventure. The followers were sworn not to survive a war leader who was slain in battle, just as the leader was expected to show in all circumstances a personal example of courage and war skills.

Young men born into noble families were not only driven by economic needs and the spirit of adventure, but also by a deep-seated psychological need for honour and recognition — a need nurtured not by nature as such, but by a cultural setting in which one's noble status was maintained in and through the risking of one's life in a battle to the death for pure prestige. This competition for fame among war band members (partially outside the ties of kinship) could not but have had an individualising effect upon the warriors. Hence, although band members ('friend-companions,' or 'partners') belonged to a cohesive and loyal group of like-minded individuals, they were not swallowed up anonymously within the group.

The most important value of Indo-European aristocrats was the pursuit of individual glory as members of their war bands and as judged by their peers. Literary works abound with accounts of the heroic deeds and fame of aristocrats — *Iliad, Beowulf,* the *Song of Roland,* and including such Irish, Icelandic and Germanic sagas as *Lebor na hUidre, Njal's Saga, Gisla Saga Sursonnar,* the *Nibelungenlied.* These are the earliest voices from the dawn of Western civilisation. Within this heroic 'life-world,' the unsocial traits of humans took on a sharper, keener, individuated expression.

It is my claim that the ultimate roots of the superior creativity of Europeans should be traced back to the aristocratic warlike culture of the Indo-Europeans. But Hewson wonders 'how unusual the Indo-Europeans were' in comparison to 'many nomadic arid-zone peoples who, like Turks, or Arabs, or Mongols, managed to conquer adjacent sedentary peoples?' He brings to attention Christopher Beckwith's observation that 'the key institution of the steppe was the war band or *comitatus* bound together by oaths of [aristocratic] loyalty and fraternity.' 'Unlike Duchesne, Beckwith holds that there was a common central Eurasian culture, encompassing all the steppe peoples.' True, in *Uniqueness,* I only made passing references to other steppe warriors, suggesting that these nomads 'came much later' after their sedentary neighbours (and the Europeans themselves) had attained a far more advanced level of civilisation than the Neolithic cultures encountered by Indo-Europeans, over which 'they were unable to superimpose their culture.' Beckwith's book, *Empires of the Silk Road: A History of Central Eurasia from the Bronze Age to the Present,* which came out while I was writing *Uniqueness,* argues that 'the most crucial element of the early form of the Central Eurasian Culture Complex was the sociopolitical-religious ideal of the heroic lord and his comitatus, a war band of his friends sworn to defend him to the death.'[318] Beckwith sees these war bands throughout the steppes, rather than exclusively among Indo-European speakers.

Yet, all in all, what he says actually solidifies my view. He agrees that the comitatus 'goes all the way back to the Proto-Indo-European times,' and that 'the true comitatus is unknown among non-Central Eurasian peoples.' Moreover, he says, if indirectly and without cognisant elaboration, that the Ural-Altaic steppe peoples evolved in a direction heavily influenced by the bordering Asian civilisations. There is a section on 'the Islamicised Comitatus,'[319] which is about 'Central Asian influence on the Arab Islamic world,' *but* which informs us that the 'comitatus system' was 'Islamicised as the *mamluk* system,' wherein the mamluks or warriors were transformed into 'a new imperial guard corps that was loyal to the ruler personally.'[320] Now, Beckwith still thinks that this system was akin to the comitatus, but the fact is that the steppe warriors who were transformed into mamluks can no longer be categorised as 'aristocratic' even if they were bound by a strong ethos of camaraderie with their peers. This is because they were not free men but slaves purchased to become loyal Muslim fighters for the personal use of a despotic Sultan. While they were eligible to attain the highest positions, and were trained with a code that emphasised courage, horsemanship and other warrior skills, they were not true peers but servants of the Sultan.[321]

Beckwith is clearer about the fate of the pastoral nomads and 'natural Warriors' known as the Hsiung-nu on the frontiers of China in the 3rd century BC. Their inability to impose themselves over the civilised Chinese let to the eventual success of the armies of the Han Dynasty 'in reducing the power of the Hsiung-nu considerably and spreading Chinese culture

---

318 Christopher Beckwith, *Empires of the Silk Road: A History of Central Eurasia from the Bronze Age to the Present* (Princeton University Press, 2009), p. 12.

319 Ibid., 23.

320 Ibid., 25.

321 James Waterson, 'The Mamluks.' *History Today* 56.3 (2006).

into the steppe zone.'[322] In contrast, as Beckwith shows, the migrations of the Indo-Europeans, particularly during the 'second wave around the 17th century BC, in which Indo-European speaking people established themselves in parts of Europe, the Near East, India, and China,' were far more influential in their effects on the lands occupied. 'By the beginning of the 1st millennium BC much of Eurasia had already been Indo-Europeanised, and most of the rest of it had come under very heavy Indo-European cultural and linguistic influence.'[323] At the same time, and also in line with my observations, Beckwith points out that the Indo-Europeans who migrated into the Anatolian highlands during the 2nd millennium were eventually assimilated to the native Hatti culture, 'growing up learning Hatti customs and language.' The Hittite rulers managed to maintain strong components of their Indo-European language for half a millennium, 'but at the end of the Bronze Age in the early 12th century BC their kingdom was overwhelmed by the convulsions ascribed to the little known Sea Peoples.'[324]

This outcome should be contrasted to the linguistic situation in the Greek mainland after the Mycenaean order ended around the same time. It remained Indo-European and would go on to produce the Homeric epics, which recounted the aristocratic and heroic ethos of the Mycenaeans. In the case of India, the Indo-Europeans would give India its national epic, the Mahabharata, with its depictions of the feats of the early warlike immigrants who herded cattle and fought from horse-drawn chariots. At the same time, as Beckwith notes, 'the local peoples of India heavily influenced' these warlike newcomers, 'who mixed with them in every way conceivable, eventually producing a new hybrid culture.'[325] By

---

322 Beckwith, p. 87.

323 Ibid., p. 30.

324 Ibid., pp. 38–39.

325 Ibid., p. 42. In arguing that Beckwith's views on non-Indo-European nomads *cannot* be seen as a challenge to my argument, I am not implying that his views on the Indo-Europeans support my view; in fact, he wrongly says that the non-Indo-European cultures (in Neolithic Europe) 'had an equally revolutionary impact on the Indo-Europeans,' through the generation of creoles via intermarriage and through linguistic symbiosis (p. 33). He offers no further words on this; but, as it is, the Indo-Europeans spread their languages throughout Europe, and the borrowings were just

the late Vedic period (after 1000 BC) the power of the aristocratic assemblies started to be replaced by a new kind of politics centred on the chief priest, the courtiers, and palace officials.[326]

Moreover, Beckwith is aware that it was the Proto-Indo-Europeans, not the Turks or the Mongols, who originated and developed the steppe toolkit, horse riding, wheel vehicles, chariots and, I would add, the 'secondary-products revolution.' Unfortunately, he barely writes about the nature and impact of these inventions on Neolithic Europe and the ancient world, other than making quick observations and stating that the Indo-Europeans 'possessed a powerful dynamism.'[327] About 150 pages of *Uniqueness* are dedicated to the Indo-European aristocratic culture, styles of fighting, heroic poetry, migratory movements, and the way their barbarian energies and tribal divisions were sublimated into more cohesive political entities (*polis*), as well as the connections of this aristocratic culture to the cultural flourishing of archaic and Classical Greece. I also show how Macedonia and Rome were rooted in the same Indo-European culture, and the way they revived the cultural and territorial dynamic exhibited by the Classical Greeks. Similarly, I emphasise the aristocratic feudal polities of the Germanic peoples and how they continued the Western legacy through the Middle Ages.

Beckwith does not even use the term 'aristocratic' but describes the comitatus as a group of peer warriors, in the course of which he erroneously assumes that the development of organised warfare in Greece and Rome, and the rise of the *polis* and the Roman senate, signalled the end of the aristocratic mind set. We need to keep in mind the aim of Beckwith's book, which is to challenge the portrayal of the steppes peoples as unduly barbaric and brutal. In this effort, he concludes with a rather bland view of 'Central Eurasians' as a people who were 'exactly as all other known

---

that, borrowings, rather than eventual subordination to the natives, as was the case outside Europe.

326 Hermann Kulke and Dietmar Rothermund, *A History of India*. (New York, Routledge, 1995), pp. 33–50.

327 Beckwith, p. 320.

peoples on earth': 'Urban and rural, strong and weak, fierce and gentle, abstainers and drinkers, lovers and haters, good, bad, and everything in between.'[328] In other words, Beckwith is a typical academic pushing an egalitarian view. My view, rather, is that the Indo-Europeans were a highly special people.

Beckwith's book, of course, is only a single source. Nevertheless, the scholarship supports the view I suggested, as I will try to show here by way of a summation of two key books with plentiful chapters by the foremost experts. They address in particular the relationship between the nomads and their sedentary neighbours, namely, *Mongols, Turks and Others: Eurasian nomads and the sedentary world*, edited by Reuven Amitai and Michal Biran, and *The Cambridge History of Early Inner Asia*, edited by Denis Sinor.[329] It will be argued that the impact of non-Indo-Europeans never came close to the deep and lasting changes associated with the 'Indo-Europeanisation' of the Occident.

From the 'Introduction' to the *Mongols, Turks and Others*, by the editors, we learn that the relationship between the nomads and their neighbours, from ancient times through the modern era, was one of 'symbiosis', 'conflict', 'trade' and 'conquest', *but* never dominion and cultural colonisation (by the nomads) in a culturally defining way. Rather, 'the ongoing contact between steppe and sown in Eurasia deeply affected the nomads themselves: their economy, political frameworks, religious life, expression and methods of warfare.'[330] While the arrival of the Indo-Europeans involved symbiosis as well, a far stronger case can be made that they thoroughly colonised Europe as 'pure nomads', with their new pastoral package of wheel vehicles, horse-riding, and chariots, combined with their aristocratic-libertarian ethos, which was superimposed on the natives. Gideon Shelach, in his chapter on the pastoral contacts of Northeast

---

328 Ibid., p. 355.

329 Michal Biran and Reuven Amitai, eds., *Mongols, Turks and Others: Eurasian nomads and the sedentary world* (2005). Denis Sinor, ed., *The Cambridge History of Early Inner Asia* (Cambridge University Press, 1990).

330 Michal Biran and Reuven Amitai, eds., p. 1.

China during 1100–600 BC, says that interaction was intensified bringing an increasing flow of goods and ideas, as attested by the archaeological records. But overall, he adds, the civilisation of China and the pastoral peoples of this period maintained their separate identities.[331]

Regarding the Cimmerians and Scythians who came into contact with their Near Eastern neighbours in the 8th and 7th centuries BC, Askold Ivantchik is very clear that these two ethnically related peoples never migrated to the Near East. Instead he suggests they only carried out raids, including military alliances and dynastic marriages, for limited periods without ever breaking off contact with their homeland situated to the north of the Caucasian mountain range.[332] Similarly, Naomi Standen observes in her study of the Liao peoples bordering north China in the 10th century that they were not interested in permanent administrative control over a piece of territory but looked to China as a raiding opportunity when trade was denied.[333] These observations should not surprise us. We are looking at nomads at a time in history in which their sedentary neighbours were occupying well-developed and populated territories which could not be easily contemplated as frontiers to be colonised. Michal Biran makes the general observation that the nomads who actually conquered Muslim lands 'either converted to Islam before the conquest, as had, for example, the Qarakhanids and the Seljuqs or, even if they conquered Muslim lands as "infidels," after decades in a mostly Muslim territory they eventually embraced Islam.'[334] Yehoshua Frenkel similarly argues, in his study of the relationship between the Turks and neighboring Muslims during 830–1055, that despite Islamic 'dependence' on the recruitment of Turkish soldiers to achieve effective government along the borders, and despite

---

331 Gideaon Shelach, 'Early Pastoral Societies of Northeast China: Local Change and Interregional Interaction during c. 1100–600 BCE' In *Mongols, Turks, and Others*.

332 Askold Ivantchik, 'Early Eurasian Nomads and the Civilizations of the Ancient Near East' (Eighth-Seventh Centuries BCE). In *Mongols, Turks and Others*, pp. 118–120.

333 Naomi Standen, 'What Nomads Want: Raids, Invasions and the Liao Conquest of 947' In *Mongols, Turks, and Others*.

334 Biran, Michal Biran, 'True to Their Ways: Why the Qara Khitai Did Not Convert to Islam.' In Mongols, Turks and Others, p. 175.

the number of Turks who became involved in Islamic politics, it was the Seljuk Turks who converted to Islam around the year 1000.[335] The Turks were Islamicised. Consequently, the outcome of the Turkic conquests of Asia Minor, the Balkans, and the Indian subcontinent was the expansion of Islam rather than Turkic nomadism (which had long come under sedentary influences).[336]

The Cambridge History of Early Inner Asia likewise shows that the peoples of the steppes did not have a lasting impact on sedentary societies. In this book with fifteen chapters, there are no countering facts or arguments which can be said to falsify the exceptionality of the Indo-Europeans in being the first steppe people to create sedentary cultures of their own, as the dominating elites, inside European lands. We learn from A. I. Melyukova that the Scythians and Sarmatians, from the end of the 7th century to the 4th century BC, carried numerous military expeditions into Western Asia from their location north of the Black Sea.[337] However, the 'relatively long period spent by the Scythians in the countries of Western Asia exerted a strong influence on Scythian society and culture.' The 'Scythian chiefs learned to appreciate luxury and *strove to imitate oriental sovereigns*' (p. 100, my emphasis). The aristocratic ideal of Indo-Europeans known as 'first among equals' or *primus inter pares*, which was exhibited by the Mycenaeans and so vividly expressed in Homer's *Iliad*, was the root base of Greece's creation of the *polis* and a culture characterised by competitive poetical displays, the Olympics, Hoplite Warfare, and the dialogical

---

335 Frenkel, Yehoshua Frenkel, 'The Turks of the Eurasian Steppes in Medieval Arabic Writing.' In *Mongols, Turks and Others*, pp. 204–208.

336 Carter Findley's *The Turks in World History*. (Oxford University Press, 2005) corroborates this assessment in the case of the Turko-Mongols further to the east within China's sphere of influence; he notes that 'interactions with non-nomadic peoples profoundly affected the steppes' (pp. 26–27); the Turko-Mongol conception of authority came under the influence of the Chinese idea of 'heaven's mandate' (pp. 31–32); the 'trade-tribute empires' of the Turks around 552–630 and 682–745 CE were centralised, hierarchical orders wherein rulers claimed to represent and embody the mandate of heaven (pp. 37–43).

337 A. I. Melyukova, 'The Scythians and Sarmatians.' In *The Cambridge History of Inner Asia*, pp. 99–100.

style of its philosophers. It was also the ethos that inclined the Romans to create a republican form of government, and the Germanic barbarians to transform their warlike organisation (that Tacitus called comitatus) into a feudal contractual form of rule based on mutual obligations by lords and vassals. The Scythians never managed to develop from their tribal/barbarian republics into a form of 'civilised' government in a republican direction. Notwithstanding their famed stand against an enormous Persian invasion about 514 or 512 BC, by way of partisan warfare, they never established dominion over their (increasingly) more advanced neighbours in the Near East. Instead, around the middle of the 3rd century AD, the Scythians were dissolved, losing their ethnic distinction. The Sarmatians suffered a similar fate in the 4th century AD, dealt by the Huns.

Ying-Shih Yu's chapter on the Hsiung-nu details in dramatic fashion the general observations of Beckwith, how 'a proud and defiant people' were forced to accept submission to the Han leadership sometime in the 1st century BC, leading to the 'Northern Hsiung-nu's collapse in the eighth decade of the 1st century AD.'[338] What about the dreaded Huns? 'No people of Inner Asia, not even the Mongols, have acquired in European historiography a notoriety similar to the Huns,' says Denis Sinor. They 'seriously challenged the equilibrium of the Western world [...] at a time when...the Roman Empire had to contend with serious internal disorders.'[339] The raid of 395–396 into Armenia, Syria, and Northern Mesopotamia traumatised the inhabitants; their destruction of the Burgundian kingdom in the 430s 'caught the imagination of generations'[340] Yet, the Huns did not exhibit any grand political designs, did not establish any permanent control over any sedentary civilisation, but remained 'a nation of warriors' always dependent on pastures available to their horses.[341]

---

338   Ying-Shih Yu, 'The Hsiung-nu.' In *The Cambridge History of Inner Asia*.p. 148.

339   Sinor, Denis Sinor, 'The establishment and dissolution of the Turk empire.' In *The Cambridge History of Inner Asia*, p. 177.

340   Ibid., p. 188.

341   Ibid., p. 204.

Colin Mackerras tells us that the Uighurs, who in the period before 744 excelled in horsemanship and archery, abandoned their nomadic past as they were impacted by the Central Kingdom. The Sogdians introduced them to a religion with a settled clergy and temples, and, 'as a result, the nomadic life became more and more difficult'.[342] A similar fate awaited the Kitans, according to Herbert Franke. The period of the 12th century AD 'showed a slow but inexorable change of the Kitan people through Chinese cultural influence.' Many Kitan emperors and their court aristocrats adopted Buddhism and became pious protectors of the Buddhist faith.[343] Similarly, the Jurchen people under the Yuan and Ming dynasties were 'absorbed into Chinese civilisation and lost their national identity' [344]

'The Mongols were by far the most successful of the steppe warriors,' writes Hildinger.[345] This is a generally held view, and it is true enough, but only so long as we pretend that the Indo-Europeans were merely a linguistic group, which is a widely shared perception.[346] The Mongols were an influential nomadic people who created the largest contiguous empire in history encompassing Mongolia, China, Korea, Russia, Iran, Iraq, Afghanistan, Transoxiana, Syria, and the Caucasus. *However*, the impact of the Mongols was felt mainly during the 13th and 14th centuries amidst their conquests and while the empire lasted. Moreover, by the

---

342 Colin Mackerras, 'The Uighurs.' In *The Cambridge History of Inner Asia*, p. 340.

343 Herbert Franke, 'The Forest People of Manchuria: Kitans and Jurchens.' In *The Cambridge History of Inner Asia*, p. 409.

344 Ibid., p. 422.

345 Erik Hildinger, *Warriors of the Steppe, A Military History of Central Asia, 500 BC to 1700 AD*. (Da Capo Press, 1997), p. 109.

346 Hildinger thus writes: 'The Scythians and the related Sarmatians are the first steppe nomads of whom we have any real knowledge' (p. 33). None of the sources/authors I cite here acknowledge them as a steppe people; *The Cambridge History of Early Inner Asia* has a chapter (by A. K. Narain) with the title 'Indo-Europeans Inner Asia,' which opens with the sentence: 'No barbarians survived so long and became so famous as those who are conventionally known as the Indo-Europeans' (p. 151). But this chapter is on the Indo-Europeans who migrated eastwards such as the Tokharian speakers and others of the Iranian ethnos, covering the period from the 2nd century BC to the 5th century AD. The Indo-Europeans who colonised the entire European continent are ignored; in *Uniqueness* I documented this academic tendency to view the Indo-Europeans as if they were merely a linguistic group.

time the Mongol and Turkic tribes experienced the leadership of Temüjin (1165–1227), the Mongolian steppe world was far from the earlier 'blood relationships between equals,' but was instead dominated by a single supra-tribe known as the *Khamag Mongol Ulus* or the All Mongol State. This State dissolved old tribal lines by regrouping them into an army based on a decimal system (units of 10, 100, and 1000); a process which was aided by a bureaucracy staffed in large measure by educated elites, obtained from the sedentary conquered populations.[347] The most significant legacy of the *Pax Mongolica* was the creation of a continuous order across a vast territory, easing the dissemination of goods and ideas throughout Eurasia. This was of course in addition to the mayhem and terror they brought to China, Persia, Russia, all of which suffered mass exterminations and famine.

The historical experiences of these steppe nomads stands in sharp contrast to the actual historical trajectory of the Indo-Europeans. Starting from their homelands in present-day Ukraine, the Indo-Europeans successfully colonised the entire European continent, whilst civilising their elemental aristocratic ways. During the course of their movements they exhibited a variety of cultural and linguistic forms, including the Yamnaya culture (3400–2300 BC), which spread across the Caspian region and moved into the Danube region. This was followed by the Corded Ware or Battle Axe culture, which extended itself across northern Europe from the Ukraine to Belgium after 3000 BC, and subsequently by the Bell-Beaker culture, which grew within Europe and spread further westwards into Spain and northwards into England and Ireland between 2800–1800 BC.[348] The Indo-Europeans also spread eastwards across the steppes as far

---

347 Timothy May, *The Mongol Conquests in World History*. (Reaktion Books, 2012). David Morgan, *The Mongols*. (Blackwell, 1986).

348 See the appropriately titled book by Marija Gimbutas, *The Kurgan Culture and the Indo-Europeanization of Europe, Selected Articles from 1952 to 1993*, edited by Miriam Dexter and K. Jones-Bley. (Washington D.C.: The Journal of Indo-European Studies Monograph Series No. 18, 1997). I have recently learned of another similar title, with close to 30 articles, entitled: *The Indo-Europeanization of Northern Europe*, edited by Karlene Jones-Bley and Martin Huld (1996). No such titles exist for the Indo-Europeans who went to the East, and for non-Indo-European nomads.

as the Tarim Basin in present-day Xinjiang, China. While these groups did have important influences on Chinese ancient culture, they were eventually absorbed by other non-Indo-European cultures.[349]

The ones who migrated into the Greek mainland went on to create the *first* Indo-European 'civilisation': Mycenae. The Mycenaean warriors comprised the background to archaic and classical Greece. The Macedonians rejuvenated the martial virtues of Greece after the debilitating Peloponnesian War, and went on to conquer Persia and create the basis for the intellectual harvest of Alexandrian Greece. The third barbarian Indo-Europeans who developed a civilisation were the early Romans. They founded an aristocratic republic, preserved the legacy of Greece, and cultivated their own Latin tradition. The fourth were the Celtic-Germanic peoples who interacted for some centuries with the Romans, and then continued the Western legacy. Despite the eventual decline of Classical Greece, the stagnation and break-up of the Hellenistic Kingdoms (out of the Western cultural orbit), and the aging despotism of Imperial Rome, the dynamic spirit of the West was sustained several times over thanks to the infusion of new sources of aristocratic peoples brought on by fresh waves of barbarians.

Andrei Znamenski, in his review of *Uniqueness*, says the book understands well that 'the aristocratic libertarian spirit of military democratic Chiefdoms' was not uniquely Indo-European, but that I only make passing references to other peoples of the steppes, and only briefly mention the native warriors of the north-western coast of North America with their own decentralised quests for heroic deeds.[350] I did not engage in any comparative assessment of the individualist-oriented ethos of Indo-European chiefdoms and the similarly organised chiefdoms of North America, but rather compared the former with the group-oriented chiefdoms of other

---

349   See the interesting collection of papers in Victor H. Mair, ed., 'The "Silk Roads" in Time and Space: Migrations, Motifs, and Materials.' *Sino-Platonic Papers* 228 (July 2012), http://www.sino-platonic.org/complete/spp228_silk_roads.pdf.

350   Andrei Znamenski, 'The "European Miracle": Warrior Aristocrats, Spirit of Liberty, and Competition as a Discovery Process.' *The Independent Review* 16.4 (2012).

non-European cultures. Znamenski provides some revealing examples of the American Indians of the Plains (Comanche, Cheyenne and others) as 'nomadic horse riders whose lifestyle and migration patterns closely resembled those of the Indo-Europeans'. The Plains chief, far from being an autocrat, sustained his status as a leader performing glorious deeds in the sight of his competitive peers.[351] These societies collapsed due to European colonisation, and so Znamenski writes: 'we will certainly never know if these Plains 'military democracies' would have evolved into something that would resemble the Athenian polis.' He also wonders why the Indo-Europeans who stayed in their homeland in the Ukraine did not evolve in the same direction as the ones who migrated to Europe. These examples tell us, he adds, that the connection from the aristocratic culture of the Indo-Europeans and the Athenian polis, Roman Republic, or the rise of the West generally, was 'far from linear.'[352]

This brings me to Hewson's impression that 'Duchesne eschews a materialist conception of history'. I understand that Hewson's main point lies in my paying little attention to certain materialistic factors such as family patterns and farming regimes that may have played a significant role. Still, I cannot help responding that the portrayal offered of the Indo-Europeans was materialistically focussed on their use of wheeled vehicles, the domestication and riding of horses, their secondary products revolution, and their geographical location in the steppes. The aristocratic ethos was explained, if too concisely, in connection to this pastoral lifestyle, which included fierce competition for grazing rights, constant alertness in the defence of one's portable wealth, and an expansionist disposition in a world where competing herdsmen were motivated to seek new pastures as well as tempted to take the movable wealth of their neighbours. This

---

351 While I did find support for this argument in the two books I consulted, namely, *The Comanches* (1952) by Ernest Wallace & Adamson Hoebel, and *Indians of the Plains* (1963) by Robert Lowie (which Znamenski references), there is more to an aristocratic way of life than political organisation; among the Indo-Europeans this aristocratic way was reflected in the nature of their gods, their heroic poetry, mythologies, individuated names, dressing styles, and burials.

352 Znamenski p. 607.

life of horsemanship, conflict and raids, brought to the fore certain mental dispositions, including aggressiveness and individualism, in the sense that each individual, in this hyper-masculine oriented atmosphere, needed to become as much a warrior as a herdsman. The perception that this is an idealistic view possibly comes from my central argument that the fight to the death for pure prestige was the primordially defining trait of aristocratic virtue. While I dedicated a section defending the findings of socio-biology, I added to this perspective the neo-Hegelian argument that a warrior's ability to overcome his natural instinct for survival, or his fear of death (whilst pursuing personal glory) was the beginning of Western self-consciousness and freedom. I contrasted the social-seeking desires of aristocrats with the ordinary pursuit of survival by humans generally. But Kevin MacDonald is correct, in that the striving for prestige and honour can also be seen within an evolutionary perspective. Indo-European individuals demonstrated their worthiness as men of virtue by risking their life for immaterial prestige, but, as my own argument shows, the Indo-Europeans did achieve great success as a genetic group. Therefore, in the words of MacDonald:

> 'prestige and honor among one's fellows is in fact typically linked with material possessions and reproductive success. Like other psychological traits related to aggression and risk-taking, the pursuit of social prestige by heroic acts is a high risk/high reward behaviour, where evidently the rewards sufficiently outweighed the risks over a prolonged period of evolutionary time.'[353]

No linear logic was intended by this emphasis on the Indo-European aristocratic way of life. The decision to trace the origins of Western uniqueness back to the prehistoric Indo-Europeans was meant to show that 'the beginnings' of the West were not in the never-explained 'Greek Miracle'. 'In the beginning' we witness warriors thirsting for individual glory, not philosophers seeking to advance original explanations of the universe. I defended at length the varying contributions of past Eurocentric historians on the

---

353 Kevin MacDonald, 'Going Against the Tide: Ricardo Duchesne's Intellectual Defence of the West.' *The Occidental Quarterly* 11.3 (2011), p. 51.

rise of the West, their emphasis on Europe's (and Greece's) geographical uniqueness, as well as their respective efforts to define and trace the rise of the West. The West did not rise point blank with the Indo-Europeans. There were many successive phases and uneven developmental dynamics with their own antecedent conditions and logics coming from different social spheres, military competition, the proximity of seas, the growth of scientific knowledge, political dynamics, innovations, literary influences, and more. For example, there was the Catholic Church's organisational structure and scholastic method of reasoning; the Gregorian reform and the systematisation of Canon law; the contractual and decentralised character of feudalism combined with the separation of society into autonomous corporate bodies; the Renaissance, the Scientific Revolution; and the Enlightenment. It would be extremely simple-minded to think that these developments were logically entailed in the aristocratic way of life of pre-historic Indo-Europeans (even if the West experienced renewed Indo-European beginnings with the Macedonians, the archaic Romans, and the Celtic-Germanic barbarians). The West is full of transitions, renaissances, and novelties, each of which was embedded to complex configurations of 'internal' and 'external' factors, unintended consequences, struggles, charismatic personalities, and environmental circumstances. At the same time, throughout these movements one finds the West's spirited and restless culture of aristocratic individualism. This does not mean, as Hewson inclines, that the continuous creativity of Westerners was the work of the aristocratic class per se. The meaning of aristocratic honour and excellence changed considerably from its barbarian origins through Classical Greek times, Christianisation, and bourgeois entrepreneurship. My book focuses on ancient Greece and medieval times with only marginal references to modern times,[354] but in the next chapter on exploration I will

---

354 Joseph Schumpeter's concept of creative destruction captures this Faustian personality in the world of business; true capitalist entrepreneurs employed their rationality for the joy of creation, to fight off competitors and conquer markets. Robber barons were creative destroyers of the existing economic conditions (Nietzsche: 'Whoever must be a creator always annihilates'). This type of capitalism personified the opposite of preservation, stagnation, the status quo: 'Capitalism, then, is by nature a form

try to capture this aristocratic soul in the history of modern exploration, arguing that i) almost all the explorers in history were European, and that ii) in the history of modern exploration we can detect in its pure form (and in a modern, peaceful way) this aristocratic desire to explore for its own sake, insomuch as explorers were no longer driven by a desire for riches, religious conversion or even scientific knowledge.

Another argument against the uniqueness of Indo-Europeans, one made by Beckwith and others, is that I fail to acknowledge the 'equally wonderful epic literature of the ancient, medieval, and modern Central Eurasians.' My book does neglect this epic literature from Central Eurasia; however there is no reason to assume robotically, without reflection and comparative analysis, that these two epic traditions were 'equally wonderful.' Having read two substantial articles, 'Mongolian-Turkic Epics: Typological Formation and Development,' and 'Mongolian Oral Epic Poetry: An Overview,'[355] I am confident in making the following distinctions:

(1)   The Indo-European epic and heroic tradition precedes any other tradition by some thousands of years, not just the Homeric and the Sanskrit epics but, as we now know with some certainty from such major books as West's *Indo-European Poetry and Myth*, and Watkins's *How to Kill a Dragon: Aspects of Indo-European Poetics*, going back to a prehistoric oral tradition.[356]

---

or method of economic change and not only never is but never can be stationary...' But Schumpeter was not optimistic, and under the influence of Weber's iron cage, saw a future in which capitalism would be replaced by a panoply of bureaucratic bodies, collectivities, regulations, and masses of [politically correct] administrators concerned with orderly management, regularity and continuity — even as the society continued to innovate and promote development. Reinert, Hugo and Erik Reinert. 'Creative Destruction in Economics: Nietzsche, Sombart, and Schumpeter.' http://www.othercanon.org/board/about- Reinert.html.

355   Rinchindorji, 'Mongolian-Turkic Epics: Typological Formation and Development.' *Oral Tradition* 16.2 (2001), and Chao Gejin, 'Mongolian Oral Epic Poetry: An Overview.' *Oral Tradition* 12.2 (1997).

356   M. L. West, *Indo-European Poetry*. (Oxford University Press, 2007). Calvert Watkins, *How to Kill a Dragon: Aspects of Indo-European Poetics* (Oxford University Press, 1995).

(2) Indo-European poetry exhibits a keener grasp and rendition of the fundamentally tragic character of life, an aristocratic confidence in the face of destiny, the inevitability of human hardship and hubris, without bitterness, but with a deep joy.[357]

(3) Indo-European poetry contains a richer repertoire of motifs and narrative stories, and a higher aesthetic level of achievement. The most basic theme of Mongolian and Turkic poetry is the search for a wife and children and fight with a demon, battle over horses, slaves, ransacking property, and clan feuds. Heroic deeds consist of overcoming natural obstacles and the evil designs of competitors en route to winning a future wife as well as fighting demons and other heroes. Similar themes can be found in Indo-European poetry, but many of these tales are richer in motifs, in the performance of greater, more adventurous and worldly deeds. The Vinland Sagas, for example, chronicle the adventures of Eirik the Red and his son, Leif Eirikson, who explored North America 500 years before Columbus, providing the first-ever descriptions of North America, recounting the Icelandic settlement of Shetland, Orkney, the Hebrides, parts of Scotland and Ireland, the Faroe Islands, Iceland, Greenland and Newfoundland. The *Iliad*, like the *Odyssey*, widely acknowledged through the centuries as two of the greatest works of literature, is a world of powerful kings living in vast, wealthy palaces, and in charge of huge armies; they are superb stories far richer in character, with heroes exhibiting complex inner contradictions, regrets, and self-criticism.[358]

(4) Indo-European epics show both collective and individual inspiration, unlike non-Indo-European epics which show characters functioning only as collective representations of their communities. Moreover, and this is a very important contrast,

---

357 Aaron Gurevich, *The Origins of European Individualism*. Blackwell, 1995) pp. 19–61.
358 Christopher Gill, *Personality in Greek Epic, Tragedy and Philosophy: The Self in Dialogue* (Clarendon Press, 1996).

further illuminating Indo-European individualism, in some Indo-European sagas there is a clear author's stance, unlike the anonymous non-Indo-European sages. The individuality, the rights of authorship, the poet's awareness of himself as creator, is acknowledged in many ancient and medieval sagas.[359]

(5) Beckwith says the Central Asian epic tradition continued to the 20th century while the Greek tradition ceased. Sure, it remained relatively stagnant in Central Asia while Homer's writings set the basis for Pindar, Aeschylus, Sophocles, Euripides, Aristophanes, and their invention of nearly all the literary patterns we use to-day: tragedy and comedy, epic and romance, and more, which the Romans eagerly assimilated. One can add to this list Virgil's *The Aeneid*, the satires of Horace and Juvenal, Ovid's *Metamorphoses*, not to mention the heroic epic of the Middle Ages all the way to Richard Wagner who is seen as the artist principally responsible for keeping the European mythological tradition alive in the modern world.

Nietzsche and Sublimation of the Agonistic Ethos of Indo-European Barbarians[360]

Finally, I would like to bring attention again to a section in my book answering the question: how do we connect the barbaric asocial traits of pre-historic Indo-European warriors to the superlative cultural achievements of Greeks and later civilised Europeans? Nietzsche provides us some keen insights as to how the untamed agonistic ethos of Indo-Europeans was translated into civilised creativity. In his fascinating early essay, 'Homer on Competition' (1872), Nietzsche observes that civilised culture or convention (*nomos*) was not imposed on nature, but rather was a sublimated

---

359 Gurevich, pp. 61–75. See also Hans F. K. Günther, *The Religious Attitudes of the Indo-Europeans*, trans. Vivian Bird and Roger Pearson (Carshalton, UK: Historical Review Press, 2001 [1963]).

360 This section draws on a section on Nietzsche in *Uniqueness*.

continuation of the strife that was already *inherent* to nature (*physis*).The nature of existence is based on conflict and this conflict unfolded itself in human institutions and governments. Humans are not naturally harmonious and rational as Socrates had insisted; the nature of humanity is strife. Without strife there is no cultural development. Nietzsche argued against the separation of man/culture from nature: the cultural creations of humanity are expressions or aspects of nature itself.

But nature and culture are not identical. The artistic creations of humans, their norms and institutions, constitute a redirecting of the destructive striving of nature into creative acts, which give form and aesthetic beauty to the otherwise barbaric character of natural strife. While culture is an extension of nature, it is also a form by which humans conceal their cruel reality, and the absurdity and the destructiveness of their nature. This is what Nietzsche meant by the 'dual character' of nature; humans restrain or sublimate their drives to create cultural artefacts as a way of coping with the meaningless destruction associated with striving.

Nietzsche, in another early publication, *The Birth of Tragedy* (1872), referred to this duality of human existence, *nomos* and *physis*, as the 'Apollonian and Dionysian duality.'[361] The Dionysian symbolised the excessive and intoxicating strife which characterised human life in early tribal societies, whereas the Apollonian symbolised the restraint and redirecting of conflict possible in state-organised societies. In the case of Greek society, during pre-Homeric times, Nietzsche envisioned a world in which there were no or few limits to the Dionysian impulses, a time of 'lust, deception, age and death.'[362] The Homeric and classical (Apollonian) inhabitants of city-states brought these primordial drives under 'measure' and self-control. The emblematic meaning of the god Apollo was 'nothing in excess.' Apollo was a provider of soundness of mind, a guardian

---

361   Friedrich Nietzsche, *The Birth of Tragedy*, trans. Ian Johnson (1872), https://archive.org/stream/BirthOfTragedy/bitrad#page/n9/mode/2up.

362   Friedrich Nietzsche, 'Homer's Contest,' in *The Genealogy of Morality*, ed. Keith Ansell-Pearson, trans. Carol Diethe (Cambridge: Cambridge University Press, 2006), pp. 174–181, 175. http://www.inp.uw.edu.pl/mdsie/Political_Thought/GeneologyofMorals.pdf.

against a complete descent into a state of chaos and wantonness. He was a redirector of the wilful and hubristic yearnings of individuals into organised forms of warfare and higher levels of art and philosophy. For Nietzsche, Greek civilisation was not produced by a naturally harmonious character, or a fully moderated and pacified city-state. One of the major mix-ups all interpreters of the rise of the West fall into is to assume that Western achievements were about the overcoming and suppression of our Dionysian impulses. But Nietzsche is right: Greeks achieved their 'civility' by attuning, not denying or emasculating, the destructive feuding and blood lust of their Dionysian past and placing their strife under certain rules, norms, and laws. The limitless and chaotic character of strife as it existed in the state of nature was made 'civilised' when Greeks came together within a larger political horizon, but it was not repressed. Their warfare took on the character of an organised contest within certain limits and conventions. The civilised aristocrat was the one who, in exercising sovereignty over his powerful longings (for sex, alcohol, revenge, and any other kind of intoxicant) learned self-command and, thereby, the capacity to use his reason to build up his political power and rule those 'barbarians' who lacked this self-discipline. The Greeks created their admirable culture while remaining at ease with their superlative will to strife.

A problem with Nietzsche is lack of historical substantiation. The research now exists to add to Nietzsche the historically based argument that the Greeks viewed the nature of existence as strife because of their background in an Indo-European state of nature, where strife was the overriding ethos. There are strong reasons to believe that Nietzsche's concept of strife is an expression of his own Western background, and his study of the Western agonistic mode of thinking that began with the Greeks. One may agree that strife is in the 'nature of being' as such, but it is worth noting that, for Nietzsche, not all cultures have handled nature's strife in the same way, and not all cultures have been equally proficient in the sublimated production of creative individuals or geniuses.

Nietzsche thus wrote of two basic human responses to the horror of endless strife: the un-Hellenic tendency to renounce life in this world as 'not worth living,' leading to a religious call to seek a life in the beyond or the Afterworld, or the Greek tragic tendency, which acknowledged this strife, 'terrible as it was, and regarded it as justified.'[363] The cultures that came to terms with this strife, he believed, were more proficient in the completion of nature's ends and in the production of creative individuals willing to act in this world. He saw Heraclitus' celebration of war as the father and king of the whole universe as a uniquely Greek affirmation of nature as strife. It was this affirmation which led him to say that 'only a Greek was capable of finding such an idea to be the fundament of a cosmology.'

The Greek-speaking aristocrats had to learn to come together within a political community that would allow them to find some common ground, thus moving away from the 'state of nature' with its endless feuding and battling for individual glory. There would emerge in the 8th century BC a new type of political organisation, the city-state. The greatness of Homeric and Classical Greece involved putting Apollonian limits around the indispensable but excessive Dionysian impulses of barbaric pre-Homeric Greeks. Ionian literature was far from the berserkers of the pre-Homeric world, but it was just as intensively competitive. The search for the truth was a free-for-all. Each philosopher competed for intellectual prestige in a polemical manner that sought to discredit the theories of others while promoting one's own. There were no Possessors of the Way in aristocratic Greece, no Chinese Sages decorously deferential to their superiors and expecting appropriate deference from their inferiors.

This agonistic ethos was ingrained in the Olympic Games, the perpetual warring of the city-states, the pursuit of political career, the competition among orators for the admiration of the citizens, and in the Athenian theatre festivals, where a great many poets would take part in Dionysian competitions. It was evident in the Sophistic-Socratic ethos of dialogic argument, and the pursuit of knowledge by comparing and criticising individual speeches, evaluating contradictory claims, collecting evidence,

---

363 Ibid., 176.

and competing by persuading and refuting others. It was also apparent in the aforementioned Catholic scholastic method, according to which critics would engage major works, read them thoroughly, compare the book's theories to other authorities, and, through a series of dialogical exercises, determine its respective merits and demerits.

Conclusion

In Spengler's language, this Faustian soul was present in 'the Viking infinity-wistfulness,' and their colonising activities through the North Sea, the Atlantic, and the Black Sea. It was present in the Portuguese and Spaniards who 'were possessed by the adventured-craving for uncharted distances and for everything unknown and dangerous.' It also lay in 'the emigration to America,' 'the Californian gold-rush,' 'the passion of our Civilization for swift transit, the conquest of the air, the exploration of the Polar regions and the climbing of almost impossible mountain-peaks' — 'dramas of uncontrollable longings for freedom, solitude, immense independence, and of giant-like contempt for all limitations.' 'These dramas are Faustian and only Faustian. No other culture, not even the Chinese, knows them.'[364]

The West has clearly been facing a spiritual decline for many years now, as Spengler observed, despite its immense technological innovations. Spengler acknowledged these, yet observed that Europe, after 1800, came to be thoroughly dominated by a purely 'mechanical' expression of this Faustian tendency. He remarked upon its remorseless expansion outward through industrial capitalism with its ever-growing markets and scientific breakthroughs. Spengler did not associate this mechanical ('Anglo-Saxon') expansion with cultural creativity *per se*. Before 1800, the energy of Europe's Faustian culture was still expressed in 'organic' terms; it was directed toward pushing the frontiers of inner knowledge through art, literature, and the development of the nation-state. It was during the 19th century that the West, according to him, entered 'the early Winter of full civilization' as its culture took on a purely capitalistic and mechanical

---

364 Spengler, *The Decline of the West*, pp. 335–337.

character, extending itself across the globe, with no more 'organic' ties to community or soil. It was at this point that this rootless rationalistic *Zivilisation* had come to exhaust its creative possibilities and would have to confront 'the hard cold facts of a late life … Of great painting or great music there can no longer be, for Western people, any question.'[365]

The decline of the organic Faustian soul is irreversible, but there is reason to believe that decline is cyclical and not always permanent — as we have seen most significantly in the case of China many times throughout her history. European peoples need not lose their superlative drive for technological supremacy. The West can reassert itself, unless the cultural Marxists are successful in their efforts to destroy this Faustian spirit permanently through mass immigration and miscegenation.

---

365 Ibid., pp. 20–21. See also Oswald Spengler, *The Decline of the West, Volume II: Perspectives on World History* (Alfred A. Knopf, 1988 [1928]), pp. 46, 44, 40.

5

A Civilisation of Faustian Explorers

Just as Ulysses, returning home to Penelope after infinite pains and wanderings, had to make one last voyage; just as Alexander, after marching to northern India, regretted there were no more worlds to conquer; so these paladins of discovery never had enough. Columbus could have settled for a castle in Spain and a pension after any of his first three voyages; but he always had to make one more. Sebastian Cabot held an honorable and lucrative position in Spain, but he had to go to sea and prove himself a sailor. Drake sailed around the world, brought home (some say) a million pounds in booty, bought a country estate, and set up as an English squire; but, at the first call, off again to sea he went, and at sea he left his bones.

SAMUEL ELIOT MORISON,
The Great Explorers: European Discovery of America (1978)

Measuring the Accomplishments of Civilisations

One argument of *Uniqueness* is that it is not any particular renaissance, revolution, or liberal institution that marks out the West, but its far higher levels of achievement in all the intellectual and artistic spheres of life. I relied on Charles Murray's book, *Human Accomplishment: Pursuit of Excellence in the Arts and Sciences, 800 B.C. to 1950*, to make this argument.[366] This book is the first effort to quantify 'as facts' the accomplishments of individuals and countries across the world in the arts and sciences, by calculating the amount of space allocated to these individuals

---

366 Charles Murray, *Human Accomplishment: The Pursuit of Excellence in the Arts and Sciences 800 B.C. to 1950* (New York: HarperCollins, 2003).

in reference works, encyclopaedias, and dictionaries. Murray concludes that 'whether measured in people or events, 97% of accomplishment in the scientific inventories occurred in Europe and North America' from 800 BC to 1950.[367]

Murray also notes the far higher accomplishments of Europeans in the arts, particularly after 1400. Although Murray does not compare their achievements but compiles separate lists for each civilisation, he notes that the sheer number of 'significant figures' in the arts is higher in the West in comparison to the combined number of the other civilisations.[368] In literature, the number in the West is 835; whereas in India, the Arab World, China, and Japan combined, the number is 293. In the visual arts, it is 479 for the West as compared to 192 for China and Japan combined (with no significant figures listed for India and the Arab World). In music, 'the lack of a tradition of named composers in non-Western civilization means that the Western total of 522 significant figures has no real competition at all'.[369]

But Murray pays no attention to accomplishments in other human endeavours such as warfare, voyages of discovery, and heroic leadership. His achievements come only in the form of 'great books' and 'great ideas.' Europeans were also exceptional in their contentious and expansionist behaviours. Their scholarly achievements, including their liberal values, were inseparably connected to their aristocratic ethos of competitive individualism. There is no need to concede to multicultural critics, as Norman Davies believes, 'the sorry catalogue of wars, conflict, and persecutions that have dogged every stage of the [Western] tale.'[370] The intellectual and artistic achievements of Europeans, seemingly peaceful as they may seem, are part of the same expansionist and disputatious psychological make-up Spengler designated as 'Faustian'.

---

367 Ibid., p. 252.
368 Ibid., pp. 113, 131–42.
369 Ibid., p. 259.
370 Norman Davies, *A History of Europe* (New York: Random House, 1997), pp. 15–16.

It has been said that when Mahatma Gandhi was asked what he thought of Western civilisation he answered, 'I think it would be a good idea.' Academics today interpret this answer to mean that the actual history of the West — the Crusades, the conquest of the Americas, the British Empire etc. — belie its great ideas, artistic beauty and claim to 'civilisation' behaviourally. In the previous chapter, I challenged this naive separation between an idealised and a realistic West, using Oswald Spengler's image of the West as a strikingly vibrant culture driven by a type of personality overflowing with expansive, disruptive, and creative impulses. This chapter will argue that the history of exploration stands as an excellent subject matter for the elucidation of this personality. Humans do not have an innate urge to explore; only European man has exhibited a keen desire to move beyond the known world into the unknown.

Current historians of exploration cannot come to terms with this difference in human psychology. In the egalitarian world of academia the deeds of great European men stand like an irritating thorn. Allowing university students (the majority of whom are now females) to learn that practically every great philosopher, scientist, architect, composer (or, simply put, everyone great), has been a male makes them uncomfortable. The thought of teaching their increasingly multiracial classrooms that these males are overwhelmingly European terrifies them. While universities cannot ignore altogether the cultural achievements of Europeans, otherwise they would have little to teach — all the disciplines, after all, were created by Europeans — the emphasis tends to be on the evolution of 'progressive' ideas, framed as if they were universal ideals by and for humanity. Egalitarians particularly enjoy teaching how these ideas have been improved upon, and continue to be, through the 'critical thinking' of teachers and activists. They envision themselves as activists fighting for the welfare of non-whites and females. This has entailed not just an emphasis on non-European experiences, but an outright depreciation and steamrolling of European greatness. But there is a problem. The greatness of Europeans is overwhelmingly substantial and pervasively present in all the fields; it cannot be effortlessly placed (equally) alongside the achievements of other cultures. We may add Chinese philosophers to the history and discipline of philosophy, but how much can one teach about Mayan epistemology and African ontology? European greatness must somehow be explained away, cut back, hidden, contextualised, and in the end held in contempt. This is what has happened in our universities.

Against Western Uniqueness

Most schools, interpretations, methodologies, and discursive analyses of the last decades have consisted of efforts to negate, implicitly or explicitly, the attainments of Europeans. Deconstruction, Orientalism, the Annales School, 'History from Below,' Feminism, World Systems Theory, Afrocentrism, Structuralism, Foucaultian Discourse Analysis, Ethnomethodology, Quantitative History and Multicultural World History may have not always advocated openly anti-Western views, but their focus has certainly been away from, or against, the high cultural achievements of Europeans.

Jacques Derrida and his pupils have encouraged the exposing of hierarchical orders, the dismantling of any rankings of values and the labeling of 'bipolar' contrasts as tenuous orderings based on unquestioned assumptions that must be unmasked. This has resulted in a fundamental devaluation of the West's high culture. Deconstruction has taught thousands of students to suspect anything that was held in high esteem or deemed to be great and noble in the past, as nothing more than 'Eurocentric' prejudice that needs to be brought down. This, in order to open the way for the 'full expression' of human talents leading to the democratic validation of all peoples.[371]

---

371 It is true, as Ernst Breisach writes, that deconstruction, in principle, calls for each culture to be challenged and eroded from within, since each culture engages in exclusions and hierarchical judgments; yet, as he adds, 'so far, Derrida and other post modernists have focused exclusively on the deconstruction of the West's understanding of the world and history. Derrida maintained that Western culture's logocentrism, with its attendant ethnocentrism, created an especially numerous and

The idea of Orientalism initiated by Edward Said has encouraged an image of Western scholars as inherently inclined to view in a negative way the cultures of the Near East, and the non-Western world at large, writing histories and developing works of art which distort the ways and achievements of non-Western peoples. The charge of Orientalism has resulted in a distorted appreciation of how much curiosity and true scholarship Westerners actually developed in their sincere attractions to the ancient cultures of Egypt, Mesopotamia and medieval Islam, and in their writing of proper historical accounts of these places and borrowing certain motifs to produce great works of art. Entire departments of Near Eastern programs, Asian and African Studies, created and financed by Europeans in multiple universities, far surpasses what these respective peoples have taught themselves.[372]

The Annales School was an excellent corrective to the notion that historical writing should be centred on the actions of the leaders of nation-states. Instead it brought to light the long lasting and powerful role of demographic and geographic forces in history, how these forces affect millions and how slowly they change, uninfluenced by politics for all the sound and fury of revolutions and wars. The lives of ordinary people are enmeshed within impersonal material realities that dictate longevity, the standard of living, and daily life.[373] But in claiming that what matters in history are the day to day lives of millions, the mortality rate, age at marriage, diseases, fertility rates, and overall material standards, this approach

---

oppressed "other" and argued against that culture's "presence." Western culture had become particularly harmful to the "other," be it the Third World or those harmed in its own society, when it attempted to order the world according to its expectations of progress' See *On the Future of History: The Postmodernist Challenge and Its Aftermath* (University of Chicago Press, 2003), p. 132. In a future book I will address how much the West stands to be blamed for its ideology of progress; my point now is that deconstruction has been singularly directed against Western culture in favor of non-Western peoples and diversification as a way of including all the 'others' excluded by European ethnocentrism.

372 Ibn Warraq, *Defending the West: A Critique of Edward Said's Orientalism* (Prometheus Books, 2007).

373 Fernand Braudel, *On History*. Trans. Sarah Matthews (University of Chicago Press, 1982).

wilfully downplayed the greatest cultural achievements of Europeans and what made them different in many ways (i.e. their immense creativity in painting, philosophy, music and literature). This portrayed the pre-Industrial West as just one more slow moving civilisation dominated by Malthusian pressures.

'History from Below' directed attention to the important roles the masses had played politically, in bringing about major revolutions. It argued that history was not an affair of the upper classes only, using the French Revolution as an example of how even its 'bourgeois' phase was driven by the actions of peasants and artisans, and how the proletariat was destined to be the main agent of history in ushering Communism.[374] This approach, advanced by Marxist historians, would be extended by feminists and cultural Marxists generally into a call for a new history that would include the 'indispensable' roles and achievements of a whole host of 'minorities' neglected by traditional academics (i.e. gays, transsexuals, lesbians, blacks etc.), all of which contained a corresponding assault, and inevitable devaluation of the one agent that stood out as unoppressed, as ultimate oppressor: white hetero males, the very beings responsible for almost all the greatest works in Art and Science.

The argument by World Systems Theory is that the 'core' countries of the West had achieved their status as advanced cultures by exploitation and holding down the 'periphery' and that a true historical narrative entailed an appreciation of the morally superior ways of Third World peoples struggling to liberate themselves from a world system controlled by white owned multinationals. This too has had an immensely negative impact on students, leading them to believe that the West only managed to modernise by extracting resources from the Third World and enslaving

---

374 George Rudé, *The Crowd in History. A Study of Popular Disturbances in France and England, 1730–1848.* New York: Wiley & Sons, 1964; Albert Soboul, *The Sans-Culottes. The Popular Movement and Revolutionary Government, 1793–1794.* Trans. Remy Inglis Hall (Princeton University Press [1968] 1980). Georges Lefebvre, *The Coming of the French Revolution.* Trans R. R. Palmer (Princeton University Press [1939] 1969).

Africans and Natives.[375] This highly influential school has missed the far more important role of modern science and liberal institutions in the industrialisation of Western European nations.

Michel Foucault and the postmodernist currents swept the academic world in the 1970s and 80s with the claim that truth was a matter of which discourse held power rather than a question of 'objectivity'. This has been used to bring down any 'metanarrative' that prioritises the role of Europeans in history, in the name of discourses expressing multiple voices.[376] This discursive assault has led students to believe that there is no way to ascertain the achievements of cultures, since reality is a construct of the discourses within which said reality is evaluated. It has led students to believe that the way to success in academia is through political influence, control of hiring and that a preoccupation with the rise of the West was no more than a preoccupation with the deeds of 'dead white males'.

Meanwhile, 'ethnomethodology' afforded a method by which to bring out the voices of the marginalised in society, the ones who had been silenced by the official discourses of 'Western social scientists'. Students were obligated to hear their folk-ways, their forms of expression, 'the silences or absences' of marginalised criminals, drug addicts, black lesbians, the mentally impaired, undocumented immigrants, African migrants, on the grounds that there was as much to be learned from their 'voices' than from the now sterile and biased works of the Western Canon.[377] Of course, the ones in charge of hearing these voices have generally been well-off academic whites, and non-whites looking to profit from white-created countries.

---

375 Immanuel Wallerstein, *The Modern World-System, vol. I: Capitalist Agriculture and the Origins of the European World-Economy in the Sixteenth Century* (Academic Press, 1974); *The Modern World-System, vol. II: Mercantilism and the Consolidation of the European World-Economy, 1600–1750* (Academic Press, 1980).

376 There is an 'industry' of discourse analyses in academia that has spread through the social sciences and humanities; see Penny Powers, 'The Philosophical Foundations of Foucaultian Discourse Analysis' *Critical Approaches to Discourse Analysis across Disciplines* 1 (2): pp. 18–34.

377 John Heritage, *Garfinkel and Ethnomethodology* (Cambridge: Polity Press, 1984).

Quantitative historians, for their part, insisted that only a history that could offer measurable data by relying on statistical and computer modelling could be trusted to give us real knowledge of the past rather than biased accounts infused by value judgments.[378] But since only certain aspects of history could be measured in this way, the result was an emphasis on such measurable issues as rates of birth, death, marriage and disease, migrations and economic trends. From this perspective, the one thing that could be known with certainty about the rise of the West was when it began to achieve modern economic growth; when it had broken with the Malthusian limits of the past agrarian order; or when it had offered workers a standard of living above the margins of existence. The philosophical creativity, artistic genius, great statesmanship and explorations of the world were interesting subjects to read about, but not the proper concern of those interested in gaining scientific knowledge about Western uniqueness. Again, as with all of these approaches, in varying degrees, quantitative history offered important insights about economic and demographic history. The reason Murray's work is very important is that he found a way to measure intellectual and artistic achievements in a comparative statistical way.

Aims of this Chapter

None of these approaches is capable of asking (let alone answering) the question of why Europeans have dominated so thoroughly the field of exploration. The only way to answer this question is through Spengler's Faustian concept. We saw in chapter four that Faustian man is animated with the spirit of a 'proud beast of prey,' like that of an 'eagle, lion, [or] tiger.'[379] Much like Hegel's master, who engages in a fight to the death for

---

378 Loren Haskins, and Kirk Jeffrey. *Understanding Quantitative History* (M.I.T. Press, 1990). There is a massive literature addressing the rise of the West strictly in terms of when this civilisation achieved modern economic growth, which focuses on quantitative evidence, as I discussed in *Uniqueness*.

379 Oswald Spengler, *Man and Technics: A Contribution to a Philosophy of Life* (Westport, CT: Greenwood Press, 1976), pp. 19–41.

pure prestige,[380] for this being 'the concerns of life, the deed, became more important than mere physical existence.'[381] This man is therefore outside the ability of all the above approaches, which are concerned with ordinary people, their daily concerns, and, yes, struggles, but not for things that are immaterial or great deeds, no matter the hardship and dangers involved. The Faustian spirit has infused every high cultural achievement of Western life. As John Farrenkopf puts it,

> 'the architecture of the Gothic cathedral expresses the Faustian will to conquer the heavens; Western symphonic music conveys the Faustian urge to conjure up a dynamic, transcendent, infinite space of sound; Western perspective painting mirrors the Faustian will to infinite distance; and the Western novel responds to the Faustian imperative to explore the inner depths of the human personality while extending outward with a comprehensive view.'[382]

Spengler writes of the 'morphological relationship that inwardly binds together the expression-forms of all branches of Culture.'[383] Rococo art, differential calculus, the Crusades, and the conquest of the Americas were all expressions of the same restless soul. There is no incongruity between the great ideas of the West and the so-called 'realities' of conflict, antagonism, and vainglory. In this chapter I will explain why the history of European exploration stands as an excellent subject matter for the elucidation of the West's singularly Faustian spirit.

Almost all the explorers in history have been European. *Concise Encyclopedia of Explorations* lists a total of 274 explorers, of which fifteen are non-European, with none listed after the mid 15th century.[384] *World Explorers and Discoverers*, a bibliographical dictionary containing profiles

---

380 The fight to the death for pure prestige is a key theme of *Uniqueness*; see in particular pp. 318–332.

381 Spengler, *Man and Technics*, pp. 19–41.

382 John Farrenkopf, *Prophet of Decline: Spengler on World History and Politics* (Baton Rouge: Louisiana State University Press, 2001), p. 46.

383 Ibid., p. 6.

384 Jean Riverain, *Concise Encyclopedia of Explorations*, introduced by Sir Vivian Fuchs (Chicago: Follet, 1969).

of 313 of the most significant individuals in the history of exploration, lists only 7 non-Europeans.[385] In the urge to explore the unknown, in the striving to claim new regions of the earth and map the nameless we can detect, in a crystallised way, the 'prime-symbol' of Western restlessness: the desire for 'limitless space' and the 'derivatives' of this prime symbol, namely 'Will,' 'Force,' and 'Supreme Deed.' We can also detect the Western mind's desire — if I may borrow the language of Hegel — 'to expand its cognitive horizon, to 'subdue the outer world to its ends with an energy which has ensured for it the mastery of the world.'[386]

As we reach the history of exploration after the 1700s, this urge to explore eventually transcended the urge to conquer other spaces, or benefit economically, becoming an urge to explore for its own sake, an intense psychological desire to reach a certain peak or goal, to be 'the first to set foot there.' By witnessing this type of exploration, driven by a desire that exceeded military, economic, or religious interests (which we commonly associate with human beings and cultures in general), we may be able to ascertain in a definite form the distinctive Faustian psyche of the West.

But in continuation with my preoccupation in prior chapters with multicultural world history, my focus in this chapter will be on one book, *Pathfinders: A Global History of Exploration*, published in 2006, authored by one of the most acclaimed historians today, Felipe Fernandez-Armesto. This book is an excellent example of how someone committed to egalitarian cultural achievements in history reacts in the face of persistent European greatness in exploration. Exploration is a subject that can be measured but it is not a subject that can be understood in measureable

---

385 Richard Bohlander, ed., *World Explorers and Discoverers* (Macmillan Publishing Co., 1992). This is a rough estimate based on an assessment of the names and possible ethnic origins. The reference book, *Who Was Who in World Exploration* (Roundhouse Publishing, 1992), by Carl Waldman and Alan Wexler, lists over 800 explorers, of which, I would say, modestly, no more than 25 are non-European. Be it noted that these sources are very keen on presenting exploration as a world-wide accomplishment.

386 G.W.F. Hegel, *Philosophy of Mind: Being Part Three of the "Encyclopaedia of the Philosophical Sciences"*(1830), trans. William Wallace (Oxford: Clarendon Press, 1971), p. 45.

terms alone; it requires a subjective appreciation of heroic will, and stamina against immense odds and hardship.

Fernandez Armesto thought it would be a subject filled with 'human connections' across the globe, testimony to the togetherness of human beings as members of one planet. But when he realised that almost all the explorers were European males, he decided to denigrate and trivialise this most honourable act of human greatness. This is yet another example of the pathology of cultural Marxism and its determination to erase European history so as to hide from our diversity curriculum its greatness. We will see yet again that the historical sources are totally on our side, though this requires acknowledging, or making explicit, the racial identities of the explorers.

The Exploratory and Geographical Activities of the Greeks

The science of geography was initiated by the Greeks. But just as pertinent is how this science was driven by individuated and contentious characters born in a culture engaged in widespread colonising and travelling activities between 800 and 500 BC. Hecataeus (550–476 BC), author of the first book of geography, *Journey Round the World*, thus based his knowledge on his exploratory travels along the Mediterranean and the Black Sea, as well as the tabulation of countless news and rumours he had heard from a long generation of colonising Greeks. To be sure, starting around the 1st millennium BC, the Phoenicians established roughly thirty colonies through the African shores in the western Mediterranean, Sardinia, Malta, and as far west as Gadir (or Cádiz in modern Spain), by the 6th or 5th century BC. However, more than thirty Greek city-states each established multiple colonies, with the city of Miletus alone establishing about ninety colonies. All in all, Greek colonies extended throughout the Mediterranean coasts, the shores of the Black Sea, Anatolia in the east, southern France and Italy, Sicily, and in the northern coast of Africa — not to mention the long colonised islands of the Aegean Sea.

A popular explanation why the Greeks launched these overseas colonies is population growth and scarce resources at home. But the evidence shows that many of these colonial operations were small-scale undertakings rather than mass migrations led by impoverished farmers. Population, in any case, was not uncontrollable in principle. Commercial interests and the incentive to gain new agricultural lands were undoubtedly motivating factors.[387] However, one cannot ignore the folklore of the times; the story of the Odyssey and other legends recounting the adventure and dangers of travelling through the Dardanelles and Bosporus, the legends of the Argonauts and Heracles, the nymph of Arethusa, and the goddess of Syracuse.[388] Centuries of overseas ventures undoubtedly produced a pioneering spirit among the Greeks. I am in agreement with A.G. Woodhead's emphasis on the 'general spirit of adventure' that permeated 'the dawn of classical Hellas', and his observation that 'many of the colonies had their origins in purely individual enterprise or extraordinary happenings.'[389] He writes: 'This personal element, indeed, probably deserves more stress than it has received. It is fashionable to look for great impersonal causes and trends which, singly or in combination, produce a human response, and the economic considerations already discussed fall into that category.'[390]

Hecataeus envisioned the world as a disc surrounded by an ocean, with the Celts placed in the west, the Scythians on the north shores of the Black Sea, Libya in the south, and the Indus in the east. But soon there would be a challenger: Herodotus, born in 484 BC, the author of Histories.

---

387 John Boardman, *The Greeks Overseas* (London: Penguin Books, 1964).

388 Robin Lane Fox's *Travelling Heroes: Greeks and Their Myths in the Epic Age of Homer* (Allen Lane, 2008) deals with how their travels from one end of their world to the other shaped the Greek myths about gods and heroes. *The Odyssey* by Homer, after all, is about the hero Odysseus' adventures, 'the eternal wanderer', as Peter Jones describes him, 'fired with a passion for knowledge and experience. Even when he returns home, he must set out again and continue wandering till death.' See Homer, *The Odyssey*, trans. by E.V. Rieu, with 'Introduction' by Peter Jones (Penguin Books, 1991), p. xlviii.

389 Ibid., p. 32.

390 A.G. Woodhead, *The Greeks in the West* (New York: Praeger, 1966), pp. 32–33.

He, too, offered numerous geographical and ethnographic insights based on his adventurous expeditions down the Nile, eastwards through Syria to Babylon and Susa, and north to the world of the Scythians and Thracians, including an expedition to Italy. In explicit awareness of his contributions, and in apparent criticism of his predecessor, Herodotus wrote: 'For my part I cannot but laugh when I see numbers of persons drawing maps of the world without having any reason to guide them, making, as they do, the Ocean-stream to run all around the earth, and the earth itself to be an exact circle as if described by a pair of compasses.'[391]

This competitive desire of individuals to stand out from others was ingrained in the whole social outlook of classical Greece.

During the Hellenistic centuries, explorers would venture into the Caspian, Aral, and Red Seas, establishing trading posts along the coasts of modern Eritrea and Somalia. Perhaps the most successful of Hellenistic explorers was Pytheas (380–306 BC). Born in the Greek colony of Massalia (Marseilles), he was the first to undertake an ambitious journey upwards through the Atlantic into the North Sea, and in so doing provided direct information on the shape of Europe. In his book, *On the Ocean*, which no longer survives but is known from quoted fragments, Pytheas recounts a journey to Brittany across the Channel into Cornwall, through the Irish Sea, the Baltic Sea, along the coast of Norway, and even to Iceland ('Thule') around 320/300 BC, as recounted later by Strabo.

These explorations encouraged astronomical and geographical scholarship leading to the full conceptualisation of the shape of the earth by Eratosthenes (276–185 BC), who not only contextualised the location of Europe in relation to the Atlantic and the North Sea, but also calculated the spherical size of the earth (within 5% of its true measure), with the obvious implication that the Mediterranean was only a small portion of the globe. This spirit of inquiry continued through the 2nd century AD, in the Hellenistic city of Alexandria, when Ptolemy wrote his System of

---

391 Barry Cunliffe, ed., *The Oxford Illustrated History of Prehistoric Europe* (Oxford University Press, 2001), p. 5.

Astronomy and Geography. In these works Ptolemy carefully explained the principles and methods required in mapmaking, and in *Universalis tabula* produced the first world map depicting India, China, South-East Asia, the British Isles, Denmark, and East Africa below the Horn of Africa. There was far less desire to explore the world's geography and landscapes among the peoples of the non-Western world. While in the 1st century BC the Han dynasty extended its geographical boundaries south into Vietnam, north into Korea, and east into the Tarim Basin, the Chinese showed little geographical interest beyond their own borders. What is striking about such Chinese maps as Chu Ssu-Pen maps of 1311 and 1320 AD is how insular they were in comparison with the much earlier maps of Ptolemy (120–170 AD). The ability of Chinese geographers to apply grids to maps to determine the positions and distances of local places is well-attested. Yet, even a 16th century reproduction of Zheng He's sailing maps lacks any apposite scale, size, and sense of proportion regarding the major landmasses of the earth. The Chinese supposition that the earth was flat remained almost unchanged from ancient times until Jesuit missionaries introduced modern ideas in the 17th century. C. Cullen writes: 'The lack of instances of arguments for a spherical earth is, of course, compounded by the lack of instances of any counter-argument at all; the flat earth remained unquestioned. This situation persisted until well into the 17th century.'[392]

In stark contrast, the argumentative Milesian philosophers of the 5th and 4th centuries BC, Thales, Anaximander, and Hecataus were already persuaded that the earth was a sphere; it is reported that they were the first to have made globes. Philolaus (470–385 BC), a Pythagorean, asserted that the earth was spherical and in motion, not around the sun, but around the 'central fire' of the universe. Aristarchus of Samos (approximately 310–230 BC), went so far as to postulate the Copernican hypothesis that all planets,

---

392 C. Cullen, 'A Chinese Eratosthenes of the Flat Earth: A Study of a Fragment of Cosmology in Huai Nan Tzu,' *Bulletin of the School of Oriental and African Studies*, University of London 39, no. 1 (1976), p. 109. Thanks to Holger Michiels for this article.

including the earth, revolve in circles around the sun, and that the earth rotates on its axis once in twenty-four hours. While the majority held Aristotle's view (384–322 BC) that the earth is immobile at the centre of the universe, and while through the Middle Ages Ptolemy's geocentric astronomy was widely accepted, Cullen is correct in reminding us of the dialogical and contested manner in which views were held in the West: 'There was, however, never any chance of such a powerful and successful hypothesis as the sphericity of the earth being abandoned so long as rational discussion continued.'[393]

The Egyptians, the Maya, and the Chinese were relatively restricted to their homeland and immediate surroundings in their movements. The Chinese ventured momentarily into the Indian Ocean, but even after European ships had sailed into the harbours of the Atlantic, the Pacific, and the Indian Oceans, 'no Indian or Chinese ship was ever seen in Seville, Amsterdam or London.'[394] Indian civilisation showed little curiosity about the geography of the world; its maps were symbolic and removed from any empirical concern with the actual location of places. Maritime activity among the relatively isolated civilisations of America was restricted to fishing from rafts and canoes. There was no contact between the two major cultural centres, the Aztecs and the Incas; the Inca Empire was crossed by two thousand miles of well-made mountain roads, but no maps were ever made of any of them. The Polynesians navigated across millions of square miles of the Pacific, but as gifted as they were in practical and experiential matters, they did not cultivate a body of geographical knowledge. The Phoenicians left no geographical documents of their colonising activities.

---

393 Ibid., p. 107.
394 Peter Whitfield, *New Found Lands: Maps in the History of Exploration* (New York: Routledge, 1998), p. 2.

The Viking Age of Exploration

The Vikings 'discovered in their gray dawn the art of sailing the seas which emancipated them' — so says Spengler.[395] During the last years of the 8th century, marauding bands of Vikings pillaged their way along the coastlines of Northern Europe. No obstacles could halt these warlords who went on to circumnavigate Spain and fight in the Mediterranean, Italy, North Africa, and Arabia. Some hauled their long boats overland from the Baltic and made their way down the great Russian rivers all the way to the Black Sea. During the 9th and 10th centuries, the Vikings (or Norsemen, to be precise)[396] continued their ventures, but increasingly their primary aim was finding new lands to settle rather than to plunder. The voyages of Norsemen far into the North Atlantic were 'independent undertakings, part of a 300-year epoch of seaborne expansion' that resulted in the settlement of Scandinavian peoples in Shetland, Orkney, the Hebrides, parts of Scotland and Ireland, the Faroe Islands, Iceland, Greenland, and Vinland (present-day Newfoundland).[397] They colonised the little-known or unknown lands of Iceland from 870 AD forward, Greenland from 980 forward, and Vinland by 1000 AD.

The Norse settlers came with their sturdily made hafskip, vessels designed to be loaded with goods, implements, and domestic animals, over the open sea for long distances and capable of sailing faster speeds in high winds than the earlier Gotstad, which were coastal vessels of shallow draught. The hafskip was the 'Knarr' of the heroic North Saga literature.[398] The shipbuilding techniques of the Norsemen were possibly

---

395 Spengler, *Decline of the West*, p. 332.

396 The terms 'Norse' and 'Norsemen' describe Norwegians and their colonies in the north, but not Danes or Swedes, who lived in the less northerly and eastern regions. These three peoples were linked by a common tradition and mythology, and the word 'Viking' may refer to all or each of them and their particular migratory movements and raids.

397 Jesse Byock, *Viking Age Iceland* (London and New York: Penguin Books, 2001), p. 7.

398 J. R. S. Phillips, *The Medieval Expansion of Europe*, 2nd ed. (Oxford: Clarendon Press, 1998), p. 158. See also Paul Jordan, *North Sea Saga* (New York: Pearson Longman, 2004).

the best at the time. The Landnamabok, a 12th century record of the Norse Atlantic settlements, contains information on a method of reckoning by which a sailor tried to steer his ship on more or less the correct line of latitude until reaching his destination.[399] The Icelandic geographers of the Middle Ages showed considerably detailed knowledge in their descriptions of the Arctic regions, stretching from Russia to Greenland, and of the eastern seaboard of the North American continent. This is clearly attested in an Icelandic Geographical Treatise preserved in a manuscript dating from about 1300 AD, but possibly based on a 12th century original. Whitfield speculates that 'some conscious impulse towards exploration and conquest' must have motivated these voyages, 'prompted by harsh living conditions at home.'[400] The most reliable account may well come from the excellent *Viking Age Iceland*, in which author Jesse Byock explains that the settlement of Iceland was led by sailor-farmers seeking to escape population pressures in the Scandinavian mainland. In turn, the settlement of Greenland was initiated by Icelanders escaping Malthusian pressures in Iceland, which by 930 AD already had an estimated population of 30,000 inhabitants. At the same time, the cultural world Byock reveals through careful reading of the famed numerous sagas associated with Viking voyages and colonial life (i.e. Njál's Saga, set in 10th century Iceland; Greenlander's Saga, written in the later 12th century; and Eirik's Saga, written in the mid 13th century). These sagas are populated by chieftains, free farmers, valorous deeds, enemies slain and territories taken, aristocratic-democratic forms of government, concerns for the honour and ethics of the individual and his family, the epic ideal of an individual's sacrifice to duty to liege lord, and the heroic experiences of sailor-farmers colonising Greenland and North America.[401]

---

399 Phillips, *Medieval Expansion*, p. 159.
400 Whitfield, *New Found Lands*, p. 18.
401 See also *The Vinland Sagas, The Norse Discovery of America*, trans. Magnus Magnusson and Hermann Pálsson (Baltimore: Penguin Books, 1965).

Marco Polo vs. Ibn Battuta

We must not underestimate Marco Polo, the greatest traveler in history: Marco Polo (1254–1324). Great ones preceded him, both in terms of longevity and distances travelled, but Marco Polo stands alone as the most influential-writer traveller and as the first one to recount his extensive travels — through what is known today as Turkey, Iran, Afghanistan, Tajikistan, China, Singapore, Indonesia, and India — in a proto-scientific manner.

Travelling through these lands (not through each single one but generally across the Mongol territories in central Asia), was not original to Marco Polo. After all, other Europeans had preceded him, such as Giovanni di Pian, who wrote *Historia Mongolorum* about his travels in the 1240s, a book which stands as yet another instance of European ethnographic curiosity going back to Herodotus and Caesar, about the ways of other people, primarily the Mongols' beliefs, marriage customs, food and drink, clothes, burial practices and divination.

Another great traveller before Marco Polo was the Fleming William of Rubruck, who also wrote in greater detail of the Great Khanate in the 1250s, estimating that a crusade against them would have been successful. And, of course, Marco's father and uncle pioneered an impressive long-term journey to the Far East, spending seventeen years in China.

What was new about Marco Polo's travels, as John Patrick Larner explains in his well-researched study, *Marco Polo and the Discovery of the World* (1999), 'was not that he visited the Far East', but that 'he produced one of the most influential books of the Middle Ages'.[402] This influence was not accidental; it grew out of the many original observations Marco made about the world of the Great Khan. The section of his book on China offered 'a total picture of a hitherto utterly unknown, prosperous world'. The sections of what is today Vietnam, Java, Sumatra fired the imaginations

---

402 John Larner, *Marco Polo and the Discovery of the World* (Yale University Press, 1999), p. 1.

of subsequent generations of Europeans, particularly Columbus; and for good reason:

> 'Never before or since has one man given such an immense body of new geographical knowledge to the West.' [403]

His observations found expression in the Catalan Atlas of 1375. While this map reflected the beliefs of medieval geographers, who espoused topographical myths and legends, and were unaware of Ptolemy's work, it was also innovative, and contained compass lines and accurately delineated the Mediterranean coasts. But more than anything, what stands out about Marco Polo was his peculiarly Faustian curiosity, the way his writing pulsated with a fascination for the unknown, the desire to tell others and incite further exploration in discovering the world around him.

Yet Marco Polo is either ignored in academia today or is portrayed in terms of Edward Said's Orientalist accusation, that Marco Polo was an ethnocentric traveller who stereotyped those who were different from Europeans as 'the Other'. This is the thesis of Syed Manzul Islam's book, *The Ethics of Travel from Marco Polo to Kafka* (1996), in which Marco Polo's travel account is portrayed as a proto-typical instance of the Western habit of construing 'discourses of othering'. In academia this means you are a bad person, and your place in history has to be questioned and replaced by others who meet the demands of diversity and equality. Not surprisingly, therefore, as the travels of Marco Polo have been degraded, the travels of the Muslim Ibn Battuta (1304–1374) have been celebrated as a 'graceful' undertaking by an 'extraordinary' man who visited more than 40 countries on the modern map and covered 75,000 miles as far east as China, voyaging for 29 years. [404]

True enough, Ibn Battuta was one of the greatest travellers. But Larner effectively argues, first, that the few hostile statements about Muslims in Marco Polo's Book must be considered in the context of the actual hostile

---

403 Ibid., p. 97.

404 Ross E. Dunn, *The Adventures of Ibn Battuta: A Muslim Traveler of the Fourteenth Century* (University of California Press, 1986).

relations at the time between Christian and Muslims; second, there are passages in the Book in which Marco Polo praises individual Muslims; and, third, the tenor of the Book is one of admiration, curiosity and intense interest in the lifestyles of others, with much praise for the Chinese.

The point here is not that Marco Polo should thus be seen in a good light, according to leftist expectations. It is rather that the 'Orientalist' charge is wrong, and that this Italian of the Middle Ages was a typical European in showing greater curiosity about other cultures, while exhibiting a unique European disposition to seek out and learn about the world.

By contrast, Larner judges that Ibn Battuta's tale 'is not a geography like Marco's work, but essentially an autobiography.' Visiting unknown or unfamiliar lands, writing about the ways of others, was not Ibn Battuta's 'overriding impulse'; rather, it was to visit 'illustrious sanctuaries'[405] in the Muslim world. He makes the crucial point that Ibn Battuta 'is always at home' in his travels, 'wherever he goes he is in the House of Islam'.

Marco, on the other hand, 'is always an alien' wherever he goes. Whereas Battuta relishes informing readers about the numerous wives he enjoyed, Marco Polo leaves out from his account his personality. Larner writes:

> 'There is something touching in all that stoic silence about his own adventures, sufferings, joys. What stands in its place is clear, serious, normally (when his admiration for the Great Khan does not stand in his) dispassionate, objective. One is tempted to say 'scientific'.'[406]

We should not however view Marco Polo as an impersonal traveller concerned with offering mere observations about the East. We should view him and his Book in light of how it inspired men like Columbus,

---

405 These words are cited by Daniel J. Boorstin in his *The Discoverers: A History of Man's Search to Know His World and Himself* (New York: Vintage Books, 1985), p. 121. This excellent survey, I should add, covers more than exploration, also scientists and others who discovered new facts and new explanations about natural/astronomical/ geographical/zoological/botanical phenomena. Again, the overwhelming number of the men discussed in this book are European.

406 Larner, pp. 97–104.

the way Columbus himself read him, not as a bookish man searching for dry knowledge, but as a man driven by an indefatigable urge to reach China by way of the sea, and, in this way, achieve something no one had done before. Marco Polo is the writer of one of the most influential books of European civilisation, a book that played a key role in energising Europeans to discover the whole world.

Portuguese vs. Chinese Explorers

Spengler writes that the Spaniards and the Portuguese 'were possessed by the adventure-craving for uncharted distances and for everything unknown and dangerous.'[407] By the beginning of the 1400s, the compass, the portolan chart, and certain shipping techniques essential for launching the Age of Exploration were in place. These included the widespread adoption of the pintle-and-gudgeon rudder at the start of the 1300s, the mizzen mast and the foremast, as well as steady increases in ship tonnage toward the 14th century's end.[408]

Under the leadership of Henry the Navigator and spearheaded by the ventures of Genoese sailors into the Atlantic and their discovery of Madeira and Azores, the Portuguese would proceed during the 15th century to round the southern tip of Africa, impose themselves through the Indian Ocean, and reach Japan in the 1540s. At first they relied on medieval maps, and possibly on Ptolemy's newly rediscovered Geography, which was translated in 1418 and mistakenly assumed that southern Africa was joined to some Terra Incognita. But soon the Portuguese would create accurate maps of west Africa as far as Sierra Leone, and then rely on Fra Mauro's new maps, one of which (1457) charted the entire Old World with unmatched accuracy while suggesting, for the first time, a navigable route around the southern tip of Africa. A mere two years after Diaz sailed

---

407 Spengler, *Decline of the West*, p. 333.

408 Lawrence V. Mott, 'A Three-Masted Ship Depiction from 1409,' *International Journal of Nautical Archeology* 23, no. 1 (February 1994), pp. 39–40, http://www.worldencompassed.com/articles/3mastedship.pdf. Thanks to Holger Michiels for sending me this article.

around the Cape, Henricus Martellus created his World Map of 1490, which showed both the whole of Africa generally and the specific locations (with assigned names) of numerous places across the entire African west coast, detailing the step-by-step advancement of the Portuguese.[409] 'What motivated the expeditions of the Portuguese?' is a classic question. Conversely, so is 'Why did China abandon the maritime explorations started by Zheng He?' Why were Zheng He's expeditions less consequential historically than those initiated by Henry the Navigator? Let's take a look at the answers found in Felipe Fernández-Armesto's *Pathfinders: A Global History of Exploration*, winner of the 2007 World History Association Book Prize — a work that mirrors the way the history of the West is taught today. Fernández-Armesto's response may be organised along the following four basic points. Firstly, Zheng He's voyages were a display of 'China's potential as the launching bay of a seaborne empire: the capacity and productivity of her shipyards; her ability to mount expeditions of crushing strength and dispatch them over vast distances.'[410] These expeditions, however, 'combined an imperial impulse with the peaceful inspiration of commerce and scholarship.' The objective was 'impressing the ports he visited with Chinese power,' as well as 'stimulating the awe of the emperor's home constituency with exotica which the Chinese classified as the tribute of remote peoples.' Zheng He's expeditions did not last, and were less consequential, because China's Confucian government assigned priority to 'good government at home' rather than 'costly adventures' abroad, particularly in the face of the more immediate danger of barbarian incursions from the north.[411]

Secondly, China was 'governed by scholars [who] hated overseas adventures.' At the same time, Fernández-Armesto portrays China's mode of exploration in rather admiring terms: her peaceful commerce, scholarship,

---

409 Evelyn Edson, *The World Map, 1300–1493: The Persistence of Tradition and Transformation* (Baltimore: John Hopkins University Press, 2007), pp. 215–216.

410 Felipe Fernández-Armesto, *Pathfinders: A Global History of Exploration* (New York: W. W. Norton, 2006), p. 113.

411 Ibid., pp. 112–114.

good government, and even 'vital contributions to the economies of every place they settled.'[412] The academic world admires this style of exploration. But did Zheng He really explore anything or was he navigating well-known sea routes in the Indian Ocean?

Thirdly, Fernández-Armesto would have us believe that the Chinese, not the Europeans, were the true explorers, on the grounds that Zheng He's expeditions along the Indian Ocean were far more difficult than European voyages through the Atlantic:

> 'The limits of Zheng He's navigation [were due to the fact that] maritime Asia and coastal east Africa form a remarkably extensive monsoonal region....[I]n the Southern Indian Ocean, or beyond southeast Asia, into the Pacific, they would be compelled to sail against the wind; or, in other directions, they would face the risk of sailing with a following wind and probably never getting home.'[413]

The termination of Zheng He's expeditions 'was not the result of any deficiency of technology or curiosity.'[414] Chinese shipping technology through the 15th and 16th centuries was superior. There was no point navigating beyond the known routes into such dangerous waters. The Chinese or any of the other navigators of this region could have gone down under Africa, but the risk was not worth the potential gains and, in any case, they already had what they needed — unlike the Europeans, who 'came as supplicants, generally despised for their poverty.' Fernández-Armesto even says that the evidence that the Chinese crossed the Pacific into the Americas 'is, at best, equivocal, it is perfectly possible that they may have done so.'[415]

Fourthly, Fernández-Armesto points out that Europeans had the motivation to explore. He makes much of the marginalised position — 'poor or of limited exploitability' and 'restricted opportunities to landward'

---

412 Ibid., p. 115.
413 Ibid., p. 116.
414 Ibid.
415 Ibid.

areas — of the maritime peoples who have engaged in exploration throughout history.[416]

There are many problems with Fernández-Armesto's analysis, starting with his overestimation of the size and capacity of Zheng He's ships. Not long ago, it was an oft-repeated statistic among Chinese scholars that the dimensions of Zheng He's flagships were 138.4 meters long and 56 meters wide, but in recent decades these numbers have been lowered. In her popular *When China Ruled the Seas*, Louise Levathes points to early Chinese calculations, stating that 'a wooden ship of this length [138.4 meters] would be very difficult to manoeuvre', adding that 'most scholars now believe that the [largest of the] treasure ships...were 309 and 408 ft long and 160 to 166 ft wide', that is, 118.9 to 124.4 meters long and 48.8 to 50.6 meters wide.[417]

Fernández-Armesto does not offer any numbers on length and width, but adopts the tonnage displacement figure of 3,000, and says that this was ten times the size of the largest ships in Europe. However, in contrast to all these estimations, Sally Church points out that in 2001, Xin Yuanou, a shipbuilding engineer and professor of the history of science at Shanghai Jiaotong University, proposed the modest measurements of 59.1 meters long by 14 meters wide as the actual size of the ships — in others words, he reduced their size to less than half of what they were formerly thought to be. I cannot help having greater confidence in Church's expertise and Xin Yuanou's estimations than in the popularly accepted estimations.[418]

The second major flaw in Fernández-Armesto's account (as in all current accounts of Zheng He's expeditions) is the unquestioned presumption

---

416 Ibid., 119.

417 Louise Levathes, *When China Ruled the Seas: The Treasure Fleet of the Dragon Throne, 1405–1433* (Oxford University Press, 1994), p. 58.

418 As Holger Michiels has communicated to me, 'the bending stress would be much too great for wooden ships well over 100 meters in length. For a ship built entirely of wood, the safe length of a seagoing ship is 70–75 meters; it might safely be 90 meters if reinforced with metal bracing.' See also, Sally Church, 'Zheng He: An Investigation into the Plausibility of 450-ft Treasure Ships,' *Monumenta Serica: Journal of Oriental Studies* 53, no. 1 (January 2005): pp. 1–42, http://www.themua.org/collections/items/show/1275. Thanks to Michiels for these articles.

that the Chinese expeditions were 'explorations' and, conversely, that the Portuguese expeditions were primarily economic in motivation. In actuality, the Chinese did not discover a single nautical mile — the Indian Ocean had been regularly navigated for a long time, unlike the Atlantic and the western coasts of Africa. The Portuguese were relatively poor and many of the sailors manning the ships longed for better opportunities, but what drove the leading men above all else was a chivalric (i.e. Faustian) desire for renown and superior achievement in the face of the economic costs, persistent hardships, and high mortality rates.

I hope to make these claims more persuasive via a debate with the more studious arguments of Joseph Needham on the incentives/disincentives in the explorations of the Chinese and the Portuguese. Needham had already observed that one of 'the primary motives of the [Chinese] voyages' was a 'desire to impress upon foreign countries even beyond the limits of the known world the idea of China as the leading political and cultural power.'[419] There was also 'a proto-scientific function,' an 'increase in knowledge of the coasts and islands of the Chinese culture-area.'[420]

Needham is impressed as well by the 'peaceful character of the Ming voyages', adding that 'the Chinese expeditions were the well-disciplined naval operations of an enormous feudal-bureaucratic state'[421]. The 'impetus' behind the expeditions was thus 'primarily governmental,' 'their trade (though large) was incidental'[422]—from which point Needham moves on to consider the reasons (motives) why the expeditions were terminated. Firstly, the Confucian landed bureaucracy was sceptical of the aggrandisement of the Grand Eunuchs tied to the Court, believing that the funds used in the expeditions could be better spent on public projects at home. Secondly, the 'serious deterioration on the north-western frontiers

---

419 Joseph Needham, *The Shorter Science and Civilization in China: An Abridgement of Joseph Needham's Original Text*, by Colin A. Ronan, vol. 3: A Section of Volume IV, Part I and a Section of Volume IV, Part 3 of the Major Series (Cambridge: Cambridge University Press, 1986), p. 130.

420 Ibid., p. 131.

421 Ibid., pp. 132, 143.

422 Ibid., p. 143.

diverted all attention from the sea.'[423] Thus far, Needham says largely the same as Fernández-Armesto, although he is more analytical.

The Portuguese expeditions, Needham continues, were driven by very different motives. First, they hoped to sail around Africa and open links with the Indian Ocean and East Indian producers of silks and spices. Historians emphasise this motivation the most; it seems to be almost self-evidently true and dovetails so well with the materialist outlook of academics. Is not human nature driven by economic need, and is not the ruling class particularly keen on accumulating more than their fair share? Second — and here the contrast with the Chinese was 'an extraordinary one' — the Portuguese set out with a warlike mindset: 'it was the settled policy of the Westerners to destroy the Arab African- Indian trade root and branch'.[424] This was accompanied by a 'conquistador mentality' and a desire to make 'one's personal fortune'.[425] Finally, missionary activity accompanied the Portuguese expeditions, so that 'by the end of the 15th century the war against all Muslims was being extended to all Hindus and Buddhists too'.[426]

'What a contrast' to the Chinese! Could not the Portuguese have behaved peacefully, going about their explorations in a bookish way, showing respect for other faiths, like Zheng He and the Chinese, who 'conversed in the tongue of the Prophet and recalled the mosques of Yunnan, in India... presented offerings in Hindu temples, and venerated the traces of Buddha in Ceylon'?[427] In a culture in which the object of learning is to 'create global citizens'[428] and promote cultural harmony, it stands to reason that the Chinese methods of exploration would be preferred over the Portuguese.

---

423 Ibid., 147.
424 Ibid., p. 142.
425 Ibid., p. 143.
426 Ibid., p. 145.
427 Ibid.
428 In *Not For Profit: Why Democracy Needs the Humanities* (Princeton University Press, 2010), Martha Nussbaum insists that the purpose of the arts is to produce academic-like, conformist, and politically correct global citizens.

But the historical truth is, the Portuguese accomplished many explo-rations, the Chinese none. A careful reading of Needham reveals this.

Needham was a Marxist writing in the 1950s, before the onset of po-litical correctness. He enjoyed greater freedom to express the truth and was not compelled to address extra-scholarly goals and the socialising obligations of multicultural teaching. Needham acknowledges, for one, that 'the Chinese achievement of the 15th century involved no revolution-ary break with the past, while that of the Portuguese was more original'.[429] While the Chinese were ahead of Europe in technology at the outset of the 1400s, their technology thereafter 'remained for the most part unchanged', whereas the Portuguese would advance continuously. Furthermore, 'the Portuguese showed seemingly more originality than the Chinese, and this was the use of the régime of winds and currents'. And, Needham adds, in contrast to Fernández-Armesto's imaginings, 'the problems they had to face were more difficult, and they rose gallantly to the challenge'[430]: 'Almost as far south as Madagascar the Chinese were in the realms of the monsoons, the 'junk-driving winds' with which they had been familiar in their own home waters for more than a millennium. But the inhospi-table Atlantic had never encouraged sailors in the same way, and though there had been a number of attempts to sail westwards, that ocean had never been systematically explored.'[431] The Chinese traversed well-known waters; their 'voyages were essentially an urbane but systematic tour of inspection of the known world'[432]

While Needham recognises that the Portuguese discovered new routes and navigational techniques, mapped out the entire western African coastline, and rounded the southern tip of Africa, he thinks that their 'mo-tives were primarily religious and economic'[433] rather than exploratory, and suggests that their voyages are therefore best understood in economic

---

429 Needham, p. 139.
430 Ibid., p. 141.
431 Ibid.
432 Ibid., p. 148.
433 Ibid.

(and in a lesser manner, religious) terms. By 'geographical explorations' Needham seems to have in mind a relatively peaceful scholarly curiosity. In suggesting that the Chinese were truer to the art of exploration because they toured peacefully while the Portuguese were driven by greed and missionary zeal, Needham sometimes sounds like Fernández-Armesto. I argue that the motives of the Portuguese explorers cannot be adequately explained in economic and religious terms without considering the feudal, chivalric, and warlike spirit of the aristocratic fidalgos (or hidalgos in Spanish). In *Pathfinders*, Fernández-Armesto actually highlights the 'chivalry-steeped world' of the Portuguese and Spanish explorers.[434] He recognises this chivalric spirit for what it was, writing that 'the glamour of great deeds thrilled' Henry the Navigator, citing Henry's words that to make 'great and noble conquests and to uncover secrets previously hidden from men' was his goal.[435] Fernández-Armesto even writes: 'we have seen evidence of one feature of European culture which did make the region peculiarly conducive to breeding explorers. They were steeped in the idealisation of adventure. Many of them shared or strove to embody the great aristocratic ethos of their day—the "code" of chivalry.'[436]

But for Fernández-Armesto, this was an ethos 'of the day' rooted in medieval romances exclusive to Portugal and Spain. And these comments on chivalry are located in a section entitled 'The European Miracle?' which argues precisely against any notion of Western uniqueness. Moreover, Fernández-Armesto does not properly explain the differences and connections between economic, religious, and chivalric motivations, but confounds them all.

---

434 Fernández-Armesto, *Pathfinders*, p. 129.

435 Ibid., p. 131.

436 Ibid., p. 145, emphasis added). Peter Russell agrees that Henry's chivalric spirit gave him the 'moral strength and the single-mindedness which made it possible for him to carry through the great enterprises of discovery associated with his name.' See 'Prince Henry the Navigator,' in *An Expanding World: The European Impact on World History 1450–1800, vol. 2, The European Opportunity*, ed. Felipe Fernández-Fernández-Armesto (Aldershot, UK: Variorum, 1995), p. 128.

The Spaniards

As I see it, the chivalric motivations of the Portuguese coloured and intensified their other motivations, and this is why they (and other European
explorers) exhibited an excessive yearning for spices and gold, a crusad-
ing zeal against non-Christians and a relentless determination to master
the seas. The chivalry of the Portuguese was a knightly variation of the
same Faustian longing the West has displayed since prehistoric times.
In its barbaric, uncivilised expression, this yearning can be described
in Spenglerian terms as the feelings of an energetic human being, the
fierceness and the joy of tension, danger, violent deed, victory, crime, the
triumph of overcoming and destroying.'[437] The willfulness of Henry the
Navigator, Bartholomew Diaz, Vasco Da Gama, and Pedro Cabral that has
been evident throughout Europe's history.

The Portuguese were not unique among their contemporaries. No
sooner did Columbus sight the 'West Indies' in 1492 than one European explorer after another came forth, eager for great deeds. In 1497, John Cabot
secured the support of Bristol merchants for a voyage during which he
discovered Newfoundland and Nova Scotia. Between May 1499 and June
1500, Amerigo Vespucci navigated up to the coast of Guyana, and then
on May 1501 sailed again from Lisbon to Brazil. By the 1520s, the Spanish
and other navigators had explored the eastern coast of the two Americas
from Labrador to Rio de la Plata. From 1519 to 1522 Ferdinand Magellan,
a Portuguese, led the first successful attempt to circumnavigate the earth
through the unimagined vastness of the Pacific Ocean. 'Magellan's energy
and vision,' writes Whitfield, 'equaled that of Columbus, and he shared
with his great predecessor the tenacity of a man driven by something
deeper than common ambition.'[438]

Between 1519 and 1521 Hernán Cortés consciously put himself at the
command of an expedition that would result in the conquest of the Aztec
Empire. Today, many regard Cortés as a kind of criminal, which is true.

---

437 Spengler, *Decline of the West*, p. 322.
438 Whitfield, *New Found Lands*, p. 93.

The campaigns he conducted against the Mexicans reached shocking levels of atrocity and barbarity. At the same time, Cortés was a proto-typical Western aristocrat or, as described by his secretary, a man 'restless, haughty, mischievous, and given to quarrelling.'[439] Cortés was born in 1485 in Medellin, Spain, one of the strongholds used in the Reconquista. His father was a poor hidalgo. Cortés studied Latin at the University of Salamanca, but, like other members of his class, he was lured by tales of new discoveries in America, and sailed in 1504 for the New World. Fifteen years later, he would go on to conquer the Aztec empire with a few hundred 'chivalrous men bred on war and adventure.'[440]

The running story on Cortés, belittled or despised in the academic world today, is that if he had not conquered Mexico someone or something else would have: the real agents were the harquebusiers, the steel swords, the horses, and the germs. Far more persuasive is Buddy Levy's fascinating account, *Conquistador: Hernán Cortés, King Montezuma, and the Last Stand of the Aztecs*. Without denying any of these external factors, Levy portrays Cortés as a man who repeatedly displayed an astonishing combination of leadership, tenacity, diplomacy, and tactical skill.[441] Even after La Noche Triste, when nearly six hundred Spaniards perished in one night, including a great number of horses, and all the cannons were lost, his men responded earnestly to Cortés' vigour, charisma and gravity of purpose.

Levy draws on Cortés' letters, the biography written in 1552 by Francisco Lopez de Gomara (Cortés' secretary), the highly readable memoirs (published in 1568 as *True History of the Conquest of New Spain*) of Bernal Diaz del Castillo (a soldier present in all three expeditions to Mexico and most of Cortés' battles), and numerous other additional sources. Levy brings out in dramatic prose Cortés' nerve, boldness, and

439 Buddy Levy, *Conquistador: Hernán Cortés, King Montezuma, and the Last Stand of the Aztecs* (New York: Bantam Books, 2009), p. 3.
440 Ibid., p. 10.
441 Ibid., pp. 328–329.

resilience. Cortés' impassioned speeches and the character descriptions of his contemporaries testify to his aristocratic ethos:

> 'I have no other favor to ask of you or to remind you of but that this is the touchstone of our honor and our glory for ever and ever, and it is better to die worthily than to live dishonored.'[442]

> '[T]he letter stated that Cortés's pursuit of the present conquest was driven by "his insatiable thirst for glory and authority," and that "he thinks nothing of dying himself, and less of our death."'[443]

> '[His] men were morally and spiritually exhausted. His only recourse was to lead them by example. He would not allow the expedition to crumble and fail. He must rally their sense of duty, pride, and above all honor…. "Victories are not won by the many but by the valiant" …. "fortune always favors the bold."'[444]

Finding gold was undoubtedly a priority for Cortés and his men from the beginning; in the words of one Nahualt Indian, as translated by a Dominican friar, 'they thirsted mightily for the gold, they stuffed themselves with it, and starved and lusted for it like pigs.'[445] However, Cortés appealed not only to the greediness of his soldiers, but also to their faithfulness and honour. These motives were, in his apt words, part of 'the same package.'[446] For all the immense wealth, estates, and eulogies Cortés came to enjoy later in life, the 'Gran Conquistador' 'never lost his adventurous spirit.'[447] Cortés discovered the peninsula of Baja California in 1536, attempted an expedition to Honduras in 1524 bedevilled with disease, mutiny, and the death of most of his men, and carried out a final, disastrous, expedition to Algiers in 1541.[448]

---

442 Ibid., p. 156.
443 Ibid., p. 203.
444 Ibid., p. 204.
445 Ibid., p. 100.
446 Ibid., pp. 224–225.
447 Ibid., p. 327.
448 Ibid., p. 329.

A similar account can be given of Francisco Pizarro. In January 1531 he embarked with 168 men (sixty-two on horseback) for Peru. Pizarro's character was moulded in a region known in Spain as 'Extremadura,' an impoverished feudal area covered in arid scrub, known for producing men 'who showed little emotion and who were known to be as tough and unsympathetic as the landscape which nurtured them.'[449] In the 1980s animated series, 'The Mysterious Cities of Gold,' Pizarro is depicted as an unscrupulous criminal who valued gold above else.

The accomplishments of Pizarro are nonetheless remarkable. An illegitimate son of a colonel of the Spanish infantry, he faced the Incas with a smaller army and fewer resources than Cortés at a much greater distance from the Spanish Caribbean outposts than could easily support him. Jared Diamond thinks it was all about 'guns, germs, and steel.'[450] I would underline the chivalric ethos of Pizarro's world, and the way Columbus' fantastic tales fired the imagination of the teenaged Pizarro, a member of the feudal nobility yet without title, a hidalgo with a superlative longing for honorific recognition. The lust for gold clearly existed among the Spanish conquerors, who dreamed of what they would do with their ingots if they survived, but the central character of this saga, Pizarro, was motivated, like Cortés, by something altogether immaterial.[451]

The same spirit that drove Cortés and Pizarro drove Luther in his uncompromising and audacious challenge to the Papacy's authority: 'Here I stand, I cannot do otherwise.' It drove the 'intense rivalry' that characterised the art of the Renaissance among patrons, collectors, and artists, which culminated in the persons of Leonardo, Raphael, Michelangelo,

---

449 Kim MacQuarrie, *The Last Days of the Incas* (New York: Simon and Schuster, 2007), p. 18.

450 Jared Diamond, *Guns, Germs, and Steel: The Fates of Human Societies* (New York: W. W. Norton, 1997).

451 'At the time of the conquest,' writes MacQuarrie, 'chivalric novels were all the vogue, one of the most popular being Amadis de Gaula, the story of a knight errant who dons armor and travels to the far ends of the earth,' *Last Days of the Incas*, p. 128.

and Titian.[452] It motivated Shakespeare to outdo Chaucer and his finely chiselled characters to create more than 120 of his own — 'the most memorable personalities that have graced the theater — and the psyche — of the West.'[453]

Let us remember that the age of the conquistadors was Spain's El Siglo del Oro, and that together with the explorations there was a veritable revolution in cartography. As early as 1507, the German cosmographer Martin Waldseemuller depicted a coastline from Newfoundland to Argentina and showed the two American continents clearly separated from Asia.[454] By 1569, the Flemish cartographer Gerard Mercator had solved the extremely difficult problem of converting the three-dimensional globe into a two-dimensional map, or projecting figures from a sphere onto a flat sheet. His world map of 1569 was the product of decades of harmonising a vast number of sources and travel narratives into a single geographic picture of the planet, including the Antarctic landmass.[455]

Human Nature Has No Urge to Explore

In the face of a list of motivations like the desire to acquire wealth and conquer new lands, it is very difficult to capture the Faustian character of the explorers. Even so, the history of exploration during and after the Enlightenment era offers an opportunity to detect and apprehend this soul. From about 1700 forward, explorers were increasingly driven by a will to discover regardless of the pursuit of trade, religious conversion, or

---

452 See Rona Goffe's, *Renaissance Rivals: Michelangelo, Leonardo, Raphael, Titian* (New Haven, CT: Yale University Press, 2004). This is an account of the passionate strivings of the greatest artists of the Renaissance to outdo both living competitors and the masters of antiquity.

453 Frank Dumont, *A History of Personality Psychology: Theory, Science, and Research from Hellenism to the Twenty-First Century* (Cambridge and New York: Cambridge University Press, 2010), p. 20.

454 John Noble Wilford, *The Mapmakers* (New York: Vintage Books, 2000), pp. 66–86. Whitfield, *New Found Lands*, pp. 53–71.

455 Nicholas Crane, *Mercator: The Man Who Mapped the Planet* (New York: Henry Holt and Company, 2003).

even scientific curiosity. It is not that the pure desire to explore exhibits the Faustian soul as such. The urge to accumulate vast riches and promote new ways to explain the nature of things may exhibit this will just as intensively. The difference is that in the desire to explore for its own sake we can see the West's psyche striving to surpass the mundane preoccupations of ordinary life, proving what it means to be an aristocrat rather an ordinary mortal satisfied with mere existence and biological longevity.

The desire to 'be the first human to set foot there' and not to yield to any obstacle provides a revealing index of (or window into) the unique dynamics of the West. In the cases of Cortés and Pizarro, it is difficult to look through this window, because their insatiable desire for great deeds was tightly wrapped up (in the 'same package') with economic and military desires we tend to regard as typical among all peoples and cultures. But when considering the 18th century we find that exploration for its own sake becomes the dominant motivation over the search for spices and gold, lands to colonise, and souls to convert, it affords the opportunity to highlight this uniquely Western Faustian impulse.

The minimisation of any substantial differences among human beings cultivated by the modern model of human nature has clouded our ability to apprehend this Faustian soul. The original outlooks of Locke and the French philosophers, themselves the product of the persistent Western quest to interpret the world anew, fostered a democratic model that regarded humans as indeterminate and more or less equal, 'white paper or wax,' malleable beings determined by outside circumstances, without tradition and culture. This egalitarian view was nurtured as well in the philosophy of Descartes, Leibnitz, and Kant, with its emphasis on the innate and equally a priori cognitive capacities of 'humans qua humans'. We also find this view in Hume, despite his emphasis on the will as opposed to reason, since he did not focus on possible cultural differences in the mode (whether individualist or collectivist) and intensity of expression of the will, but spoke of intentional actions as the immediate product of the 'human passions'.

It should come as no surprise that historians constantly write of passions and motivations as essentially alike across all cultures. In terms of exploration, we are typically informed that 'the desire to penetrate and explore the world's wild places is a fundamental human impulse.'[456] Frank Debenham's *Discovery and Exploration*, a broad survey published in 1960, is subtitled *An Atlas-History of Man's Journeys into the Unknown*. The text has the air of many published in the 20th century dedicated to the edification of the lay public (i.e. *The Ascent of Man, The Great Ages of Man, The Great Thoughts of Mankind* etc.). The introduction to *Discovery and Exploration*, written by Edward Shackleton, son of the great explorer Sir Ernest Shackleton, states:

> Man has always been inquisitive. Sometimes he has crept, and sometimes he has marched boldly to the limit of his known environment; then some have been courageous enough to risk going beyond…The real story of discovery and exploration begins with those early travelers who went in search of trade, who felt compelled to disseminate religious ideals, and who wanted to claim new lands for the glory of their country. Yet many explorers have set out without such apparent motives, and if we ask why these particular men went travelling, we might just as well ask why man undertakes anything. Sometimes they went out of simple curiosity, which is the basis of scientific exploration today.…It is the striving to know, this inquisitiveness that lies deep in man's nature that has been a mainspring of discovery and exploration.[457]

There are three thoughts running through this passage:

(1)   Certain exploratory motivations such as trade, missionary work and 'scientific' knowledge drive men into exploration.

(2)   However exploration appears to be driven too by 'simple curiosity', which is not clearly distinguished from the pursuit of knowledge but is nevertheless something else, possibly 'inquisitiveness'.

---

456   Whitfield, *New Found Lands*, 186.

457   Frank Debenham, *Discovery and Exploration: An Atlas-History of Man's Journeys into the Unknown* (London: Paul Hamlyn, 1960), p. 6.

(3) These non-exploratory motivations and exploratory/inquisitive motivations are part of 'man's nature'.

However, later on, in trying to explain the end of 'Cheng Ho's' voyages, Debenham says that the Asians 'apparently lacked an urge to explore.' In the next sentence, he falls back on the standard explanation why they had 'no need' to seek out new trade routes, and thus to explore: they were already a 'self-sufficient' and highly civilised people.[458] Yet, much of *Discovery and Exploration* is about (modern and wealthier) Europeans hiking across the globe for no apparent reason other than the urge to explore the unknown. An appendix, 'Famous Explorers and Their Routes,' lists a total of two hundred and three names, of which only eight are non-Western.[459]

Similarly, in Peter Whitfield's *New Found Lands*, every explorer mentioned after Zheng He is Western. In the last two sentences, as if finally aware of this overwhelming statistical reality, Whitfield almost says outright that exploration is uniquely European 'in spirit' and not intrinsic to the 'oriental spirit,' citing an 'oriental sage' for whom: 'The next place might be so near at hand that one could hear the cocks crowing in it and the dogs barking, but one could grow old and die without ever wishing to go there.' After which he concludes: 'This [Oriental] spirit is fundamentally opposed to the European drive for knowledge and for the power that knowledge brought with it. All the various phases of European exploration [military, commercial, scientific, romantic…] form a revealing index to the dynamic but flawed psychology of European civilisation.'[460]

Current academics reject *ab initio* any notion of an exclusively 'European psyche.' Yet the existing sources, biographies, encyclopaedias, and histories tell us that almost all the explorers were European. Robin Hanbury-Tenison, an explorer, filmmaker, and conservationist, recently edited *The Great Explorers*, to which an 'international group of distinguished travel writers, broadcasters, and historians' contributed short

---

458 Ibid., p. 123.
459 Ibid., pp. 214–236.
460 Whitfield, *New Found Lands*, pp. 195–196.

biographical essays on the foremost explorers of the oceans, the land, rivers, polar ice, life on earth, and new frontiers. Only one of the forty biographies is about a non-Westerner, Nain Singh (1830?–1882), who mapped the great plateau of Tibet.[461] Nonetheless, the inside jacket of *The Great Explorers* opens with this sentence:

> It has always been mankind's gift, or curse, to be inquisitive, and through the ages people have been driven to explore the limits of the worlds known to them — and beyond.' Similarly, Piers Pennington's *The Great Explorers* 'tells the story of the world's great adventures into the unknown,' yet the fifty-plus explorers listed are all from the Occident.[462]

Fernández-Armesto vs. Faustian Man

Europe's singular achievements are unbearably disconcerting to promoters of diversity and to white academic men who seek approval from their feminist colleagues. In the first page of *Pathfinders*, Armesto informs us that he will write about this subject as if he were an imaginary cosmic observer, not just any observer, but a 'goddess' standing on high with a gift for judging the affairs of men on earth:

> Imagine a cosmic observer [Armesto], contemplating humankind from immensely remote space and time, seeing us with the kind of *objectivity* that we — who are enmeshed in our history — are unable to attain. Imagine

---

461 Robin Hanbury-Tenison, ed., *The Great Explorers* (London: Thames & Hudson, 2010).

462 See also Helen Delpar, ed., *The Discoverers: An Encyclopedia of Explorers and Exploration* (New York: McGraw-Hill, 1980). Charles Pasternak's book, *Quest: The Essence of Humanity* (Wiley, 2004), takes questing, the thirst for knowledge and adventure in the sciences and in exploration, 'beyond basic needs and personal comfort' as that which makes humans unique, but other than some general statements about the migration 'out of Africa,' and the development of civilisations, actions which fit within the basic needs of survival and comfort, all the scientific discoveries and acts of explorations he brings up are European. This projection of European drives and ambitions onto humanity should clearly be categorised as 'Eurocentric' with all the bad connotations that term carries, but it never is; the very multicultural postmodernists who otherwise dislike Europeans who universalised Enlightenment values, seem to like universalising European achievements to all humans.

asking *her* — for, perhaps on the basis of *my own experience* of home life, I see omniscience and omnipresence as *female* qualities — how *she* would characterize the history of our species on our planet. Imagine her answer.[463]

Armesto is happy and enthusiastic in his role as a goddess in the opening chapters as he recounts 'the first trail finders' from prehistoric times, the migrations of Lucy's 'descendants' out of East Africa, the 'communications' between civilisations, the Polynesian exploration of the Pacific, and the navigators who learned to decode the monsoon system in the Indian Ocean. He really appeared to be offering us a survey 'of humankind's restless spirit,'[464] as a *New York Times* reviewer describes his book. It all seemed so global and 'stirring' — never mind that Armesto was confounding two very different subjects: migrations and explorations. Never mind either that the explorations of the Greeks and their invention of the science of geography and cartography were barely mentioned, and that the territorial expansion of the Mongols and the Silk Road trade were loosely defined as exploratory, while all European territorial and commercial expansions were left unmentioned. On the plus side, Armesto does afford his readers with lively anecdotes about a Japanese woman's maritime diary.

But as his narrative reaches the modern era, with only European explorers holding centre stage and outperforming the Chinese, there is a conspicuous change in attitude toward the whole business of exploration. The goddess is noticeably upset. Indeed, just when the European voyages take on a more scientific and humane character; the tenor of *Pathfinders* becomes extremely cynical and disparaging. Chapter 8, which deals with the period between 1740 and 1840, opens with this sentence: 'What good came of all this exploration?' After which Armesto uses Diderot's words to denounce the 'base motives' that drove the explorers: the 'tyranny,

---

463 Fernández-Armesto, *Pathfinders*, p. 1.

464 Benjamin Healy, 'Cover to Cover,' *Atlantic Monthly* (December 2006), http://www.theatlantic.com/ magazine/archive/2006/12/cover-to-cover/5370/; Candace Millard, 'Fantastic Voyages,' New York Times, December 3, 2006, http://www.nytimes.com/2006/12/03/books/review/Millard.t.html?pagewanted=print.

crime, ambition, misery, curiosity'[465]. The most illustrious member of this emerging group of 'criminal' explorers was Captain Cook. But who really was Cook? Armesto merely notes a few facts about his voyages. The historical record shows that, on the contrary, Cook was part of a new breed of explorers that began to adopt more humane methods of exploration. As a young apprentice on a navy merchant ship, Cook applied himself to the study of algebra, geometry, trigonometry, navigation, and astronomy. During the course of his three legendary Pacific voyages between 1768 and 1779, Cook showed that New Holland and New Guinea are two separate lands or islands, dispelled belief in the long-imagined southern continent, discovered New Caledonia, charted Easter Island, and discovered the Hawaiian Islands. It is said that Cook explored more of the earth's surface than any other man in history. His methods were 'painstaking, practical, and humane,' and he prided himself on feats achieved 'without loss of life among his crew as in the discoveries themselves.'[466] Cook was undoubtedly a heroic figure filled with a zeal for greatness and adventure, a man with 'indomitable courage.' In his own words, what Cook wanted above all else was the 'pleasure of being first': to sail 'not only farther than man has been before me but as far as I think it possible for man to go.'[467]

Armesto's disapproving tone takes on a heightened character regarding the most benign forms of exploration, those to the Polar Regions and the interior of Africa during and after the 19th century. As he bluntly puts it at the end of *Pathfinders*, 'almost all the explorers who have featured in this chapter [from 1850 to 2000] were failures... hampered by characteristic vices: amateurism, naivety... credulousness...bombast, mendacity... sheer incompetence.'[468] David Livingstone, arguably one of the greatest land explorers of all time, is portrayed as a buffoon:

Livingstone...had a strong sense of his own 'Channel of Divine Power', but how

---

465 Fernández-Armesto, *Pathfinders*, p. 290.

466 Whitfield, *New Found Lands*, p. 123.

467 Cited in Robin Hanbury-Tenison, ed., *The Oxford Book of Exploration* (Oxford University Press, 1993), pp. 490–503. This is an anthology of the writings of explorers.

468 Fernández-Armesto, *Pathfinders*, p. 394.

much of a missionary vocation he ever really had is doubtful. Notoriously, he is supposed only ever to have made one convert who soon reverted to paganism... He tackled slavers and Boers and intractable native chiefs with gusto...The expedition failed in all its objectives: no trade, no converts, no suitable sites for British colonization, *no new geographical discoveries resulted*...His meanderings took him nowhere useful.[469]

This is a shameless caricature. At the age of ten, Livingstone started working in a cotton mill for 12-hour days, while putting himself through medical school, later landing in Algoa Bay in 1841, and until his death thirty two years later in 1873. He travelled thousands of miles every year, for a total of about 30,000 miles (!), mostly alone, 'a solitary white man with a nucleus of faithful [African] attendants', enduring sickness and dangers of every kind, at times during the rainy season and even once desperately sick with dysentery. His legacy includes discovering the southern end of Lake Tanganyika, and the locations of Lake Mweru, Lake Bangweulu, Lake Nyasa and the Victoria Falls. Contrary to Armesto's claim that his missionary efforts involved no compromises with Africans, he lived with them, learned their local language, vehemently condemning and working against the cruelty of the slave trade inside Africa.[470]

Armesto has nothing to say about Ernest Shackleton's incredible voyage to the South Pole, except that it was a 'failure,' 'pointless.' Of Henry Morton Stanley (1841–1904), the first European, and possibly the first person, to circumnavigate Lake Victoria, to connect the Lualaba River to the Congo River, and add many new place names to the map of Africa, Armesto simply says that Stanley did nothing worthwhile except 'spent his patron's wealth and his men's lives with equal profligacy...Stanley worked for millionaires or governments.'

---

469 Ibid., pp. 353–354.

470 As Clare Pettitt writes, 'David Livingstone did not just explore Africa and then come home again, he lived there and worked alongside Africans...Much of his writing is from Africa looking at Europe and the 'old civilized countries' as from a distance.' See 'David Livingstone, Africa Coast to Coast' in Hanbury-Tenison, *The Great Explorers*, p. 151. For similar assessments of Livingston, see Frank Debenham, *Discovery and Exploration*, pp. 170–175; Whitfield, *New Found Lands*, pp. 170–172.

He describes Robert Peary's identification of the location of the North Pole as an achievement that 'was much disputed...unverifiable,' 'remains a matter of doubt.'[471] Armesto is equally dismissive of Amundsen's explorations, describing them as futile, even though he was the first to traverse successfully the fabled Northwest Passage, where he learned from Inuit's techniques, which he then used to become the first to reach the South Pole. According to Russell Potter, Amundsen's achievements 'stand unequalled.'[472] But Armesto is not impressed: 'Amundsen demonstrated the paradox of the Northwest Passage. The American Arctic was navigable between the Pacific and Atlantic — but uselessly so.'[473]

Among the many biographies of Amundsen is a recent one by Stephen Brown, *The Last Viking* (2012), fully cognisant of Amundsen's Faustian longing. From his youth, Amundsen 'had visions of vanquishing against great odds, geographical chimeras, enduring incredible suffering in the process and emerging a hero.'[474] In Amundsen's words, in *The North West Passage* (1908): 'Strangely enough the thing in Sir John Franklin's narrative that appealed to me the most strongly was the suffering that he and his men endured. A strange ambition burned within me to endure those same sufferings.'[475]

Armesto's mindset is paradigmatic of what is going on in academia today in the face of the great achievements of European males. We are dealing with a world renowned historian who has carried the title 'Principe' (Prince) in his academic positions, the recipient of multiple prizes, including titles associated specifically with navigation and geography, the Caird Medal of the National Maritime Museum (UK), the Premio Nacional an

471 Fernández-Armesto, *Pathfinders*, pp. 379–380.

472 Russell Potter, 'Roald Amundsen, A Burning Ambition to Reach the Poles,' in *The Great Explorers*, p. 181.

473 Fernández-Armesto, *Pathfinders*, p. 380.

474 Stephen Brown, *The Last Viking The Last Viking: The Life of Roald Amundsen* (Da Capo Press, 2012), p. 8.

475 Cited in Russell Potter, 'Roald Amundsen, A Burning Ambition to Reach the Poles,' p. 181.

Investigacion of the Sociedad Geográfica Española, and the John Carter Brown Medal.

The most glaring expression of Armesto's contempt for European achievement is his cynical and cowardly account of Robert Falcon Scott's tragic expedition to the South Pole in 1911–1912. He writes:

> Scott was an irresponsible commander...He jeopardized his men by refusing to recognize the obvious symptoms of scurvy...Scott's final message with its pathos and patriotism, its historic nostalgia and its unspecific religion, was perfectly calculated to appeal to British sensibilities and match the common notions the British share of themselves.[476]

Not a single one of the many biographies written on this iconic British figure is referenced; in fact, there are barely any sources cited in Armesto's book. Scott was a revered figure during the first half of the 20th century, with more than 30 monuments and memorials set up during the first dozen years following his death. But in the last decades of the 20th century, as the cultural Marxists took over our institutions, Scott became a figure of controversy and even ridicule. This is particularly true after the publication of Roland Huntford's 1979 biography *Scott and Amundsen*, where Scott is portrayed as a reckless, sentimental amateur responsible for the death of his men. Armesto does not cite this biography. He is completely unaware of subsequent attempts to rescue Scott's reputation from Huntford's interpretation. Sir Ranulph Fiennes's 2003 biography *Captain Scott*, which defends Scott as a great historic hero, has been praised by reviewers as a stinging rebuttal of Huntford's 'story of a living liar.'[477]

Armesto references Scott's famous diaries, the 1913 edition by L. Huxley, published as *Scott's Last Expedition*. Citing Scott's legendary last letters to his family and country, Armesto comments: '[D]espite the fine words, they had died demoralised, unwilling or unable to go on, though

---

476 Fernández-Armesto, *Pathfinders*, pp. 381–384.

477 Jasper Rees, 'Ice in Our Hearts,' *The Telegraph* (December 19, 2004). I should add that, in fairness to Huntford's biography, *Scott and Amundsen*, its intention was to draw attention to the long neglected achievements of Roald Amundsen, which had been obscured by the British patriotic preoccupation with Scott's failed mission.

they were only 11 miles from food sources...The suspicion abides that they were virtual suicides, who preferred to die dramatically rather than live in obscurity. Scott's *excuse* for failure was bad luck.'[478]

To set the record straight: when Scott and his party of five men were 21 miles from the depot, he wrote in his diary: 'We have had more wind and drift from ahead yesterday; had to stop marching; wind NW, force 4, temp. -35. No human being could face it, and we are worn out nearly...My right foot has gone, nearly all the toes.'[479] A few days later, one of the explorers, Lawrence Oates, who was barely able to walk and knew he would be a burden, willingly left the tent and walked to his death. When they were some 11 miles away from a food depot, held up by a blizzard that howled relentlessly for nine days, with their supplies almost out, Scott wrote his final words, 'Message to the Public,' defending the expedition's organisation and conduct and adducing weather conditions for the party's failure:

> We took risks, we knew we took them. Things have come out against us, and therefore we have no cause for complaint, but bow to the will of Providence, determined still to do our best to the last...Had we lived, I should have had a tale to tell of the hardihood, endurance, and courage of my companions which would have stirred the heart of every Englishman.[480]

Armesto imputes that the deaths were orchestrated by Scott and his men as 'the best career move.'[481] But the meteorologist Susan Solomon, in *The Coldest March, Scott's Fatal Antarctic Expedition* (2001), has factually defended Scott's message, attributing the failure of the expedition to the extreme weather condition of February and March 1912.

The *Wall Street Journal* review of *Pathfinder* informs us that Armesto writes with 'gusto and panache'. Armesto certainly delights in the use of mocking phrases against Scott's sombre expressions of patriotic duty.

---

478 Fernández-Armesto, *Pathfinders*, p. 383.

479 Robert Scott, 'Final Diaries and Letters,' in Hanbury-Tenison, ed., *The Oxford Book of Exploration*, p. 508.

480 Ibid.

481 Fernández-Armesto, *Pathfinders*, p. 396.

Scott was dutiful alright, says Armesto, 'until the glare of the ice got in his eyes and the scent of the quest in his nostrils. Then he forgot his plain duty.'[482] Max Jones offers a far more incisive assessment of the significance of Scott, less as a 'great' explorer than someone who 'composed the most haunting journal in the history of exploration…a last testament of duty and sacrifice.'[483] Jones extols the captivating power of the journals, the mounting tension, the constant anxiety as the ship battles to reach the Antarctica coast, and the epic account of the relentless march to the Pole.

Jones situates Scott within a wider cultural setting, tracing the intellectual influences on Scott's writing: his immersion in polar literature, his awareness of characters in major novels who sought to prove themselves, his copy of *On the Origin of Species* and Scott's 'bleak vision of the universe as a struggle for existence,' the literary influences of Henrik Ibsen and Thomas Hardy and their fascination with the dependency of the human will on the indifferent power of nature and necessity.[484]

Overall, the pervading idea of the journals is the heroic vision of exploration as a test of individual worthiness and national character. From his early manhood, Scott was filled with anxiety and doubts about his adequacy in life's struggles: 'I write of the future; of the hopes of being

---

482 Ibid., p. 395. Armesto's repeated used of the word 'useless' in reference to European explorations post-1850s betrays either a complete lack of knowledge or a mind warped by resentment and hatred of European men, since the opposite is true. This is attested by the books I have consulted here, but see in particular Edward J. Larson's *An Empire of Ice. Scott, Shackleton, and the Heroic Age of Antarctic Science* (Yale University Press, 2011), for a strong case showing that British expeditions of the late Victorian and Edwardian era were organised as 'grand enterprises of science. Simply reaching the head of the Nile, the high Himalayas, or the South Pole was not enough.' While Amundsen's expeditions were about the joy and grandeur of exploration, 'Scott brought along more scientists than any prior Antarctic expedition.' Larson rejects Eric Hobsbawm's opinion (Marxist admirer of Stalin eulogised in academia) that Scott's was just a 'hapless' character who attempted to reach the pole without any practical aims in mind; rather, 'in fields ranging from climate change and paleontology to marine biology and glaciology,' Scott's expedition, as well as Shackleton and others, were ground breaking (pp. 2, 5, 293–294).

483 Max Jones, introduction to *Journals: Captain Scott's Last Expedition*, by Robert Falcon Scott (Oxford and New York: Oxford University Press, 2008), p. xvii.

484 Ibid., pp. xxxiv–xxxvii.

more worthy; but shall I ever be — can I alone, poor weak wretch that I am bear up against it all.'[485] Expedition narratives through the 19th century became ever more focussed on the character of the explorer rather than the economic externalities, as exploration became an inner journey, 'a journey into the self, nowhere more so than in the emptiest of continents, Antarctica.'[486] Scott understood this: 'Here the outward show is nothing; it is the inward purpose that counts.'[487] There was nothing to meet in the center of Antarctica except the reflection of the inner Western quest to face the struggle of life in a heroic fashion.

The last chapter of *Pathfinders*, 'Globalizing, 1850–2000,' is not just full of dismissals but actually ignores almost all the European explorers of this era. A consultation of the Smithsonian publication, *Explorers: Great Tales of Adventure and Endurance*,[488] and *The Great Explorers*, cited earlier, quickly brings home the numerous great explorers Armesto wilfully hides from students. Roughly speaking I counted about 75 'great' European explorers in the period from about 1800 to the present, men (and a few women) who dedicated themselves to the discovery of the unknown. They sought out deserts, rivers and lakes, climbing the highest mountains, penetrating into the deepest crevices of the oceans and high above in space. Armesto's book is a complete travesty and a direct testimony of the deceitfulness of academics determined to spit on the greatness of European history, solely for the sake of enforcing a make-believe world of equality and racial mixing in the West. The history of the West has been virtually banned in academia, and nowhere is the history of exploration being taught other than as a history of imperialism and 'othering'. This is a most unfortunate affair. For the history of exploration provides us with a profoundly revealing index of Western heroic self-fashioning that should

485 Ibid., p. xix.

486 Ibid., p. xxxiv.

487 Ibid., p. xxxv.

488 *Explorers: Great Tales of Adventure and Endurance* (Royal Geographical Society, 2010). With a Foreword by Sir Ranulph Fiennes.

be taught to male students increasingly bored by their cultural Marxists professors.

This would not be a history to elicit self-satisfaction among students but to teach them the meaning of endurance and hardship and the inimitable European thirst for adventure and risk. It would be a history celebrating 'the perverse, obsessive, often destructive urge [of European males] to go beyond the boundaries of human experience.' Education has been made boring for European males. Books of explorers at many levels of education would be a wonderful way to get boys to realise that learning can be exiting and male-oriented. There is a high varying number of explorers with different Faustian personalities coming from changing historical backgrounds.

There is Samuel de Champlain (1580–1635), founder of the French Empire in North America, the first European to explore and describe Lake Huron and Lake Ontario, the first European who chose to live and die in Canada, a noble man whose entire life was 'a battle against fainthearts, the mean-spirited, the avaricious, the sensual', who published maps of his journeys and accounts of what he learned from the Indians, who endured three harsh winters in Nova Scotia and New Brunswick, before founding Quebec, the oldest city in North America outside the Spanish sphere, and who eventually settled to become the first Governor of New France, and thus the Father of Canada. Morris Bishop captures precisely the indomitable Faustian spirit of Champlain:

> The passion of his mind was exploration, discovery. He was possessed by the old *libido sciendi*, the lust of knowing. His lust turned to the great unknown of his time, the white void on sailors' maps. He looked, longing, to the west, the land of mystery...More than ease, more than security, he desired the knowledge of strange and perilous lands.[489]

There is Louis Antoine de Bougainville (1729–1811), who embodied the rational, scientific mode of exploration of the Enlightenment while sailing

---

489 Morris Bishop, *Champlain: The Life of Fortitude* (Carleton Library/McClelland and Steward Limited, 1964), p. 74.

around the world accompanied by naturalists, establishing a colony for France in the Falkland Islands, and proving that Espiritu Santo was an island rather than a part of Terra Australis Incognita. There are also the heroes of the American West, Meriwether Lewis (1774–1809) and William Clark (1770–1838), who identified more than 100 new species; and the German Alexander von Humboldt (1769–1859), who climbed what was then believed to be the highest peak in the world, Chimborazo (19, 286 ft.), mapped the course of the Orinoco River (1,500-mile), collected 12,000 specimens, while almost starving to death and being reduced to eating ants, and finally completed his life with a massive 25 year work, *Kosmos*, describing the universe.[490] There are Wilfred Thesiger's (1910–2003) dangerous journeys from Sudan across Sahara to Tibesti, and through Syria, Arabia, and Indonesia, driven by the 'lure of the unknown and the challenge to resolution and endurance', and many more explorers.

But if I may end this Faustian account of the West with a lesser known explorer, Gino Watkins (1907–1932), who may speak directly to young men today. Described as 'effete, slight, and blond, with a taste for dancing and sports cars',[491] but who could not stand the drab dullness of his

---

490 von Humboldt was a traveller-explorer in the same vein as Marco Polo, and Charles Darwin. World historians today, on realising that there are hardly any non-European explorers, have started identifying mere travellers, people who travel to places already known, even hobos from China who spend days drifting in the streets, as explorers. It is not always easy to distinguish a traveller-explorer from a mere traveller, but one criteria I use, is that the traveller has visited areas not known in the geographical sense, or not categorised in cartographic terms. The true traveller-explorer is also someone who writes about his travels exhibiting an ethnographic aptitude as well as bringing new knowledge of the topography, climate, customs, geology, etc., of the areas. A very important traveller-explorer in this respect is Darwin, his fascinating *Voyage of the Beagle*, first published in 1839. As the subtitle of the book says, this was a "Journal of Researches." Darwin's stories of his six years of travelling at sea and into the lands of South America and across the Pacific, evinced a keen scientific mind, though he was a young man in his twenties, influence by Charles Lyll's celebrated *Principles of Geology*, published while Darwin was travelling. His astute ethnological observations, both affectionate and Anglocentric, would have occasioned academics today to cut his future scientific investigations short. See Charles Darwin, *Voyage of the Beagle*. Edited with an introduction by Janet Browne and Michael Neve (Penguin Classics, 1989).

491 Jeremy Scott, 'Gino Watkins' in The Great Explorers, p. 267.

contemporary England, decided at the age of 23, in a thirst for adventure and risk, 'to do something big', to investigate the shortest air route over Greenland's ice cap, linking Europe to America. This expedition entailed enormous depravations, an entire winter in the Arctic, 40 days of continuous storms. Later it was determined that the plans for this expedition, were reckless, unfit equipment and improper clothing. Still, they overcame 'appalling setbacks' and experienced conditions described by Arctic experts as 'at the limit of human endurance'. Clearly, what drove him was not the knowledge to be gained about some air route; it was his 'addiction to risk'. Watkins dreaded the thought of 'mundanity and a 9 to 5 job', so after returning from this expedition, he left for the Arctic again, from which he did not return, dying at the young age of 25.

These are the characters cultural Marxists hate, and it is they who gave the West its glory. These men can still be found today, most evidently in 'extreme sports', in rock climbing without ropes or harness, hiking in extreme weather, aggressive inline skating, kitesurfing, snowboarding, base jumping, diving, parachuting... Almost all the men involved in these high risk undertakings are white.[492] The Faustian spirit lives even if the West is in decline culturally, geopolitically, and economically. What really threatens this spirit, smothering it forever, is mass immigration and race mixing. This is why the concept of a European sub-race is essential to a full understanding of the Faustian soul of Western civilisation, and the imminent danger facing this soul.

---

492 We still have explorers today; Adam Shoalts' new book, *Alone Against the North* (Random House, 2015), narrates his explorations in Canada's north. Shoalts, who contacted me some years ago praising an article I wrote on exploration as the most insightful rendition of the psychology of exploration, is a very courageous young man who regularly goes by himself on long explorations, which have been recognised as highly valuable and original by The Royal Canadian Geographic Society, including his mapping of the little known Again River. He is currently preparing for a five-month journey across the Arctic in 2017.

Index

OTHER BOOKS PUBLISHED BY ARKTOS

	Understanding Islam
	Why We Fight
Daniel S. Forrest	*Suprahumanism*
Andrew Fraser	*The WASP Question*
Daniel Friberg	*The Real Right Returns*
Génération Identitaire	*We are Generation Identity*
Paul Gottfried	*War and Democracy*
Porus Homi Havewala	*The Saga of the Aryan Race*
Rachel Haywire	*The New Reaction*
Lars Holger Holm	*Hiding in Broad Daylight*
	Homo Maximus
	Incidents of Travel in Latin America
	The Owls of Afrasiab
Alexander Jacob	*De Naturae Natura*
Jason Reza Jorjani	*Prometheus and Atlas*
Peter King	*Here and Now*
	Keeping Things Close: Essays on the Conservative Disposition
Ludwig Klages	*The Biocentric Worldview*
	Cosmogonic Reflections: Selected Aphorisms from Ludwig Klages
Pierre Krebs	*Fighting for the Essence*

OTHER BOOKS PUBLISHED BY ARKTOS

PENTTI LINKOLA   *Can Life Prevail?*

H. P. LOVECRAFT   *The Conservative*

CHARLES MAURRAS   *The Future of the Intelligentsia*
                                & For a French Awakening

MICHAEL O'MEARA   *New Culture, New Right*

BRIAN ANSE PATRICK   *The NRA and the Media*
                                Rise of the Anti-Media
                                The Ten Commandments
                                of Propaganda
                                Zombology

TITO PERDUE   *Morning Crafts*
                                William's House (vol. 1–4)

RAIDO   *A Handbook of Traditional Living*

STEVEN J. ROSEN   *The Agni and the Ecstasy*
                                The Jedi in the Lotus

RICHARD RUDGLEY   *Barbarians*
                                Essential Substances
                                Wildest Dreams

ERNST VON SALOMON   *It Cannot Be Stormed*
                                The Outlaws

TROY SOUTHGATE   *Tradition & Revolution*

OSWALD SPENGLER   *Man and Technics*

TOMISLAV SUNIC   *Against Democracy and Equality*

OTHER BOOKS PUBLISHED BY ARKTOS